1998

MEDIEVAL TEXTS AND STUDIES

General Editor

John A. Alford

MEDIEVAL TEXTS AND STUDIES

General Editor

John A. Alford

THE SOUL'S ADDRESS

TO

THE BODY

The Worcester Fragments

Edited by

Douglas Moffat

COLLEAGUES PRESS

1987

Medieval Texts and Studies: No. 1

ISBN 0-937191-01-9
Library of Congress Catalog Card Number 86-72187
Copyright © 1987 Douglas Moffat

Published by Colleagues Press Inc.
Post Office Box 4007
East Lansing, MI 48823

Printed in the United States of America

CONTENTS

ACKNOWLEDGMENTS

Many people must be thanked for their help in bringing this work to its final form. Professors C. B. Hieatt and Peter Auksi directed the initial dissertation, while its examiners, Professors John Leyerle, Donald F. Chapin, Richard Firth Green, and Robin Jones, each contributed valuable suggestions for improvement. Dr Ashley Crandall Amos aided me a great deal with the discussion of language, and Professor E. G. Stanley, in conversation, helped settle a crucial point about fragment order. Professor Roberta Frank also read a later version of the work. Finally, Professor John Alford and the anonymous readers of Colleagues Press were both attentive and expeditious in their treatment of my submission.

I must also acknowledge the expert advice of Dr B. S. Benedikz of The University of Birmingham and the assistance of the Dean and Chapter of Worcester Cathedral, particularly The Reverend Canon J. R. Fenwick, during my examination of Worcester Cathedral MS F. 174.

I would like to thank the Department of English of The University of Western Ontario, the J. B. Smallman fund of the University of Western Ontario, and the Social Sciences and Humanities Research Council of Canada for their support during the writing and publication of this work. Finally, I must thank my family, especially my wife, Elaine, for all their patience and their encouragement.

ABBREVIATIONS

ASPR	*The Anglo-Saxon Poetic Records*
BT	Bosworth and Toller, *An Anglo-Saxon Dictionary*
BT Supp.	Bosworth and Toller, *An Anglo-Saxon Dictionary: Supplement*
EETS (O.S.)	Early English Text Society (Original Series)
ES	*English Studies*
JEGP	*Journal of English and Germanic Philology*
ME, eME	Middle English, early Middle English
MED	*Middle English Dictionary*
MLN	*Modern Language Notes*
MLQ	*Modern Language Quarterly*
MP	*Modern Philology*
MS	*Mediaeval Studies*
OE, eOE, lOE	Old English, early Old English, late Old English
OED	*The Oxford English Dictionary*
PL	*Patrologia Latina*
PMLA	*Publications of the Modern Language Association*
PQ	*Philological Quarterly*
SN	*Studia Neophilologica*
SP	*Studies in Philology*
SWML	Southwest Midlands
WML	West Midlands
WS	West Saxon

INTRODUCTION

THE MANUSCRIPT

The fragments which remain of the *Soul's Address to the Body* (*SA*) are found on folios 63ᵛ–66ᵛ of Worcester Cathedral MS. F. 174, currently located in the Chapter Library of Worcester Cathedral. This manuscript also contains a much excised version of Ælfric's *Grammar and Glossary*, ff. 1–63ʳ,[1] and a short fragment of rhythmical prose on the state of learning in England beginning "*Sanctus Beda was iboren her,*" f. 63ʳ.[2]

Physical Characteristics

1. *Size and Quality of the Sheets.* The sheets used in F. 174 were of various sizes and shapes when the text was written and the manuscript compiled. For example, f. 19, which has survived intact, is 198 x 185 mm. and contains twenty-three lines of text; f. 12, which is also intact, measures 276 x 175 mm. with thirty-one lines of text; f. 59, on the other hand, has a writing area that measures about 215 mm. across—that is, significantly larger than either ff. 12 or 19—despite its having been trimmed along one of its edges. Folios 63–66, which contain *SA*, have each been trimmed across the top and down their free (as opposed to bound) edge. Folio 63ᵛ in its current state contains twenty-seven lines of writing and a writing area 205 mm. in width at its largest point; f. 64ʳ has thirty lines, the width of the writing space approximately 193 mm.; f. 64ᵛ, thirty lines as well, 195–200 mm.; f. 65ʳ, thirty lines, about 195 mm.; f. 65ᵛ, twenty-nine lines, about 200 mm.; f. 66ʳ, twenty-eight lines, 190 mm. at the top broadening to 200 mm. at the bottom; f. 66ᵛ, thirty lines, 187 mm. at the top, 197 mm. near the bottom.

Given the abuse they have received (see pp. 3–5), the extant leaves of F. 174 have survived remarkably well, particularly those toward the end of the manuscript where the poetical leaves are found. Nevertheless,

ff. 63–66 are thin and fragile, yellowish in color, and somewhat translu-
cent. A number of small holes and the occasional tear are present — the
latter often the result of ruling; also, on f. 64, two creases have occurred
along the free edge of the leaf at some time after the writing had been
completed.

2. *Foliation*. In the nineteenth century the leaves were numbered 1
through 66 in the upper right-hand corner of the recto side. Because
of trimming at the top of some leaves, these numbers sometimes appear
between the lines of the text.

3. *Gatherings*. In its original form the manuscript would appear to have
been quaternion, the leaves arranged in each gathering so that hair side
faced hair, flesh side faced flesh; in some gatherings, if they were indeed quaternion, the recto of the first leaf is a hair side, in others, a
flesh side. Ker is of the opinion that f. 1 and the misplaced f. 10 are
a bifolium and that the six leaves are missing that were originally between them.[3] This would appear to be true: f. 1ᵛ ends on p. 8 of Zupitza's edition of Ælfric's *Grammar*, f. 10ʳ begins at the top of p. 31, and,
on the average, one folio of the manuscript corresponds to about four
pages in Zupitza. It is also assumed by Ker that Ælfric's preface to the
Grammar, pp. 1–3 of Zupitza, was never included in this copy;[4] Floyer
and Hamilton suggest, however, that two leaves are missing from before
current f. 1.[5] One might then assume, along with Ker, an original collation of I⁸ (ff. 1 and 10; 2–7 missing), II⁸ (ff. 2–9), III–IX⁸ (ff. 11–66),[6]
but the subsequent damage to the manuscript makes certainty impossible. See pp. 3–6.

4. *Binding*. The manuscript is currently in a nineteenth-century binding which must date from after 1879. See pp. 3–4. Each folio is interleaved
with paper.

The Scribe

1. *Script*. The manuscript is considered to be wholly the work of an
anonymous scribe whose distinctive, quavering script has been named
by scholars the "tremulous hand." The letters tend to slope backwards,
the strokes are thick rather than fine, and the size of the letters can change
quite substantially from one leaf to the next, though on the whole they
are fairly large. The "tremulous hand" is found in a number of
manuscripts, almost always in glosses, and it is clear from their provenance that he was working at Worcester. Further, Ker has shown that

additions in the "tremulous hand" to a marginal index in Bodleian MS. Hatton 114, f. 10, probably date from the second quarter of the thirteenth century.[7]

F. 174 is the only extant manuscript in which the "tremulous hand" is the primary script, and it is interesting to note how variable the hand can be. Of particular interest is f. 1, where the script is characterized by smaller letters produced with finer strokes than elsewhere in the manuscript, especially in the verse sections, ff. 63–66. On f. 1 occurs the letter form *ð*, for example, *habbeð*, l. 10 of f. 1ᵛ; it is not usually found in the work of the "tremulous hand" but does appear in his copy of the Nicene Creed, reproduced in facsimile by Crawford (1928). Ker mistakenly says *ð* does not occur in F. 174.[8] Also, Carolingian *g* on f. 1 has a tail which ends with a downward turn, e.g. *englisc*, l. 12 of f. 1ᵛ. In the verse sections the tail of Carolingian *g* turns upward to the line and joins with the body of the letter; it resembles a lopsided 8.

2. *Ruling*. The manuscript is ruled with a pencil. There are no vertical lines demarcating margins, though the scribe left a 5–10 mm. margin on the left-hand side of each leaf, recto and verso. It would appear from ff. 57–58, from which, uncharacteristically, the bound edges have been trimmed, that the scribe used short, ink strokes placed along the free edge of each leaf as a guide in drawing the horizontal lines. These lines are drawn right across the page from one edge to the other. Long lines, as opposed to columns, are an old-fashioned feature in an early thirteenth-century manuscript, according to Ker.[9]

3. *Spacing*. As mentioned above, the size of writing in works in the "tremulous hand" can vary from leaf to leaf. On average, the height of the minims on the poetical leaves of F. 174 is 4 mm.; that of the ascenders and descenders, 2–3 mm. The height of the interlinear space varies from 1–3 mm.

History

The manuscript was written at Worcester and apparently has always remained there. It is the only manuscript containing work of the "tremulous hand" still at its place of origin. Nevertheless, it is not mentioned by Patrick Young, who compiled in 1622–1623 the earliest extant catalogue of the Chapter Library, because it had been disassembled and used in the binding of another manuscript in the Library. Ker suspects this disassembly took place in medieval times.[10] It does seem probable that it took place before the visit to Worcester of Archbishop Parker, c. 1565, for it is likely he would have taken the work from the Library along with other Anglo-Saxon manuscripts, even though it was probably from the outset a rather plain, undistinguished piece of work compared to other productions of the Worcester scriptorium.[11] Sir Thomas Phillipps, who discovered the fragments and in 1838 published the first edition of *SA*, along with a portion of the Ælfric material and the "*Sanctus Beda*" fragment, has the following to say about their condition: "The Fragments, having been found in the cover of an old book (of which they, with some other fragments, constituted the sole stiffening), had been so much smeared with a brown paste to make them adhere together, that it required much washing to make some of them in the least degree legible."[12] The identity of the "old book" remains a mystery despite the efforts of N. R. Ker and B. S. Benedikz. Dr. Benedikz deduces from their present condition that the fragments were "cover-stiffeners for some large volume (such as the A-class muniments, that is, Act Books and Registers)," and his deduction is given weight by Phillipps' statement in a letter to George Murray, Bishop of Rochester, that he found the fragment among the "Chapter's Muniments at Worcester."[13] The cleaned and perhaps reordered leaves of what was to become F. 174 — though still unbound — were apparently misplaced again and not rediscovered until 1879, when Zupitza found them while searching for all extant copies of Ælfric's *Grammar and Glossary* in preparation for his edition of that work.[14] The current binding was probably done shortly after this rediscovery.

Though the leaves of the manuscript have survived quite well, some damage has occurred. As a result of leaves being pasted together, the offset of letters from other leaves is found throughout the manuscript. Perhaps as a result of the cleaning carried out by Phillipps, the ink in some words is very faded. More serious is the trimming of the top edge and the free edge of most of the leaves. (Some were also cut along the bottom; three were trimmed along the bound edge rather than the free edge; a few were cut in two; some were left uncut.) Folios 63–66 have been trimmed along the top and down the free edge. It is impossible to ascertain exactly how much is missing from the leaves because of trimming at the top. Five to seven lines have been lost from the *Glossary* at the top of f. 63^r. We might, therefore, assume that a similar amount of text is missing from f. 63^v where *SA* begins. But whether this space contained only lines from *SA*, or a conclusion to the "*Sanctus Beda*" passage of f. 63^r, or both, cannot be determined. Also, because of the varying

sizes of the leaves, one can only estimate the loss from the tops of ff.
64–66 to be about five lines of text, give or take two or three lines, that
is, between two and eight lines.

The previous editors state that only one or two letters are missing from
each line of writing because of the trimming of each leaf's free edge.[15]
However, because of the lack of uniformity in the size of the sheets both
before and after the manuscript was disassembled, it is impossible to
make such a general statement. The scribe left a fairly even left-hand
margin of 5–10 mm. on each page but no right-hand margin; therefore,
since the free edge of each leaf was trimmed, it is clear that more text —
the width of the margin — is missing on the recto side. The best method
for estimating how much has been lost from each leaf is to find other
occurrences of a word that is almost certainly the one missing from the
beginning or end of a given line and to measure the relevant portion
thereof. This method yields the following results:

> f. 63ᵛ, *fleoþ* would seem to be the word missing in A37. It has
> an estimated length of 15 mm.
>
> f. 64ʳ, *puncheþ* is almost certainly required in B38. The missing
> *pun* probably measured about 14 mm.
>
> f. 64ᵛ, the last three letters of what must be *wurmes*, C43, prob-
> ably measured 11–12 mm.
>
> f. 65ʳ, *licame* plus a point, D26, *beornen*, D14, and *fæderes*, D23,
> all seem to be missing about 19 mm. of writing apiece.
>
> f. 65ᵛ, *deope*, which is almost certainly the word missing in E8,
> probably measured about 17 mm.
>
> f. 66ʳ, the missing portions of both *sunfule*, F8, and *makunge*,
> F41, probably measured about 17–18 mm.
>
> f. 66ᵛ, *tunge*, G15, measured 16–17 mm.

With the exception of portions of f. 64, there is room for more than one
or two letters to be missing from each line of the poetical leaves. However,
the figures are approximations. The width of the margin varies from
5–10 mm.; the scribe did not always write to the right-hand edge of the
page, though generally he comes very close to it; the size of the writing
can vary somewhat from leaf to leaf.

The disassembly of F. 174 coupled with the trimming of its leaves has
created another problem for the editor of the *SA*. Because there are other
extant versions of Ælfric's *Grammar and Glossary*, the order of the leaves
in that part of the manuscript, that is, ff. 1–63ʳ, is easy to establish.
The poetical leaves present a much more difficult task: there is no source

or analogue sufficiently close to *SA* to serve as a clear-cut pattern, and further, the trimming of the top of each leaf has resulted in the loss of material that might have allowed the editor to join the fragments together in the correct order on the basis of continuity of subject matter.

Of the leaves that contain *SA*, we can be certain that f. 63 has been correctly positioned: the Ælfric *Glossary* ends on f. 63^r. We can also be certain that recto has been correctly distinguished from verso on the final three leaves, ff. 64–66. As previously mentioned, on ff. 57 and 58 (two leaves from which the bound edge was trimmed instead of the free edge) ink markings appear that served as guides in the ruling of the leaves, markings which have been lost on the leaves from which the free edge has been trimmed. Since these markings do not occur on ff. 64–66, we can assume that the free edge was trimmed from all of them, and it follows that, if any significant trimming took place, the left-hand margin of 5–10 mm. the scribe always allowed himself will occur only on the recto side of these leaves. In the current, Phillipps order, this left-hand margin does, in fact, occur on the recto side of ff. 64–66. Further, ff. 63–66 are arranged so that hair side faces hair side, flesh side faces flesh side; f. 63^r is a flesh side, 63^v, hair; f. 64^r is a hair side, 64^v, flesh; f. 65^r, flesh, 65^v, hair; f. 66^r, hair, 66^v, flesh. It would appear, in other words, that ff. 63–66 do form, as Ker's collation suggests, the last half of a quaternion gathering in which the first leaf, f. 59, is flesh side, recto, and hair side, verso. The physical evidence would appear to support the Phillipps order.

However, we must not lose sight of the fact that we are dealing with fragments, and this fact of fragmentation undermines significantly the certainty we might be inclined to feel about any evidence derived from the manuscript in its current state. Furthermore, the fact that ff. 63–66 occur at the end of the manuscript should serve to increase our uncertainty about the validity of this physical evidence: it is at the outer extremes of medieval manuscripts, at their beginnings and ends, that damage and loss are most frequent. In regard to Worcester Cathedral MS. F. 174, as already mentioned, six leaves have been lost after f. 1; it is possible, though by no means certain, that some leaves have been lost from before f. 1. In the discussion of "Sources and Structure" to follow, I shall argue that if the current order of the leaves is accepted, at least one leaf must be missing from after f. 66; I shall further argue, however, that this current order of the leaves is, in fact, incorrect.

LANGUAGE

Richard Buchholz offers a very thorough description of language in his 1890 edition of *SA*.[16] He views it almost wholly from an OE perspective, listing all the orthographic reflexes of OE phonological and morphological features found in the poem. Except for his discussion of new diphthongs, he does not attempt to redefine or reclassify these OE features in order to fit them more closely to the later linguistic context of *SA*. In the treatment of nouns, for example, whereas d'Ardenne, in her analysis of the AB dialect (1961), finds only four declensions and three cases that are morphologically distinct, Buchholz, employing the format of standard OE grammars, divides the nouns according to their Germanic roots and into declensions of four or five cases each. With the morphology in particular, this strict adherence to OE categories can obscure rather than clarify the quality of the language in such a late work. Nevertheless, Buchholz's analysis remains very useful, particularly when read in conjunction with both Zupitza's review of the edition (1890), in which a number of small errors are pointed out, and Hall's also quite thorough assessment of the language in his *Early Middle English* (1920). In what follows I shall first attempt to describe the language briefly in a fairly traditional manner, concentrating on features of importance which, in my opinion, Buchholz either neglected or underemphasized.[17] Then, I shall offer some evidence, based on an examination of the whole of Worcester Cathedral MS. F. 174, with which we can begin to differentiate between the language of the scribe and that of the poet, and begin to achieve thereby a clearer appreciation of our version's linguistic texture.

Phonology

Stressed Vowels

1. OE ĭ remain substantially unchanged.
2. OE ĕ remain substantially unchanged, though rounding to ø̆, written *eo*, is found in some forms.
3. OE æ̆ are spelt *e* or *æ* for the most part, indicating narrowing to ĕ. æ, the i-umlaut of Prim. Ger. ā, appears more often as *æ* than *e*, while æ from Prim. Ger. æ occurs more frequently as *e*. The usual form of OE *wæs* is *was*, however.

4. OE ā̆. ă appears as *a* except before nasals where the presence of *o* indicates the WML development to ŏ. The *a/o* variation in spelling, and the dominance of *o*, shows that OE ā has moved to ō, also a WML feature. *eo* occurs for OE ā in *greoneþ*, A25, *greoning*, A15, perhaps in *weowe*, A7, and variations of *seoruhful*, as well as in the nominative plural demonstratives *þeo*, beside *þa*, and *þeos*. Professor Stanley's view is that *eo* simply cannot represent a phonological reality when it stands for OE ā in the Caligula *Brut* (1969); rather, its presence must represent an archaizing tendency on the part of the scribes or of Layamon himself. He attributes the same tendency to the "tremulous hand," but in *SA* there is evidence that *eo* does indeed represent the reflex of OE ā. In A15 and A25 occur the apparently rhyming pairs *greoning/woaning* and *greoneþ/woaneþ*. In both roots the vowel derives from OE ā: therefore, we must conclude that for the poet the words served as exact rhymes. *oa* is a common ME representation of ō from OE ā and it seems inescapable that, given the *oa* spellings and the etymological similarity from OE, *eo* must have represented for the scribe, if not the poet, the sound ō; otherwise he would be guilty of falsifying a rhyme in his exemplar, which seems a very unlikely error. It is possible that ǿ, the monophthongization of OE ēo, was very close in sound to ō, the WML development of OE ā: there may, in fact, have been some overlap of the phonemic boundaries in the scribe's idiolect. If this were the case, *eo*, a living digraph in the orthographic system of the WML in eME, could legitimately serve for ō, just as *o*, the usual graph for ō, could serve for ǿ (see nos. 10 and 11 as well as the analysis of scribal features below).

5. OE ō̆ retain their OE quality, by and large.

6. OE ū̆ appear from spelling to be unchanged.

7. OE ȳ̆ retain rounding and are spelt *u*, for the most part. In the neighborhood of palatals, unrounded forms prevail, e.g., ȝet, C2, G7, etc., ȝerde, A33, *chirche*, E25. Exceptional in this regard is the unusual ȝeoddede, G21 (see the explanatory note for this line).

8. OE ĕa. Except following certain consonant groups, OE ĕa appears to have moved through æ̆ to ĕ. Before r-groups, *ea* is usually written, *e* occurring occasionally. Before l-groups, nWS lack of breaking is the rule: *a* is written except before the lengthening group -*ld* where *o* appears, in keeping with the movement of ā to ō. Before palatal j, *e* plus glide (*ei*) is usual; following palatal *sc*, *ea/e* spelling variation is the rule, though all present forms of "shall" show nWS simple back vowels, e.g., *schal*, A9. Remarkable examples of OE ĕa are *markes*, B6, which shows

a lowering characteristic of more northerly and easterly dialects, and *heldan*, C35, which shows ẽ from æ from broken WS ĕa instead of the usual *o*.

9. OE ēa, for the most part, has monophthongized to ẽ, as the spelling variation *ea/e* attests.

10. OE ĕo appears most often as *eo* before r-groups and *o* following palatals. Before palatals, *i* is the rule. *u* from lWS ȳ appears in forms of the word "self" as well as in mutated *afursed*, E6 and 37.

11. OE ēo is primarily written *eo*, though, before lengthening r-groups, *o* sometimes appears. Before palatals, ēo shows smoothing to ē and a further movement to ī: *driæn*, B36, beside *dreiʒen*, G6, and *lihte*, C48.

12. Before the palatals j and h, OE short and long front vowels, including the diphthongs ĕa and ĕo, are generally written *ei*. æ̃ do appear as *æi*, however. j, spelt *ʒ*, may or may not follow this new diphthong; h, spelt *h*, always does.

13. Before the OE voiced velar fricative, written *ʒ* in OE, the OE back vowels retain their traditional spellings. This fricative has apparently joined the w phoneme and is primarily written *w* in *SA*, though *u* occurs occasionally. Before the voiceless velar fricative, which has become an allophone of h, OE back vowels are primarily written as *ou*, with some variation in *o*. OE back vowels before w, in words in which syllable shift had occurred, are written variously *ow, ou,* and *ouw*.

Low-stress Vowels

14. Phonological levelling of unaccented vowels to schwa, written *e*, is very much in evidence medially and finally. Nevertheless, many old spellings remain, particularly *a* when covered in an inflectional ending. The infrequent presence of *æ* in the same position may be owing to deliberate archaistic spelling on the part of the scribe, as Professor Stanley believes (1969); however, it may also be evidence of back spelling of *e* to *æ* in the scribe's exemplar. For the most part, prefixes maintain their OE forms, though *ʒe-* has become *i-*. Shortening in low-stress words is graphically attested in *þauh*, G27, 28, from OE *þeah*, and in *me*, D10, beside *mon*, A33. Weakening after accent shift is apparent in *hore* and *ham* from OE *heora* and *heom*; *heom* also occurs. Parasiting is largely confined to cases where r or l precede the velar fricative written *w* or *h* in *SA*, e.g., *seoruhfule*, A8, beside *seorhful*, A15. Loss of medial i has occurred in *chirche*, E25.

Consonants

15. The consonants do not show a great deal of change from OE. Doubled consonants occur medially, but finally only -ll occurs: *all*, Gb and 13, and *iwill*, G3. Some unsteadiness is apparent in the case of the fricative θ. It appears for OE d in the forms *iworþen, iwurþen*, F45, 46, and is replaced by d in *lod⟨liche⟩*, C48. Unvoiced t appears for θ once, *mænet*, A7. f occurs finally for θ in *hauef*, G26, a spelling that may indicate an early stage in the movement from θ to the sound written *gh*. þ is written for medial h once, *puþte*, B12. This form may be a scribal error, but many similar spellings occur in *Brut*, particularly the Otho version, perhaps as a result of French pronunciation.

Also important is palatal j. Initially it is distinguished from velar g by writing, i.e., *ȝ/g*. Medially — unless followed by voiceless consonants, especially t — OE j appears to have merged with the preceding tautosyllabic vowel; *ȝ* is sometimes written, sometimes not, e.g., *unheiȝe*, C30, beside *heie*, G40. When followed by voiceless consonants, especially t, OE j is consistently written *h*. It would appear that in this position, as well as finally, OE j has become an allophone of h. In the OE suffix *-iȝ*, however, simplification to ī has occurred; *lutiȝ*, B2, beside *luti*, D28, is the only instance of *ȝ* written finally in *SA*.

Non-Alphabetic Signs

16. *Punctuation graphs.*

The point is used throughout the work to separate verse from verse and line from line, that is, it would appear to be a metrical rather than syntactical sign. The colon (it may, in fact, be a *punctus elevatus*, i.e., ⁊) that appears in A6 does not seem to function differently from the point. At three places in the poem, points are used to separate items of a list, a task for which they were employed in some OE poetical manuscripts as well: *þu were wedlowe · and monsware · and [....] hund inouh*, D47; *þu scalt rotien · and brostnian · þine bon beoþ bedæled*, E9; *heouene · and eorþe · luft · and engles, / wind · and water*, F38–39. And, in at least one instance, it would also appear that points have been used to set off a word of one letter from the surrounding words, probably to achieve graphic clarity: *wendest þu la erming · her · o · to wunienne*, D18.

17. *Tachygraphs.*

In the English lines, a tilde over a vowel is used sporadically to indicate a following nasal, e.g., *into*, B28, *in*, E52. ƥ is used throughout to indicate *þet*, though the word is often written out in full as well. *þ* meaning *þurh* occurs twice, F47, C44, but usually the word is written out in full. *p̷*, meaning *pri-*, occurs three times in Fragment F, in 22, 27, and 31; *pri-* is written out in full in 21 and 32 of the same fragment.

In the Latin lines, a tilde over a letter is used to indicate missing letters that generally precede the marked letter, e.g., *omīa* for *omnia*, F44, *redditī* for *reddituri*, E41, and sometimes follow it, e.g., *eternū* for *eternum*, E46, particularly if the following letter is a nasal. *p* stands for *pe* in F2. *ꝑ* for *pro-* in E41. A stroke over a letter indicates missing following letters, e.g., *q̄* for *qui*, E50, *t̄* for *-ter-* in *eternam*, E50, and *p̄* for *-pri-*, as in the English lines, in *propriis*, E41.

18. *Word signs.*

There are two word signs used throughout the work, both for the conjunction "and" — *⁊* and &. The word is never written out in the English lines. In the Latin lines, *et* appears in F44 and E50; & is written in F2 and 49.

Grammar

19. *Nouns*

1. *Gender.* Levelling of vowels in inflectional endings largely obscures OE gender distinction in the nouns themselves; however, preservation of gender in the pronouns (personal, demonstrative, and relative) allows for at least a partial assessment of its survival in the nominal system. Some movement toward natural gender is apparent: neuter *hit* may refer to inanimate nouns which were either masculine or feminine in OE, e.g., *iwill/hit*, G3; plural *wrecches*, G22, beside the OE weak form, *wrecchen*, C23, probably is indicative as well of a tendency toward natural gender. However, examples of grammatical gender also occur. *middenearde/him*, A2, *muþ/hine*, C17, etc., and perhaps *dream/he*, E23, show preservation of the masculine gender in inanimates, while *tunge/heo*, G15, etc., shows preservation of the feminine. *bearn/hit*, A6, etc., and *wif/þet*, A41, reveal the preservation of the neuter in animate nouns.

2. *Case.* (a) Nominative and accusative singular forms cannot be distinguished from one another, nor can nominative and accusative plural forms. As a rule, the singular forms are uninflected or retain a reduced *-e* from an uncovered OE vowel. Exceptional are the feminine o-stem nouns which consistently show unetymological *-e*. The

plural forms in all genders show evidence of the attraction to either -*es* or -*en*, the latter appearing not only with OE weak forms but also with nouns such as *lawen*, G50, and *sunnen*, F11, etc. There is also evidence, however, for feminine o-stem plurals in -*e*. Though a reconstruction, *soule*, E42, is apparently plural, as is *wæde*, B9, and *isceafte*, F47, beside *isceæftan*, A2. A small number of uninflected, ablaut plurals are also found, e.g., *men*, C16, *teþ*, G9, *bec*, F35, etc.

(b) For the most part, genitive singular forms are marked by -*es*, genitive plurals by -*e*. Genitive nouns tend to occur before the nouns they describe, i.e., they may be fairly looked on as attributive adjectives. Exceptional in this regard is *weolan*, B32, and perhaps *feonde*, C12. The use of the *of/æt* periphrasis for the genitive is sparse; it is confined to appearances after the verbs *bidæled* and *birefen*, both of which took objects expressed in the genitive in OE, e.g., A22, B16, E9. When the *of/æt* periphrasis is used, the object of the verb appears in either the accusative or dative case. In E20 and G12, however, *birefen* takes objects expressed with the inflectional genitive.

(c) Dative singular forms are almost all inflected -*e*. The common dative plural form is -*en*; however, there are six examples of plural forms in -*es* after prepositions that in OE and elsewhere in *SA* govern objects in the dative: *mid* five times, E48, F17, 22, G11, 38; *bi* once, B6. These examples seem to show a breakdown in the distinction between the nominative-accusative case on the one hand and the dative on the other. (Of course, -*en* from OE -*um* cannot be distinguished from -*en* by analogy with nominative-accusative forms in -*en*: the loss of a separate form for the dative plural may be more widespread than is apparent.) Nevertheless, dative plural *wurmen*, C28, does occur beside nominative-accusative *wurmes*, B41, etc., that is, a distinct dative plural form has not been lost altogether. The indirect object is expressed once with a *to* periphrasis, E22: *þe ⟨wel⟩ tuhte his hearpe and tuhte þe to him*. Otherwise, the inflectional dative is used. The adjective *loþ*, F17, etc., governs the dative case, as it did in OE, and the verbs *helpen*, C25, and *cwemen*, G21, continue to take objects expressed in the dative.

20. *Adjectives.*

As a rule, only nominative singular adjectives are uninflected. Otherwise -*e* occurs, except in the following cases: genitive singular -*es* occurs twice in strong constructions, E20, G12, and once in a weak construction, F41; genitive plural *alre* occurs three times in superlative constructions, for example, E7, *on alre horde fulest*; strong feminine dative singular -*re*, three times, G1, G26, G46; strong masculine accusative singular *-ne* twice, B19, C4. *wrecche*, G6, may lack *-ne* by analogy with the many similar lines in *SA* in which this word occurs in weak position. Comparative forms are marked by *-re*; superlative forms by *-est, -st*.

21. *Adverbs* are marked by either *-liche* or *-e*. It is interesting to note that *-liche* is never reduced in *SA*, nor does unetymological *-e-* ever intrude between this suffix and the root noun or adjective from which the adverb was formed.

22. *Pronouns*

1. *Personal.* Full paradigms of the forms in *SA* can be found in the Glossary under *ic, þu*, and *he*. There is some variation of form in the accusative and dative third person plural. The close relationship of the feminine and plural forms of pronouns may account for the single accusative plural occurrence of *heo*, A5, beside the more usual *ham*. Alternatively, *heo* may be an archaic form in this case. Also archaic in appearance is *hi*, apparently an accusative plural in both B14 and D22, though the latter instance offers some difficulties. For the variation *heom/ham* in the dative plural, see the discussion of scribal features below.

2. *Demonstrative.* The demonstrative pronoun remains largely intact from OE; for a full paradigm, see the Glossary, *þe*. There is some evidence, however, that the OE system is beginning to disintegrate. In the nominative, accusative feminine singular as well as in the nominative, accusative plural, the analogical and possibly phonological variants *þa/þeo* occur alongside the unetymological *þe*, for example, feminine *þe sowle*, A28, and plural *þe ban*, A21. Also, *þet* can appear before non-neuter nouns, for example, *þet soule*, A9. However, whether *þet* in these instances reveals the emergence of a comprehensive demonstrative form, "that," or the weakening of nominal gender distinction (see no. 19.1) or a combination of both developments cannot be known. In some ambiguous cases, *þet* may, in fact, be a conjunction.

3. *Relative.* *þe* is the most common relative pronoun in *SA*; *þeo* often appears with feminine and plural antecedents, e.g., B43, C39; *þet* appears occasionally for nouns of all genders and for indefinite pronouns, e.g., B27, C34. *þa*, the analogical and possibly phonological equivalent of *þeo*, occurs once, E18, with a plural antecedent. It is clear that gender distinction is beginning to break down in the usage of relative pronouns. In identical lines, feminine *lore* is the antecedent for *þe* on one occasion, G14, and *þeo* on the other, E21. Some evidence of a movement toward distinguishing between animate *þe* and inanimate *þet*, which McIntosh finds in the AB dialect (1947), is also apparent in

SA, e.g., OE masculine *fontstone/þet*, G37, OE neuter *wif/þe*, A41, and *team/þe*, G51.

4. *Other.* The six occurrences of the OE demonstrative *þes* (see Glossary) all conform to OE usage; nominative plural *þeos* may derive from the OE feminine nominative singular form (but see no. 4 above). There are three instances of reflexive pronouns: dative singular *þe sulfen* twice, C27, F28; dative singular *him sulfen* once, F23. Interrogative *hwi, hwui*, occurs three times: B17, D22, G4. The indefinite pronouns that appear are *al, hwo, nammore, nowiht/nouht, mon/me*, and *oþre* (see Glossary).

23. *Numbers.*

Three cardinal numbers occur: *one*, A33, F46, and *seouene*, F40. The single ordinal is *seoueþe*, F35.

24. *Prepositions.*

In form as well as function, the prepositions are largely unchanged from OE. The preposition *on* is still used to indicate more than surface location, i.e., it has not been superseded by *in*: e.g., *on deope sæþe on durelease huse*, B40, E8, and *isæid hit is on þsalme*, G19. *at* apparently occurs twice with the meaning "of," A23, C8, but in both cases there are textual problems. *mid*, which governs the dative or instrumental cases in OE, governs plural forms in *-es* five times, that is, forms which do not appear to be dative; *bi*, which is also associated with the dative or instrumental in OE, governs a plural form in *-es* once (however, see no. 19.2c above). The traditional distinction between motion (accusative) and location (dative) is maintained, by and large; e.g., *in þet eche fur*, E48, i.e., "into the eternal fire," and *on heouene*, G42, i.e., "in heaven."

25. *Verbs.*

While it must be admitted that the amount of evidence is not great, it may still be fairly stated that the OE verbal system, for the most part, survives intact in *SA*. Class II strong *forleosen*, for example, shows full maintenance of the OE ablaut: pret. 1s. *forleas*, G33; pret. 2s. *forlure*, G43; pp. *forloren*, G51. *-i-* of Class II weak verbs is almost always retained. There are two clear cases of verbs shifting from their OE classes: *slepen* has moved from Class VI strong to Class I weak; *ringen* has moved from Class I weak to Class III strong. Most of the unusual verbal forms in the poem are the result of phonological, rather than morphological, change, e.g., *heldan*, C35, beside pret. 1s. *heold*, D21, and pp. *holden*, G32 (see no. 8); *iworþen/iwurþen*, F45, 46 (see nos. 5 and 16).

1. *Infinitives* are usually marked by *-en*. *-i-* is retained in OE Class

II weak verbs in all instances but one, *fostren*, D2, beside *fostrien*, G54.

2. *Present.* The inflections are: 1s., uninflected, *-e*, or *-ie* (Class II weak verbs); 2s., *-t*, *-st*, *-est*; 3s., uninflected, *-þ*, *-eþ*; p., *-aþ*, *-eþ*, *-ieþ* (Class II weak verbs); s. subj., *-e*, *-ie* (Class II weak verbs); p. subj., *-en*; prp., strong verbs, *-inde*, weak verbs, *-iende*. Contraction is not the rule, but does occur occasionally. *-i-* of Class II weak verbs is generally preserved. *-ing* occurs twice as the ending for verbal substantives in A15; it does not actually appear with a present participle.

3. *Preterite.* The inflections are: 1s. and 3s., unmarked in strong verbs, *-de*, *-ede*, in weak verbs; 2s., *-e* in strong verbs, *-edest*, *-dest*, *-test* in weak verbs; p., *-en* in strong verbs, *-den*, *-eden* in weak verbs; pp., *i-* or some other prefix and *-en* in the strong verbs, *i-* or some other prefix and *-d*, *-t*, or *-ed* in the weak verbs. The only possible unprefixed strong preterite participle is *rungen*, E27. The combination of *-est* with enclitic *þu*, i.e., *-estu*, does not occur in *SA*; however, the unusual *mostes þu*, E26, may result from a tendency toward such a form. Orthographically archaic *licode*, G14, occurs beside *likede*, E21.

4. Reflexive verb forms appear in B14, D13, E22, and F8. The impersonal verb *þunchen* occurs five times, never with the formal subject expressed. The OE impersonal *licien* occurs three times: twice in relative clauses, E21, G14, with a dative object; once, C40, with the subject expressed and a periphrastic construction, *for heom þin flæsc likeþ*. Impersonal *grisen* occurs once, C18. Only a few subjunctive forms are found in the poem, and they occur in unexceptional circumstances, e.g., *come*, B11, in an object noun clause of a verb of volition; *cume*, E39, in a temporal clause introduced by *ær* and expressed in the present tense. There are many periphrastic constructions involving modal verbs and nonfinite verb forms that are to be construed as subjunctive, however.

26. *Rhyming and Assonant Lines.*

A number of lines in *SA* are composed of verses whose final stressed syllables are either rhymes or assonances. Most of these correspondences are compatible with OE phonology, e.g., *greoning/woaning*, A15, from OE ā (see no. 4 above); *fuse/huse*, B15, from OE ū; *forscutted/fordutted*, E38, from OE ȳ. The wordplay in C27, *þu wurpe cneow ofer cneow ne icneowe þu þe sulfen*, is also based on identical OE sounds: *cneow/icneowe* from OE ēo. In a number of instances, however, the correspondence is not so exact.

1. The apparent assonance of *lif/siþ*, both vowels from OE ĭ, occurs nine times in the poem (see the explanatory note for A29). *wif/siþ*

occurs twice, A41, 43. If, however, the occurrence of *f* for θ in *hauef*, G26, is indicative of some conflation of the f and θ phonemes, then these assonant pairs may be closer to rhyme than they appear (see no. 15).

2. In A23 and D20, OE ȳ may be in correspondence with OE ŭ, *wunne/wunede* and *cunne/icunde*. In D48, 50, and F26, OE ȳ may be in correspondence with OE ĭ, *sunne/wiþine*, *sunne/wiþinne*, and *fullen/wille*. If these are indeed assonant pairs, this would show some division in the development of OE ȳ (see no. 7).

3. If *bowe/howe*, C4, is a rhyme, this would indicate that ŏ in OE *boʒa* had undergone lengthening in order to correspond to OE ō in *hoh*.

4. If it forms an assonant pair with *blisse* in D37, *paradis* must have ĭ.

5. The correspondence of *helewewes* and *sidwowes*, C30, almost certainly should be considered a rhyme, though this appears unlikely from their forms. The first *e* of *-wewes* appears to derive from broken ĕa, the *o* of *-wowes* from unbroken OE ă (see no. 8).

6. In G43, *ʒif þu hit ne forlure   þuruh þæs deofles lore, forlure/lore* probably is an example of consonance only.

Definitive statements about phonology cannot be made on the basis of the comparatively few rhyming words in the poem. In some cases what might be rhyme may, in fact, be consonance, and what might be assonance, simply wordplay.

I have not been able to date the composition of *SA* through any reference to external events or practices. The *terminus ad quem* is the approximate date which Ker (1937) has supplied us for the work of the "tremulous hand," that is, the first half of the thirteenth century—the end of his long career coming perhaps as late as 1250. Certain linguistic features in the text, to be discussed below, seem to point to a somewhat older version of the work than we now possess, and the Englishness of the vocabulary might be used to justify a much earlier date of composition: only *messe*, B23, can be of French origin, and this, in the context, must be considered doubtful. While the dialect of the original work cannot be established with certainty, the dialect of our version is predominantly WML in nature with a sprinkling of SW forms (see, for example, nos. 8, 9, 10 above). We might expect to find this sort of mixture in ME Worcestershire: as Sundby has demonstrated (1964), the dialect boundary separating WML from SW ran through this region. In other words, there is little reason to argue against the view that, by and large, we are dealing in *SA* with the language of the "tremulous hand" rather than that of the poem's author. It would be useful, of course, to know more precisely what specific linguistic characteristics are scribal, and with this in mind I have studied the whole of Worcester Cathedral MS. F. 174, the only complete manuscript in the "tremulous hand," paying particular attention to the reflexes of a select number of OE features in three separate sections of it: ff. 11ʳ-20ʳ, ff. 40ʳ-50ʳ (both in the Ælfric *Grammar*), and ff. 63ᵛ-66ᵛ (*SA*).

A word should be said about the evidence that is to follow. In every category, variant spellings of certain forms occur in OE, and in the case of æ, ȳ and æ̆ before l-groups, these variant spellings often reveal dialectal distinction. For the Ælfric material my method has been to follow the spellings in the Zupitza edition of the *Grammar*, that is, to take lWS as the norm. In the case of æ̆ and ā, no grave difficulties arise. In the case of æ, we must assume that a number of forms recorded below as variants in *e* would, in WML, have been usually spelt *e*, e.g., *þer, were, ded*, that is, forms from Prim. Ger. æ̆. Likewise, a number of forms which show, for one reason or another, ȳ in lWS, would have had variant spellings in *e, i*, etc. in a nWS area such as the WML. Commentary on the evidence will follow. I have made no effort to indicate the precise location in the manuscript of the forms given; in the case of *SA*, the Glossary will provide this information. If a form occurs more than once, it is followed by a number indicating how many occurrences there are; for example, "æfter3x" means "*æfter* appears three times."

OE æ̆

ff. 11ʳ-20ʳ	æ:	æfter3x, æker-, ærest, æt, cræftca, fæder, fæȝernesse, stæfifeiȝe, þæs3x, þæt, (beside þet and frequent þ), wæstm-2x
	e:	creft-4x, efter5x, etform, feste, festhouel, heueþ, hweþer, kert2x, leswe, olekunge, reil, irimkrefte, stefifeiȝe, stepe2x, þes2x, iþeslic, þet (beside þæt and frequent þ), unþeslic, welhreow
	a:	habbe, hafþ, haueþ, hwas, hwat4x, nafþ, naueþ2x, was, water
ff. 40ʳ-50ʳ	æ:	afæstan, æfter3x, æt5x, ætferan, ætgædere, befæste, cræft-2x, dæi, fæder, færst2x, fæstniende, frætwiȝe, hæfde2x, hæfþ, hræd-4x, hwæt, ilæsw-2x, mæi, mæinþrunesse, næfþ3x, olæce, ismæcche, stæpe4x, þæt (beside þet5x, þat, and frequent þ)

e: bestan, -crefte, cweþ3x, fretwiȝe, hweþer, ilecche, stefifeiȝe, þet5x (beside þæt, þat, and frequent þ)

a: at, dai7x, farþ, habbe, hafþ2x, haueþ2x, hwat3x, mai4x, naueþ, salmærie, þat (beside þæt, þet5x and frequent þ), was2x

o: hwonne5x

SA   æ: æt2x, æfter, -fæder-3x, gæder-5x, goldfæten, hæfd-, mæi, sæiþ3x, isæid2x þæs10x, wæs

e: creft, efter6x, et, feire2x, heuedest4x, messe, nenne, nes, seiþ4x, -seid-4x, þet12x (beside frequent þ)

a: at2x, dai, hafd-, hauest4x, haueþ5x, nafst2x, was20x, water2x

other: leiȝe, nis

WS æ

ff. 11ʳ-20ʳ   æ: æffre, æht-2x, ælc-3x, ær, ærfrumþe, dæle, gælsa, næren, onræs, ouæt, tæle, widsæ

e: adrefde, clene, -del-15x, eihte, eiþer8x, enne2x, foreseide, geþ8x, keie, lennesse, imene, mest, nelde, redeþ, iseid, speche, techeþ, þer3x, þere20x, uniþwere, wei-3x, weren

other: iferlaihte, þeoles

ff. 40ʳ-50ʳ   æ: æfen, æfre3x, æȝhær, ælc-3x, ær4x, ærest, ærne, ærren, ætslide2x, broþorædenne, cwæþon, -dæl-8x, færunge, forgæge, ihwær, -læche-3x, ilær-5x, iliþwæcce, lustbære, -mæle4x, imænliche, mærsie, mæþful, mæþliche2x, næȝe, næfre3x, ræd-3x, ræt, sæide, sæl 3x, iswæsl-, tæc, tæch-, þære24x, wiperæde, wæte

e: -del-3x, ef(f)re2x, eiþer3x, ene, geþ6x, helend, nenne3x, red-7x, iseid, teche, weie, were, weren2x

a: hwar4x, hware

SA   æ: æf(f)re6x, aræreþ, ær10x, belæfed, -dæl-5x, flæsc-2x, forlæten, grædi-2x, ilærede, ilæsteþ, -mæne-4x, næffre, tæcheþ, þær-7x, þære4x, wæde, wære e: arerdest, beden2x, bilefdest2x, clei-2x, clene2x, clensien, -dede-7x, -delen-4x, efre10x, eni, geþ, gredi, leden, ilered, ilest-2x, lettest, mest, nefre7x, ofermete, offered, reste, resten, sete-2x, sleptest, þer-5x, unleþe, were 13x, weren5x

other: æihte, betæiht, hwar5x, keiȝe

OE ā

ff. 11ʳ-20ʳ   a: axest, hwa2x, hwa, hwam, lateow, manfull, na, nãmo(re)5x, irade7x, -stan, twã4x, þã6x (beside þen30x)

o: aloten, also21x, goþ4x, hod-16x, holie, horung, hotene2x, hoteþ, lom, lorþeaw-2x, monfull, no, nõ, non2x, none, on-35x, orleas, orwurþe, oþswara, owene, so32x, ston-2x, -ston, tocna, itocneþ3x, tocnowen, itocnunge, two-10x, werhod

eo: þeol4x, þeos12x

oa: moa

ff. 40ʳ-50ʳ   a: axung, ia2x, la, ma, na, nãmore3x, nates, twam, þã2x, þam

o: also17x, blokienne, brod, cnowen, go2x, goþ6x, hod-6x, hol, holi, hom5x, ihoten(e)6x, hotheortnesse, hwo, lor-2x, mo, more, no, nohwar, non3x, none, on2x, one5x, ones, oþ, so39x, tocne, itocneþ, itocnunge, two3x, þo8x, woclicost, wost, wot

eo: þeo25x, þeos18x

other: auht, nout2x, nouþre

SA   a: a, aȝan, ahte2x, ban, facen2x, fakenliche, la, lac, ma, -mare, nãmore2x, þa8x, wa

o: also4x, bon-4x, blowen, cloþes2x, cold-3x, idol2x, -foh, -gon-6x, gros, holi6x, holiwatere, ihoten, hwo, loc, lodliche, lore5x, loþ8x, mo, monsware, more3x, nãmore2x, non, none4x, nouht, nowiht2x, o, ohtest, one2x, one, orlease2x, oþes, owen, so 16x, -ston, swo, sor-19x, soule-12x, stirope, swopen, þo, unhol, wo2x, woneþ, woniende, wot

eo: greon-2x, þeo 13x, þeos, ?weowe

    other: onȝean, weasiþ, woan-2x

lWS ẏ

ff. 11ʳ-20ʳ   u: awurdnesse, æfrumþe, icunde, cunn/kunn16x,
                  endeburdesse, hwulces, lutel, muchel 2x, imundi,
                  orlute, put, rune, rure, iscrut, sulf21x, surwan,
                  þulliche, uncusti, wrums (OE wyrm), wrusm (OE
                  wyrm)

              i: andȝit, first, girla, ȝif5x, hwilc-9x, ilk-21x, six,
                  swift, itwisan, underȝitten, wiln

              e: beli, -helle, welle

            eo: cleop-4x, tweoneþ

        other: blase, euenlotte, fall, healt, ihwlc

ff. 40ʳ-50ʳ   u: beburie, betwux, -burd-2x, ibureþ, -buri-2x,
                  cnutte, cumaþ5x, cumþ, icund, cunn/kunn16x,
                  cust-3x, dude3x, fulie, fulleþ, furhtu, ifurn,
                  ȝursten2x, hwuder, hwulc-2x, lust-3x, lutel,
                  mæinþrūnesse, muchel 2x, nulle, ouerluttrie,
                  ougulde, runel, iscuppe, scuppend, sulf,
                  sulfwilles2x, sund-3x, sungie2x, swulche, swuþ-3x,
                  þulliche2x, þwur, þwurnesse, ufele4x, umbecluppe,
                  wurche, wurs

              i: andȝite, flihþ, ȝif8x, ȝiue, hicge, ilke, king, micclū,
                  niþer-4x, six2x, twinunge, þider2x

              e: ibecnie, bern-2x, cherre, formelte, ȝet7x, -selt-3x,
                  werme2x

            eo: eorne, ȝeorne, neoþemest, seoþþen5x, þreo-

        other: hlote, salte, seorteþ, soþþen2x, warie, warmie

SA   u: afursed2x, burewen, icunde2x, cunne, dreamþurles,
                  dude, fordutte3x, forscutted, frumþe, -fulle-5x,
                  grulde, guldene, gultes2x, huned, luft, luti-2x,
                  muchel-3x, murie, nulleþ3x, ruglunge, sulfen3x,
                  sunfule, sunne-10x, tuhte3x, þuncheþ2x, ufel,
                  wunne, wurchen, wurme-6x, wurst2x

              i: chirche, ȝif2x, ȝiuen, king, kinemerke

              e: amerdest, bidernan, biȝete, erming2x, ȝerde, ȝet6x,
                  scerpeþ

eo: ?ȝeoddede, seoþþen6x

Prim. OE ǣ before l-groups

ff. 11ʳ-20ʳ   a: al-19x, alderman, also21x, befalleþ, burhaldor, halue, walles

o: bold, holdeþ3x, olde2x, -tolde-2x, -uold-39x

e: wellæs

ff.40ʳ-50ʳ   a: al-20x, also17x, halue7x

o: iholde, isold2x, -uold-4x

ea: ealra

e: seld-3x, welle

SA   a: al-37x, also4x

o: hold2x, holden2x, molde, monifolde, nolde-6x, scold-8x, wolde-3x, iwold

e: diȝelliche, formelten, heldan

eo: sceold-2x

This survey of forms reveals a number of things. First of all, it is clear that the scribe was neither a mirror copyist nor a wholesale "translator" of his exemplar.[18] The archaic treatment of OE æ in ff. 40ʳ-50ʳ, where *æ* spellings prevail decisively over the *e* spellings that predominate in the other two sections, shows an ability (exhibited for whatever reason at this point in the manuscript) to preserve older spellings (see no. 3 in the discussion of Phonology, above). This conservative tendency is also apparent in the treatment of some other linguistic features in this portion of the manuscript, particularly inflectional endings. But set against this potential to preserve old spellings, probably those of the exemplar, we find a clear tendency toward regularization of certain phonological and lexical features. Even in the more conservative ff. 40ʳ-50ʳ, for example, lengthened, unbroken *o* appears before *-ld* and unbroken *a* before other l-groups; OE ā is predominantly written *o*; the third person plural present form of "to be" is *beoþ*; the third person nominative plural personal pronoun is primarily *heo*, the demonstrative *þeo* — all of these forms recur throughout the manuscript. In the case of at least three words, metathesized forms have been substituted for OE originals: *nelde* for *nædl*, *kert* for *cræt*, and *bold* for *botl*. In the case of at least two words, wholesale substitution has taken place: *steel* for *isen* and *euere* for *symle*.

It seems reasonable to assume that these and other linguistic features, which appear with regularity throughout the manuscript, represent the language of the scribe. (Whether or not all of them exist in the manuscript because of scribal "translation" is a less easy question to answer: some may have been present in his exemplar.) We can say with assurance, for example, that, for the "tremulous hand," OE ā has become ō (see no. 4 in Phonology), because of the preponderance of *o* spellings throughout F. 174: a ratio of roughly five *o* spellings to one *a* spelling is about average. The movement of OE æ to ɛ is less firmly established, because of the remarkably conservative spellings in ff. 40ʳ–50ʳ; it is instructive, however, that in two of the metathesized forms mentioned in the previous paragraph, *nelde* and *kert*, OE ǽ appears as *e*. Noteworthy in regard to the treatment of æ is that the common forms *was* and *haueþ* most often show *a*. OE ȳ is usually written *u*, but in the Æfric material, at least, other spellings, especially unrounded *i* and *e*, occur in the neighborhood of palatals, liquids, and nasals: there appears to be some unsteadiness in the development of this sound, though infrequent is the sort of variation in spelling of a single word that one finds with OE æ (see examples on pp. 18–19). Also appearing with remarkable consistency throughout the manuscript is *o* before *-ld* and *a* before the other *l*-groups, indicating lack of breaking for Prim. OE ǽ and, in the case of the *o*-spellings, lengthening.

Certain words that occur frequently throughout the manuscript can probably be attributed to what Benskin and Laing (1981) call the scribe's "repertory." The metathesized and substituted forms mentioned above likely belong here. Among the personal pronouns, singular *he*, *hine*, *his*, *him*, *heo*, and *hit*, the OE forms in other words, all occur, though only *he* and *hit* appear often. Plural forms are more common:

ff. 11ʳ–20ʳ   nom. heo21x, hi2x
                acc. —
                gen. hore11x
                dat. hā3x

ff. 40ʳ–50ʳ   nom. heo22x, ?he, ?hoe
                acc. —
                gen. hora8x, heora
                dat. ham

SA   nom. heo28x
              acc. heo, ham5x, hi2x
              gen. hore7x
              dat. ham5x, heom6x

Clearly nominative plural *heo* and genitive plural *hore/hora* predominate. Among the demonstrative pronouns, nominative masculine singular *þe*, accusative masculine singular *þene*, dative masculine singular *þen*, and nominative plural *þeo* occur almost without exception. The more modern spelling of ff. 11ʳ–20ʳ shows *þes* for *þæs*, *þere* for feminine singular *þære* and genitive plural *þara*, and *þen*16x beside *þā*5x for the dative plural. The more traditional ff. 40ʳ–50ʳ has feminine singular *þære* (as does *SA*), genitive plural *þera*, *þerœ*, and *þæra*, and dative plural *þam*4x and *þā* (genitive and dative plural forms do not occur in *SA*). The nominative plural of the other demonstrative pronoun, that is, "these," appears as *þeos* throughout the manuscript. Among the common words found almost without exception in a single form are *ȝet*, *ȝif*, plural *beoþ*, *sulf*, *ilke*, *also*, *so*, and inflected *alle*.

This clearer designation of what we can call scribal in F. 174, though by no means complete, also enables us to see with more clarity what in the language of our only version of *SA* is nonscribal, if not authorial. The form *swo*, B4, for example, I have not found in the Ælfric material. *ȝeoddede*, G21, is remarkable because of its unusual paleographic form, *ȝeoddde*, the rounded vowel, where one might expect either *e* or *i* from OE ȳ, heightens its peculiar nature. These individual forms, and others such as *lutiȝ*, B2, and *licode*, G14, probably derive from a previous copy of the poem in which orthographic conventions more archaic than those of the "tremulous hand" prevailed.

The reflexes of WS æ and lWS ȳ have the potential to reveal with more precision the phonological character of both the scribe's and the poet's dialect. In the WML we might expect the reflex of Prim. Ger. æ to be *e*, and this form does, in fact, predominate. All seven forms of the word "deed" in *SA*, for example, show *e*. But other forms containing Prim. Ger. æ reveal variation in spelling, e.g., *grædi/gredi*, *wære/were*. One possible interpretation of this variation is that the *æ*-forms survive from an older version of the poem written in a language that must ultimately have derived from WS where Prim. Ger. æ remained æ. However, the evidence may also indicate a tolerance for *æ*-forms on the part of the scribe, a tolerance which in turn may indicate the lack of a clear phonological distinction between the two kinds of OE æ in his idiolect.

In the case of lWS ў as well, words such as *ʒet, ʒif,* and *seoþþen* point to a dialect of nWS origin, but words such as *sulf, muchel,* and *swuþe,* which are clearly part of the scribe's "repertory," must derive from WS. The consistency with which the scribe spells the reflex of æ̆ before l–groups in the Ælfric material reveals that he was sensitive to what was probably a clear phonological distinction between his own idiolect and what he found in his exemplar. The mixture of forms in the case of æ from Prim. Ger. æ and lWS ў probably should be seen, therefore, as reinforcement of our understanding of ME Worcestershire as a dialectal frontier area where WML and SW forms could coexist.

One other phonological feature is remarkable — the *eo* spelling for OE ā. In the Ælfric material the nominative plural demonstrative pronouns are *þeo* and *þeos* throughout, as they are in *SA.* However, I have found no other instance of *eo* for OE ā in the *Grammar* or *Glossary,* and it could therefore be argued that these two forms reveal not a phonological reality but rather a development by analogy with feminine singular forms, a development evident elsewhere in transitional texts. In *SA,* on the other hand, *eo* also appears for OE ā in *greon*–2x and perhaps in *weowe* and *seoruhful*6x as well. This spelling may reveal a deliberate, archaizing tendency on the part of the scribe, as Professor Stanley believes (1969); however, there is some evidence to suggest that *eo* for OE ā may, in fact, represent a phonological reality in this scribe's dialect (see no. 4 in Phonology, above).

The Ælfric material, by its very nature, offers limited evidence about morphology. In regard to the personal pronouns, it is interesting to note that dative plural *heom,* which alternates with *ham* in *SA,* does not occur in either ff. 11^r–20^r or ff. 40^r–50^r. Where it is found, therefore, it may well represent the language of the exemplar. In the Ælfric material inflectional endings are quite variable: for dative plural nouns, for example, they range from *-ū,* through *-am* (once), *-an, -en,* to *-es* (occasional). In *SA* only the last three of these occur, and *-an* appears only once. If we assume that the apparently random preservation of older endings in the Ælfric material would also be reflected in *SA,* if its exemplar contained such endings, then the fact that only relatively modern forms are found in the poem may indicate that they predominated in the exemplar as well. It seems possible that the evidence for the maintenance of grammatical gender in the poem (see no. 19.1 in Grammar above) reveals authorial rather than scribal usage; the instances in which feminine o-stems form their plurals with *-e* are probably authorial as well (see no. 19.2a, above).

It is hazardous to guess about dialect and date for the original version of *SA*. The consensus among previous commentators is that the poem is SW or SWML from the last half of the twelfth century. Only Hall argues for a "Middle South" provenance; he believes the original dates from the first half of the thirteenth century.[19] The above information leads me to believe the scribe's exemplar, at least, represented a more archaic version of a dialect not too different from his own.

PROSODY

In his edition of *SA*, Buchholz attempts (pp. lxii–lxxiv) to categorize the English lines of the poem in the following manner: A i. lines with alliteration, but no end-rhyme (subcategorized according to number and position of alliterating elements); A ii. lines with alliteration and end-rhyme; A iii. expanded lines; B i. lines with end-rhyme, but no alliteration; B ii. lines with neither end-rhyme nor alliteration; C. short lines, that is, three unaccompanied half-lines, one of which has been eliminated from this edition (see explanatory notes for A27–28), two of which, A19 and G41, still remain. He lists many examples under each heading. However, although he strives for only a basic descriptive analysis, Buchholz acknowledges that a number of lines in the poem do not fit neatly into these reasonable categories. And his method raises other problems: for example, at what point does rhyme shade into off-rhyme and off-rhyme into consonance? Or, to what extent do elements that would not bear alliteration in earlier OE verse alliterate in *SA?*

Prosody in *SA,* like so many other aspects of the poem, is a vexed issue, though in this case the difficulties of analysis extend to other metrical and quasi-metrical compositions of lOE and eME origin: for example, the rhythmical prose of Ælfric, Wulfstan, and other homilists, the *Brut,* the Katherine group, and so forth. N. F. Blake (1969) calls these works examples of "rhythmical alliteration"; Angus McIntosh (1982) calls them "metrical structures"; Derek Pearsall (1977) locates them along a "continuum of alliterative writing": the terminological problems reflect the analytical ones. The relation between these works and "classical" OE verse,

to use McIntosh's term, has not struck many observers as being particularly close, though some relation there must be.[20] Rather, the OE
prosodical antecedents of *SA,* at any rate, seem to be not *Beowulf* or
Cynewulf but Ælfric and Wufstan. In fact, my impression is that, in
terms of rhythm, *SA* differs only slightly from the most rhythmical
passages in Wufstan and Ælfric. Why *SA* is usually thought of as verse
and Wulfstan, for example, as prose probably has less to do with the
quality of the lines than with the consistent production of them from
one end of *SA* to the other. This relation to OE rhythmical prose will
be more fully developed below within a discussion of what I believe is
the rhythmical nature of the work.

Though usually categorized as an alliterative work, *SA* is, as Buchholz's
efforts make clear, a prosodical hybrid. A clear majority of its English
lines divide into half-lines which are linked together by alliteration on
one or more of their stressed syllables. Two stresses per half-line is the
rule; occasionally three occur. However, approximately forty-five lines
in *SA* show half-lines joined by rhyme, off-rhyme, or some other
phonological device acting on the last or, in the case of inflected forms,
next to last syllable. Sometimes this method of linkage is accompanied
by alliteration, but usually it is not. Though we latter-day critics (and
perhaps the poets of "classical" OE and of fourteenth-century alliterative
verse, as well) might find this particular combination of rhyming and
alliterative lines indecorous, even annoying, it would appear that the
writer of *SA* — and the writers of other "alliterative" works from the period
of transition between OE and ME — found the combination both pleasing and useful. We cannot avoid judging the verse of *SA* from the perspective of its more august alliterative relatives, but to insist on that perspective
alone is to insist on seeing the work for what it is not. For this reason
I shall try primarily to examine the verse of *SA* as its writer might have
perceived it.

Let us begin with the "rhyming" lines. The number of such lines given
above, forty-five, is somewhat misleading, because it includes all occurrences where a rhymed, or off-rhymed, pair recurs in what is substantially the same line; *lif — siþ* occurs eight times; *agon — fornon,* three times;
efre — nefre, twice; *sunne — wiþinne* (?), twice. The recurrence of these pairs
offers one clue to the use of rhyming lines in the poem. On each occasion when the *lif-siþ* pair, or the *agon–fornon* and *efre–nefre* pairs occur,
they halt the progress of the description in the alliterative lines; often
they also signal a modulation in the focus of the work. In other words,
the poet seems to be employing at least some of his rhyming lines to

delineate structural changes in his poem. This use of rhyming lines and of recurring lines, rhyming or otherwise, is more fully considered in the discussion of Style to follow.

Did the poet of *SA* perceive his rhyming lines to be rhythmically distinct from his alliterative ones? His use of some rhyming lines rhetorically, to accentuate sections of his work, bespeaks an awareness on his part of some difference between them and the surrounding alliterative verse. Further, there is no evidence that rhyming lines could have served as a prosodical alternative to alliteration. And certain of these rhyming lines, e.g., D37–39, resist scansion according to even a very relaxed version of the traditional OE rhythmical types. They seem far more amenable to what we might call an accentual scansion:

$$
\begin{array}{ll}
\text{fŏr}||\text{lórĕn þŭ}|\text{háuĕst}|\text{þĕo écĕ}|\text{blíssĕ} & \text{bĭ}||\text{númĕn þŭ}|\text{háuĕst}|\text{þĕ} \\
 & \text{pár}|\text{ădís} \\
\text{bĭ}||\text{númĕn}|\text{þé ĭs þĕt}|\text{hólĭ}|\text{lónd} & \text{þĕn}||\text{déoflĕ}|\text{þú bĭst ĭ}|\text{sóld ŏn}|\text{hónd} \\
\text{fŏr}||\text{nóldĕst þŭ}|\text{néfrĕ}|\text{hábbĕn}|\text{ĭnóuh} & \text{bútĕn þŭ}|\text{héfdĕst}|\text{ún}| \\
 & \text{ĭfóuh.}
\end{array}
$$

Arguments could be advanced against specific foot divisions and placement of lifts and dips in these lines. What seems inescapable, however, is a four-feet-per-half-line division, each foot comprising two or three visual syllables (elision is possible in some cases). Also remarkable in this particular passage is the tendency for each half-line to be rhythmically identical to its pair, especially in regard to the first two feet. The poet must have been aware that lines such as D37–39, or B17 or E39, stood out from the alliterative verse not only by means of rhyme but also by their distinctive rhythm.

Nevertheless, the poet also employs traditional OE rhythms — falling, rising, or clashing, i.e., types A, B, or C — perhaps as many as eleven times in lines that also contain rhyme, e.g., A25, *þĕo||módĕr|gґeonĕþ ắnd þ(ĕt)|béarn wòanĕþ*, or E49, *béornĕn þĕr|éfrĕ||éndĕ nĭs þĕr|néfrĕ*. Further, alliteration itself occurs in nine lines that also show rhyme, e.g., *heo weren monifolde   bi markes itolde*, B6, or *and mid his reade blode   þ(et) he ʒeat on rode*, B27; and by no means do these nine lines fall into the group that show rhyme and traditional alliterative rhythms. When we examine the rhyming and off-rhyming lines of *SA* as a group, they do not, in fact, form a self-contained unit distinct from the alliterative lines. Rather, they comprise a heterogeneous collection of rhythmic possibilities extending from traditional OE patterns to clearly non-OE ones.

Recently Angus McIntosh has argued for the introduction of two new terms to describe the rhythmic character of what he chooses to call the "metrical structure" of the transitional period:

> ..., I shall use *heteromorphic* to designate rhythmical material in which the basic 'foot' units have a number of different forms (in a manner brought out for Old English by the various classifications from Sievers onward) and in which it is usual for these to succeed one another in no fixed order. *Homomorphic* will designate material where there is only one basic foot-unit and in which (apart from reasonably well defined minor deviations) lines and larger entities are made up of a continuous succession of examples of this unit.[21]

The distinction is a useful one, perhaps particularly when the object of scrutiny is a prosodical hybrid such as *SA*. One might anticipate that the rhyming lines of *SA* would form a homomorphic rhythmic group distinct from the predominating alliterative and heteromorphic lines. But, in fact, as we have already seen, the rhyming lines of *SA* as a group reveal a blurring together of homo- and heteromorphic types. Some of the lines, especially those susceptible to what we have previously called accentual scansion, seem to fall into the category McIntosh designates homomorphic. The feet into which they can be divided, while not rigorously identical to one another, are nevertheless very distant from traditional OE rhythms. With lines such as A25 or E49, however, the poet brings together rhyme, a feature we can associate with homomorphic rhythm, and the traditional heteromorphic rhythms. In his rhyming lines, then, he exhibits a relaxed view of the rhythmically distinctive types McIntosh points out. Is he more strict, rhythmically speaking, in his composition of alliterative lines?

The poet of *SA* may have inherited something of the versemaking techniques of the "classical" OE poets, but prosodically his work is much closer to the alliterative line of *Gawain and the Green Knight* and other fourteenth-century alliterative works than to *Beowulf* or even the lOE *Soul and Body*. While the three most common patterns of alliteration in OE verse — ax:ay, aa:ax, xa:ay — predominate in *SA,* for example, every other conceivable pattern is found as well.[22] Unlike OE, particles and finite verbs appear capable of receiving both stress and alliteration at any point in a verse, e.g., *he walkeþ and wendeþ   and woneþ oftesiþes,* A12, *him scerpeþ þe neose   him scrinckeþ þa lippen,* A18. Also, among the alliterating staves, a number of changes from OE appear: *sc* may alliterate with *s; st, sw,* and (in every case but one) *gr* alliterate only with themselves; palatal *ʒ* does not alliterate with velar *g.*[23]

Looking specifically at rhythm, we find numerous examples of falling, rising, and clashing types among the half-lines of the work, verses which could be denominated A, B, and C, for example:

falling (A)	líf ǎnd|sóulě	A4b
rising (B)	ǎc þǣr bǐþ|sór ǐdòl	A5b
clashing (C)	sǒ þěo|béc sèggěþ	F35b

The two other characteristic OE verse rhythms, however, types D and E, are virtually absent; and what is apparently another rhythmic type — one sometimes called rising/falling or B/A because it seems to combine features of those two OE rhythms — is very common, as it is in *Gawain*:

ǎnd\|állě þěo ǐ\|scéæftǎn   þě\|hím tǒ\|scúlěn
ǎnd mǐd\|múchělě\|créftě   þěně\|món hě ǐ\|díhtě

A2-3.[24]

It might be argued that verses such as these fit a new rhythmic pattern which the poet used along with the traditional A, B, and C rhythms to construct his poem, that is, that so-called B/A ought to be given the status of a rhythmic verse-type. The problem with this view is that it introduces into a scheme of basically four-part types a five-part type as a rhythmical equal. In other words, the sum of lifts, half-lifts, and dips in all the traditional rhythmical types, A through E, equal four: /x/x (A), x/x \ (B), x/\ x (C), //x\ and //\x (D), /\x/ (E).[25] In B/A this sum is five — x/x/x. If the rhythmic character of our poet's verses was established by the clear differentiation between lift and dip, as we think was the case in OE, I find it hard to believe that he could have perceived a B/A verse as rhythmically equal to A, B, or C verses. That he could employ such a rhythm alongside the more traditional ones may show, in fact, that his verses were not established solely by a dynamic differentiation between lift and dip.

Rigorous analysis according to the strictures customarily placed on "classical" OE verse is not applicable to the verse of *SA*. However, a less rigorous method adumbrated by McIntosh (1949) and developed more fully by Funke (1962) in their work on Wulfstan's prose can be used to reveal a number of interesting features about *SA*'s prosody. McIntosh himself has more recently advocated the use of this method with verse works, including *SA* (1982). Besides their stressed elements, each of the verses in the poem can be divided into two or three constituent parts: the central portion of the verse containing the low-stressed syllables between the two main stresses, if any such syllables occur; the low-stressed syllables in anacrusis, if any occur; the low-stressed syllables in the cadence following the final main stress, if any occur. Two of these constituent parts — in a metrical context we could use the term "dip" — can be found in almost every verse. It will be apparent that in this method of analysis the measure system of OE prosody is ignored. Also, phonemic resolution, a fundamental feature in the prosodical analysis of OE verse, is not taken into account, even though resolution must have occurred in some forms. The analysis is based on a count of visual syllables; no account is taken of grades of stress.

The typical cadence of the verses in *SA,* as in the rhythmical work of Ælfric and Wulfstan, is /x, for example,

> and alle þeo iscéæftãn   þe him to scúlẽn
> and mid muchele créftẽ   þene mon he idíhtẽ
>
>   A2-3.

Only *sculen* in A2b might be subject to phonemic resolution. Monosyllabic endings, as in both verses in A6, *þ(et) bodeþ þ(et) bearn   þonne hit iboren biþ,* are considerably more common than they are in Wulfstan,[26] but perhaps not quite as common as in Ælfric. The assessment here depends on whether or not rhyming lines are to be considered as a separate group. About fourteen percent of the alliterative lines end in monosyllables; the figure climbs to twenty percent if rhyming lines are included, a figure identical to the one given for Ælfric's rhythmical prose.[27] An examination of cadences in the verses of the poem generally confirms that nominal compounds and nouns with heavy formative suffixes have become, for the most part, words with a single main stress followed by two, three, or four low-stressed syllables, a situation linguistically predictable. Examples are *pineþ þẽnẽ lícãmẽ,* A11b; *þurh sópẽ bíréousũngẽ,* F12a; *õn hólíẽ wísdõmẽ,* F43b; *ímétẽn þínẽ mórþdẽdẽn,* E15a; *〈f〉rõm déaþẽs dímnẽssẽ,* E33a. Alternative scansions from the point of view of OE prosody might be proposed in these and other cases, but they would be unjustified linguistically, particularly in regard to suffixes, and would also serve to swell the already large number of verses in the poem with anacrusis.[28]

Nevertheless, it would appear that some compounds in the *SA* must receive two heavy stresses in order that the verses in which they are found not be deficient. Certain cases are *ẽt þẽn fóntstónẽ,* G37a; *þú háuẽst kínẽmérkẽ,* G41a; *héo wérẽn mónífóldẽ,* B6a; *þínẽ dréampúrlẽs,* E30b.[29] Verse B29a, *ãc þú fẽngẽ tõ þéowdómẽ,* may also be included because of the alliteration on *d* in the off-verse; however, one is tempted to stress *fenge* in this verse as well. In the use of compounds, the writer seems willing to have them pronounced with stress patterns that suit the requirements of a particular verse, though, in fact, no identical compound in the poem receives in one verse two heavy stresses and in another only one. *Þeowdome,* B29a, and *wisdome,* F43b and 48a and E43a may demonstrate this apparent fluidity. The presence of compounds with two significant stresses seems to invite comparisons with "classical" OE verse on the one hand, though they are few in number, and only one, *hellewite,* actually occurs in the ASPR; on the other hand, the number of cadences composed of trisyllabic compounds with one heavy stress negates the validity of comparisons to OE verse where such cadences would not usually occur.[30]

Verse B29a brings to the fore another feature of the prosody of *SA* that concerns the central part of each verse, that is, the low-stressed syllables between the two main stresses. The number of syllables in this part ranges from zero, in verses with clashing rhythm, e.g., *þíné dréampúrlés,* E30b, to six, e.g., *lú⟨þér⟩líché éart þu förlóren,* B35a, and *sóríliché tó híré lícáme,* D17b and E3b.[31] In the vast majority of cases, there are two main stresses in a verse, but in certain instances there seem to be three. It might be argued that in B29a, *ac þu fenge to þeowdome,* the verb *fenge* ought not to be stressed, but, as a rule, finite verbs in *SA* must be stressed along with infinitives and participles. (Auxiliary verbs are problematic; it is often difficult to decide whether they should be stressed or not.) A number of examples of three-stress verses occur in rhyming lines, but some do not, e.g., *för úfél ís þéo wrécché lúfé,* A44a; *þéo sóulé résté önföþ,* F12b; *þurúh hólíé lúfé cristés,* G45b; *héo wúlléþ fréten þíné fúlé hóld,* C41a. Among the examples in which a finite verb probably bears stress are *né héold íc þín⟨é éiȝén⟩ ópéné,* D21a, *déredést cristéné mén,* D29b, and both verses of E11, *brékéþ líp fróm líþé   líggéþ þé bón stíl⟨lé⟩.* In the last three examples, alliteration seems to demand that the finite verb be stressed.

Funke, following McIntosh, remarks that anacrusis in the prose of Wulfstan seems to be compensatory: it almost always occurs when the main stresses of the verse form a pattern like the second measure of an OE B or C verse, i.e., /x \ or /\x; the number of syllables in anacrusis is, for the most part, inversely proportionate to the number of syllables in the rest of the verse.[32] A similar situation exists in the *SA.* Only two verses in the poem that end with a stressed monosyllable lack anacrusis: *éfré má éft,* F18a, and *gódnéssé ánd ríht,* B3a. Verses without anacrusis usually contain a central part, or dip, of three, four, or five low-stressed syllables, e.g., *sóftlíché hé héo ísóm⟨néde⟩,* A5a; *sórlíché ídælén,* A9b; *þínéþ þéné* lícămĕ, A11b; *sĕorŭhlĭchĕ bĕrĕauĕd*, A22b. Verses whose length from the first main stress to the end is seven syllables or longer have only one syllable in anacrusis in nearly every case in which there is any anacrusis at all, e.g., *mĭd sĕorŭwĕn ăl bĕwŭndĕn* A27b; *mĭd clŭtĕs pŭ ĕrt fŏr⟨bŭn⟩dĕn*, F17a. Exceptional is *pŏnnĕ pĕ lícămĕ ănd pĕ sówlĕ*, A28a, with trisyllabic anacrusis. Verses whose main part is six syllables in length generally have one syllable in anacrusis and sometimes two, if anacrusis occurs, e.g., *ănd ăttĕrnĕ bĭhíndĕn*, G17b; *nŭ hĕo wŭnĭĕþ ŏn éorþĕ*, D24a. If the main part of a verse contains five syllables, anacrusis occurs frequently. About half the time the anacrusis in this case is monosyllabic; di- and trisyllabic examples are also frequent, e.g., *hĭm déauĕþ þă ærĕn*, A17a; *ănd mĭd mŭchĕlĕ cré⟨ftĕ⟩*, A3a; *ănd pĕnĕ sĕorŭhfŭlĕ síþ*, A8a. Verses whose main part contains four syllables occasionally have one syllable in anacrusis, but two or three syllables are much more common, e.g., *ŏn déopĕ sæpĕ*, B40a; *þ⟨ŭrh⟩ þæs déoflĕs lórĕ*, E21a; *fŏr pínĕ fŭlĕ sŭnnĕ*, G5a. Verses whose main part is only three syllables in length always have anacrusis and rarely only one syllable. Two syllables in anacrusis are usual in such verses; three or four syllables are common, e.g., *þŭrh sópnĕ scrĭft*, F10a; *sŏ þĕo béc séggĕþ*, F35b; *ăc þær bĭþ sór ĭdól*, A5b; *pŏnnĕ hĭt ĭbórĕn bĭþ*, A6b.[33]

I believe that this relation shown to exist between the number of syllables before and after the initial main stress in the verse is crucial to our understanding of the rhythmical nature of *SA*. No strict pattern emerges, but my reading of the evidence is this: while the dynamic relation between lift and dip was undoubtedly important in the establishment of each half-line's rhythmical character, duration — the amount of time needed to utter the half-line — was also a rhythmical factor. Some of this time may have been occupied by the length of vowels, particularly in stressed elements, but syllables in anacrusis (perhaps pretonic syllables would be a better phrase) often provided another means of filling out the half-line. The poet must have possessed a sense of minimum and maximum duration for a typical verse; in terms of visual syllables, however, the range seems quite large: as low as four, as high as ten. I believe the poet had a stronger sense of the relation between the two half-lines of each long line, a relation I would describe as roughly isochronous. Where one verse is short, for example, four syllables, its companion is usually four, five, or six syllables, and this relation holds through to the longer verses as well. I have noted above how some rhyming lines show repetition of the rhythm of the on-verse in the off-verse. A similar repetition occurs often in the alliterative lines, at least once, A17-18, with absolute precision in order to accentuate rhetorical balance:

hĭm déauĕþ þắ ǽrĕn   hĭm dímmĕþ þĕ́ éiӡĕn
hĭm scérpĕþ þĕ néosĕ̆   hĭm scrínckĕþ þắ líppĕn.[34]

This consciousness on the part of the poet of a rhythmical similarity between the two verses of the long line, or between all the verses of the poem, does not mean that the rhythm of *SA*'s alliterative lines is homomorphic, by McIntosh's definition. However, it does reveal, to my mind, a movement toward a sameness in rhythm and away from the heteromorphic quality of "classical" OE verse. This tendency toward a standard rhythm provides a framework in which the dynamically peculiar five-part B/A verse can coexist, through durational equivalence, with the traditional four-part verses. And further, it points to a closer rhythmical relationship between the alliterative and rhyming lines than we might perceive if we insist, in particular, on an OE perspective: in other words, the hybrid nature of *SA*'s prosody becomes more understandable.

Why this development would take place is a matter for speculation. Perhaps one solution to the problem of composing traditional alliterative verse in long lines, without the traditional tools, was to strive to achieve balance between the two half-lines in order to give the impression of regular, measured utterance sufficiently distinct from prose that it might be called verse. This solution would certainly allow a writer to avoid the uneven doggerel of some of the *Chronicle* verses. However, it also leads inevitably to a kind of dull sameness in the lines and also, I think, to rhyming lines as well where a phonological device can accentuate the rhythmical similarity between the half-lines. In other words, because a fundamental rhythmical change has occurred, it may be that the effort to write in the traditional manner ironically leads the poet away from the tradition rather than back to it. It remains possible that the poets of transitional verse may indeed have imported the idea of using rhyming lines from Latin or elsewhere, but the implication of the view expounded above is that they were neither as helpless not as hopeless in the composition of alliterative verse as they have often been portrayed.

STYLE

The author of *SA* has not been accorded much praise for his stylistic achievements.[35] He is not, however, quite so artless a poet as it might at first appear. The portrayal of a soul addressing its body after death obviously involves an expanded use of *prosopopoeia,* a rhetorical figure which medieval writers and audiences found particularly fascinating. In the English literature that precedes *SA, The Dream of the Rood* comes to mind as an outstanding example of the use of this figure along with the *Exeter Book* riddles and, of course, the Old English *Soul and Body.* In the context of "body and soul" literature, however, a speaking soul (and a speaking body, in the case of debate) consitutes not so much a rhetorical device as a convention, a fundamental feature of the form, which creates opportunities for the use of certain rhetorical devices while limiting possibilities for the use of others. The author of *SA* avails himself of a number of rhetorical figures and devices in the composition of his poem, and he achieves a style which is distinctive, if not exalted.

The most striking stylistic feature of *SA* is repetition. Though examples of other basic types of rhetorical devices can be found in the work (some of which will be listed below), it is clear that the poet sought to move his readers or auditors, and to convey to them the import of his work, primarily through the repetition of words, phrases, and whole lines. And by examining patterns of repetition, particularly those of significant words, one can understand, to some extent, the compositional strategy or impetus which lies behind the poem. Each of the fragments can be divided into quite clearly defined subsections (not marked in the manuscript) in which the focus of the poet's commentary (in Fragment A) or the soul's address (in Fragments B through G) is accentuated by the repetition of key words and sometimes by other devices, especially kinds of balance and antithesis which are themselves often established by repetition. It seems clear that the poet was consciously employing rhetorical devices to define these subsections of his work: the repeated elements change with the usually abrupt shifts in focus, and brief sum-marizing statements, often rhyming or assonant lines, usually signal the end of one subsection or the beginning of the next. As a rule, in the soul's address proper, the focus of the subsections alternates back and forth between the current state of the body and its actions in life. However, though one can generally detect these shifts in focus without difficulty, the precise reason for many of the developments in the work remains unclear.

Perhaps the finest passage in *SA* from the point of view of style, and one which displays the characteristics of that style at its best, is the soul's relation of the body's refusal to take communion while living:

Noldest þ⟨u ma⟩kien lufe   wiþ ilærede men,   20

ȝiuen ham of þine gode ... þ(et) heo þe fo⟨re⟩ beden.
Heo mihten mid salmsonge ... þine sunne acwenchen,
mid ⟨ho⟩re messe ... þine misdeden fore biddæn;
heo mihten offrian loc ... leofli⟨che⟩ for þe,
swuþe deorwurþe lac, ... licame cristes; ... 25
þurh þære þu were alese⟨d⟩ ... from hellewite,
and mid his reade blode ... þ(et) he ȝeat on rode.
Þo þu we⟨re⟩ ifreoed ... to farene i(n)to heouene,
ac þu fenge to þeowdome þ(urh) þæs de⟨ofles⟩ lore. ... B20–29.

The first two lines establish the context of what follows: the refusal of
the body to give anything to the priests so that they might intercede for
it after death. One can see a three-fold balancing of B22 and B23: *mid
salmsonge / mid ⟨ho⟩re messe, þine sunne / þine misdeden, acwenchen / biddæn,*
and further, *fore biddæn* in B23 echoes *fo⟨re⟩ beden* in B21, both occurring
in final position in their respective lines. Line 24 repeats the opening
phrase of B22, *heo mihten;* and *loc,* in final position in the on-verse, balances
both *salmsong* and *messe* of the previous lines. The term *loc* also both in-
tensifies the beneficial nature of that which the soul has lost and introduces
the idea of Christ's sacrifice. The beneficial nature of the host is amplified
by 24b, *leofli⟨che⟩ for þe,* and by the phrase *swuþe deorwurþe,* which precedes
the repetition of *loc,* i.e., *lac* in B25, once again in final position in the
on-verse: the host's sacrificial attribute is made explicit in 25b, *licame
cristes.* Lines 26 and 28 balance one another in the on-verse by means
of *anaphora —þu were alese⟨d⟩ / þu we⟨re⟩ ifreoed —*and also, in the off-verse,
through the restatement of the same idea from antithetical viewpoints —
from hellewite / to farene i(n)to heouene. Line 27 introduces the other key
element of the communion sacrament, the blood, with rhyming verses,
blode / rode, so that B26 and 28, besides balancing one another, each follow
a line in which one of the eucharistic elements is named. In B29 the adver-
sative *ac,* the movement from subjunctive to indicative mood, and the
word *þeowdom* in the same position as the participles of opposite meaning from B26 and 28, *alese⟨d⟩* and *ifreoed,* mark the end of the passage,
an abrupt return from what might have been to what is. The citation
that follows signals a shift in focus to the avaricious nature of the body.

This subsection of *SA* is unusual for its density of rhetorical patterning, however. Very different is the following subsection, B30 to the end
of the fragment, one of the most diffuse in the poem. The focus shifts
rapidly from the greedy nature of the body, to the disgust of the friends,
to the grave and worms, to a pair of rhyming lines contrasting the tran-

sitory nature of earthly joy with the eternal nature of suffering in hell. The chiastic pattern of the concluding rhyming lines, B44–45 (*swetnesse, b⟨ittere⟩ / bittere, swete*), the repetition in B40 (*on deope sæþe   on durelease huse*) and the repetition of *lufedest* in final position in the off-verse in both B35 and 43 (*epistrophe*) are all striking rhetorical features, but repetition and other devices are, nevertheless, comparatively rare in these fifteen lines. That this scarcity of repetition coincides with an impression of diffusion and rambling is probably not accidental.

Other passages clearly established by the repetition of key words and phrases are F1–15 on the refusal of the body to confess its sins; F22–33, the amplification of the hedgehog simile expressed in F20–21; C23–37 concerning the house of the living body and that of the dead; C38–50 and D1–8 on the assault of the worms on the corpse; E12–52 on the Last Judgment, particularly towards the end of the passage, and, embedded in it, E17–35 on the ears of the body which refused, while living, to hear the various signals that might have led to salvation and will now hear instead the *heard dom* on Judgment Day.

Among the other particularly noteworthy rhetorical features in the poem are the following:

> 1. *Asyndetic isocolon* with *epanaphora*: A17–21, *Him deaueþ þa æren, him dimmeþ ⟨þa⟩ eiʒen, / him scerpeþ þe neose,   him scrinckeþ þa lippen,* etc.
> 2. *Prosopopoeia*, the personification of death: A11, D44, E38, F16.
> 3. The extended amplification of the hedgehog simile: F20–33.
> 4. Chiastic patterns: B44–45, C48–49, F12–13, F21–22.
> 5. Citation of authority, mostly examples of *oraculum*: C20–22, E40–42, E45–46, E50, ? F2, F43–45, F49, G19–21, G34–36.
> 6. The *ubi sunt* (or *quid profuit*) passage: B4–11.
> 7. *Zeugma*: D12–14, F8–11.
> 8. *Ecphonesis*, i.e., exclamations expressing emotion: A13–14, B19, C10, F4, G3.
> 9. Puns: A23, C27, D20, E51, G51.
> 10. *Isocolon* with intensive alliteration: E33, ⟨f⟩*rom deaþes dimnesse   to drihtenes dome.*
> 11. *Ploce*, i.e., repetition of a word with a new meaning after the intervention of one or a few words: E22, *þe ⟨wel⟩ tuhte his hearpe   and tuhte þe to him.*
> 12. *Polyptoton*: F48, *wisliche/wisdome/wiseþ*; E43, *wisliche/wisdome*; ? B7, *goldfæten/guldene.*

13. *Periphrasis*: most examples, such as *hellewite*, B26, *fonston*, G37, *salmsong*, B22, *heauedponne*, D5, and *bedstrau*, D14, are commonplace; a few, *earfeþsiþ*, A41 and 43, *soulehus*, A22, and perhaps *goldfæt*, B7, may derive from OE verse; *dreamþurl*, E30, and the problematical *qualehold*, B42, may be original coinages of the poet.

Also of interest from the point of view of style are a number of verses and whole lines that occur more than once in the work. Some of these may have a formulaic or quasi-formulaic stature: for example, *on deope seaþe   on durelease huse*, B40 and E8; *þu were leas and luti   and unriht lufedest*, B2 and D28; *wowe domes   and gultes feole / oþre birefedest rihtes istreones*, E19–20 and G11–12, *þurh þæs deofles lore*, B29, E21, G13 and G43; *þe drihten weren loþe* or *he was drihten ful loþ*, E23, G18, and G50. Other repeated lines indicate stages in the development of the work. Variations of the line *ʒet sæiþ þeo soule   soriliche to hire licame* mark changes in the focus of the soul's address: C2, D17, D26, E3, and E36. Whether the repetition of this line was employed to produce a cumulative, climactic effect or to impel forward to a conclusion an already long work is not clear. From the standpoint of style, however, the repeated rhyming or assonant lines are of particular importance in *SA*, for they fulfil not only a structural but also a thematic function by expressing in a brief, almost proverbial, manner summations of the significance of particular passages in the work and of the work as a whole.

The opening twenty-eight lines of Fragment A, portraying the birth and death of a man in general, conclude with the line *þonne biþ þ(et) wrecche lif   iended al mid sori siþ* which separates them from the ensuing description of the preparation of the corpse for burial. Variations of this line recur throughout the work, always in similar pivotal circumstances: C15 between the description of the corpse's new house, the grave, and the portrayal of the worms' assault on the corpse; C37 dividing a revelation of the ingratitude of servants and friends and a most thorough description of the worms' voracity; D9 between the description of the worms' voracity and the cleansing of the body's former residence; D16 between the passage on the cleansing of the house and the soul's description of the body's blindness to its eventual fate; D42 as the culmination of six rhyming or assonant lines all dealing with the loss of eternal bliss and the prospect of eternal woe; F19 between the soul's description of the body's refusal to confess and the simile of the hedgehog; and finally G6 between a passage on the damnation of the soul and one on the particular sins of the body's tongue. The line serves, as Dorothy Everett suggests, as a kind of refrain which "emphasizes a main idea of the poem,"[36] and it works quite successfully as a striking counterpoint to the repetitive and sometimes overlong subsections of the poem it concludes or introduces.

The other repeated rhyming or assonant lines in the poem seem to serve a similar function. The line *so þu weˌ⟨re⟩ mid sunne   iset al wiþinne,* F26, is used to divide vehicle from tenor in the amplification of the hedgehog simile; as D48 it may be viewed either as a summation of the previous five lines on the fractious nature of the living body or as an introduction to the next passage, the last two lines of Fragment D and what has been lost from the beginning of Fragment E. It also "emphasizes a main idea of the poem" as do the lines, *þet swetnesse is nu al agon, þ⟨et⟩ b⟨ittere⟩ þe biþ fornon / þ⟨et⟩ bittere ilæsteþ æffre,   þet swete ne cumeþ þe ⟨næffre⟩.* As B44–45, this pair of lines seems to serve as a conclusion to a rather diffuse subsection of Fragment B, i.e., B30–45; as D40–41, it appears as part of the series of rhyming or assonant lines mentioned above, D37–42.[37] Each of these six lines in itself encapsulates one of the key themes of the poem; together they act as the emotional climax of the work because of their terse quality and their distinctive prosodical form. The poet clearly intended that they should perform such a function and therefore grouped them together in this manner.

The use of repetition and other rhetorical devices, coupled with the employment of rhyming and assonant lines, defines the style of *SA.* However, mention must be made of one feature remarkable for its rarity. The poet tends to avoid words and phrases of description, amplification, and embellishment. Certain terms in keeping with the tone of the work occur with some frequency, for example, *ful* "foul," *luþer* "loathsome," *wrecche* "wretched," and variations of "sorry," "sorrowful," etc. Variations of the latter occur seven times in the first twenty-eight lines of Fragment A; *ful* ("foul") is used three times in E5–7, and in 5 the verb *afulen* occurs as well. For the most part, however, the poet either leaves his nouns undescribed or uses adjectives so worn that they have little impact on the imagination: for example, *dimme eʒen,* A42, *on holie wisdome,* F43, *mid hearde worde,* G22; somewhat stronger are *on durelease huse,* B40 and E8, and *hungrie feond,* C39. As a result, his work takes on a stark, almost ascetic quality. This lack of description may arise from an inability to handle the more intricate rhetorical figures in a metrical context. Certainly the amplification of the hedgehog simile, F22–23, is a labored and unpromising affair. It must be allowed, however, that the poet might have made a conscious decision to reduce the aesthetic appeal of his work by keeping amplification to a minimum, thereby enhancing his overriding didactic purpose. If this was his intention, he has certainly succeeded; there are very few passages in the poem where the manipulation of language is such that one might be seduced into disregarding the moral import of what is being said.

SOURCES AND STRUCTURE

The definitive work on medieval "body and soul" literature remains a *desideratum*. Batiouchkof's 1891 monograph, though flawed and incomplete, is still the most comprehensive study. Hans Walther's magisterial examination of Latin debate literature in the Middle Ages (1920) provides additional information; Rudolph Willard (1935), concentrating on the English tradition, refines our understanding of precisely when, in relation to death, souls might address their bodies; Eleanor K. Heningham, in her edition of the Latin *Royal Debate* (1939), offers a considerable improvement on Batiouchkof's complex theory for the development of the debate format. A useful synthesis of scholarly comment on the theme can be found in Gail D. D. Ricciardi's essay on sources in her collective edition of English "body and soul" poems (1976). However, much remains to be done: even a quick glance at F. L. Utley's bibliography of primary and secondary material on the "body and soul" theme (1972) suffices to reveal both its size and its complexity as an area of study. Although more recent work does not abound, articles by Ackerman (1962) and Bossy (1976) and portions of Rosemary Woolf's *The English Religious Lyric in the Middle Ages* (1968) cannot be overlooked.

For the most part only the existence of *SA* is noted in the abovementioned works; exceptional, relatively speaking, are Ricciardi and Woolf. The only study devoted wholly to the poem is Eleanor K. Heningham's "Old English Precursors to the Worcester Fragments" (1940). Scholars generally agree that the medieval "body and soul" poems have their antecedents in the prose versions of the theme, and Heningham demonstrates at great length that this also holds true in the case of *SA*.

A disturbing number of rash and unconvincing statements mar Heningham's appraisal, but her main contention is sound: the many stylistic
and verbal parallels between *SA* and OE homiletic material point, in
a general way, to the poem's position in an OE tradition of prose writing
(though our knowledge of the Latin backgrounds of OE prose is not so
thorough that we can dismiss a relation to Latin as readily as Heningham
does). Particularly striking in this regard is a homiletic exemplum in
which a damned soul claims to have been *"Godes dohter, and œngla swistor
gescapen, "* a statement which closely parallels G31 of *SA: "Ic was godes douhter,
ac þu amerdest þ(et) foster. "*[38] Also of interest are a few correspondences of
detail between *SA* and the fourth *Vercelli Book* homily,[39] though I believe
Heningham, characteristically, gives the impression of a much greater
degree of resemblance than actually exists. In the explanatory notes I
shall indicate what seem to me to be the clearest correspondences of this
kind between *SA* and other "body and soul" works, English or non-English.

Eager as she is to prove continuity, however, even Heningham does
not argue for a direct relation between any specific OE prose version
of the theme and *SA*. Nor should we expect to find such a relation. As
Rosemary Woolf points out, important changes occurred in the treatment of the theme in the transition from prose to verse, changes of significant structural consequence:

> In the Anglo-Saxon homiletic tradition the meeting of Body and Soul
> was presented as an episode in a long sermon that often contained other
> themes of death. . . . But in the twelfth century a development took place
> in the Body and Soul tradition . . . whereby the theme, instead of be-
> ing a short and isolated anecdote, became a large and flexible
> framework, with all the traditional death themes accumulated into the
> reproach of the soul. This transition was of very great importance, first-
> ly, because through it separate themes became organized into a dramatic
> whole, and, secondly, because the tone inevitably changed, for what
> before had been a rhetorical and objective description of a preacher
> became, when spoken by the soul, entirely filled with a personal vin-
> dictiveness and horror.[40]

The rambling addresses of both a blessed and a damned soul in the fourth
Vercelli homily serve to qualify Woolf's statement to some extent; nevertheless, it is reasonable to say that, as a literary form, the address of
the soul to its body was transformed in the movement from prose to verse.
And it is not surprising, therefore, if we turn our attention away from
particular verbal similarities to larger questions of structure, that the

prose versions, OE or otherwise, fail to provide us with significant parallels. In particular, if we attempt to examine the order of the fragmentary leaves which contain *SA* from the point of view of the poem's structure, we must look instead at the poetic versions of the theme, especially the other English addresses.

A few "body and soul" poems possess a relationship to *SA* which is borne out by clear verbal parallels. The OE *Soul and Body* is not one of these: the similarities indicated by Oakden result from two English poets treating an identical theme, not from direct influence of the older work upon the later.[41] In *The Grave*, however, a short fragment of roughly the same date as *SA*, some lines occur which remind one of specific passages in the longer poem.[42] Especially striking are ll. 9–10 of *The Grave*, *Đe helewaȝes beoð laȝe, sidwaȝes unheȝe; / þe rof bið ibyld þire broste ful neh*, compared to C30–31, *lowe beoþ ⟨þe⟩ helewewes,   unheiȝe beoþ þe sidwowes, / þe rof liiþ   on þine breoste ful ⟨nei⟩h*. Also of interest are B39–40, *ær þu beo ibrouht þær þu be⟨on⟩ scalt, / on deope sæþe,   on durelease huse*, in relation to ll. 5 and 13 of *The Grave*, *Nu me þe bringeð þer þu beon scealt* and *Durelease is þet hus   and dearc hit is wiðinnen*. These verbal correspondences do indicate some connection between the works, but the nature of this relation cannot be precisely determined.[43] Though it certainly does contain many of the features associated with "body and soul" poetry, there is, in fact, no overt proof that *The Grave* should be so classified; nor is its distanced, universal tone typical of an address of a soul to its body.[44] *The Grave* provides very little evidence as to the original structure of *SA:* comparisons between a work of some twenty lines and one of 350 are clearly of limited value.

A more promising analogue to *SA* is the early thirteenth-century *Latemest Day*.[45] Like *The Grave*, it contains a number of significant verbal echoes of the earlier poem: for example, l.76 of *Latemest Day*, *Me wule suopen þin hus*, and D10 of *SA*, *nu me wule swopen þine flor;* l.79, *Nu þe sculen wormes wunien wið–inne*, and C28, *þ(et) þu scoldest mid wurmen   ⟨wu⟩nien in eorþan;* l.45, *Ne schaltu neauer sitten on bolstre ne on benche*, and C26, *ac þu sete on þine benche   underleid mid þine bolster.*[46] The poems also share a number of similar features: an *ubi sunt* passage (*SA*, B4–11, and *Latemest Day*, ll.49–56); a description of the grave and the worms (*SA*, especially C29–50 and D1–8, and *Latemest Day*, ll. 83–92); descriptions of the attitudes of the living to the dead (*SA*, B10–16, B37–39, C16–18, C32–36, and D10–15, and *Latemest Day*, ll. 37–38); an extensive treatment of the theme of judgment and damnation and a portrayal of the Last Judgment (*SA*, E40–52, and *Latemest Day*, ll. 101–24). However, if *SA* served as a primary source for *Latemest Day,* the later poet largely recast the structure, eliminating virtually all references to the creation of the soul and its implantation in the body (found primarily in Fragments F and G of *SA*) as well as the long prologue on the death and burial of the particular man whose soul addresses its body after death (the substance of Fragment A). The later poet also increased the emphasis on the pain of hell concentrated at the end of the work. Facile, to my mind, is Heningham's assertion that the later poem is "little more than a condensed version" of the earlier one.[47] It might be argued, in fact, that the soul's address in *Latemest Day* has become a feature in a larger apocalyptic work: in each of the four manuscripts where it occurs, *Latemest Day* is preceded by the poem *Doomsday.*[48]

This increased emphasis on hell torment and Last Judgment in *Latemest Day* parallels developments in the twelfth- and thirteenth-century "body and soul" debates such as the Latin *Royal Debate (Nuper huiuscemodi visionem somnii),* the Latin *Vision of St. Philibert (Noctis sub silentio),* the French *Un Samedi par Nuit,* and the English *Desputisoun (Als y lay in a winters niȝt)* and *In a thestri stude.*[49] Thematic parallels also occur between *SA* and these debates, both English and non-English. However, address differs significantly from debate in structure, and since it is structural similarity that we seek, the debates prove not especially useful to this line of investigation. Nor do they contain much in the way of significant verbal parallels which might encourage us to explore them further. There is, in fact, no close source or analogue that can serve as a pattern to help us reorder, incontrovertibly, the fragments of *SA.*

One method by which this investigation into the order of the *SA* fragments can proceed, however, involves the comparison of the material on each individual fragment with the features one finds in other poems of the "body and soul" tradition, particularly the English addresses. Some of the features typical of "body and soul" poems have been mentioned already in the brief comparison drawn above between *SA* and *Latemest Day.* An *ubi sunt* passage, for example, is found in all the Middle English and Latin versions of any length, though not in the Old English *Soul and Body.* Descriptions of the grave and worms occur throughout medieval "body and soul" literature. Portrayals of the attitudes of the living to the dead are also ubiquitous, as are descriptions of the body's sins in life (*SA,* B20-21, B32-34, C23-28, D27-36, D45-48, E18-28). Also common to all poems, though of increased importance in the works subsequent to *SA,* are descriptions of hell torment and the Last Judgment. In terms of the relative position of these features in "body and soul" poems, the following conclusions can be drawn: the earlier in the work that the *ubi sunt* passage and the most intense descriptions of the grave and worms occur, the later the work's date of composition;[50] the apocalyptic vision, on the other hand, always occurs at the end of the work followed by a usually brief return to the framing device with which the poem began. This framing device is another typical feature of "body and soul" poems. In *SA* the fullest expression of these features common to the tradition — the *ubi sunt* passage, the description of the grave and worms, and the apocalyptic vision — is found without exception on ff. 64 and 65, Fragments B, C, D, and E in the current order.

Concentrated on ff. 63ᵛ and 66 of *SA*, Fragments A, F, and G of the current order, are a number of features that must be judged unusual from the point of view of the extant "body and soul" material. Some of them do occur in prose versions but, by and large, without the development they receive here. The poem in its present form begins with the end of what must have been a short statement on the creation which served as a preamble to the depiction of the joining of body and soul. Mention is made in other poetic versions of birth and the body's condition at birth, but no version treats as extensively as *SA* the image of birth and the relation of the pain felt then to the pain of death. This concern with creation in general and with the joining of body to soul is amplified considerably on f. 66 where we find passages dealing with the creation of the soul in the context of the universal creation (F34–50) and the marriage of the soul to the body at baptism in which reference is made both to the soul as the daughter of God and to the lost children of the soul and body, probably their good deeds (G27–56). The soul's creation and its familial relation to God are briefly discussed in the OE homilies mentioned above; neither figures importantly in the English poems, however, though brief references to the creation of the soul occur in the Old English *Soul and Body* as well as in the *Vision of St. Philibert*.[51] To judge from what remains, this poet is, atypically, as concerned with the creation and origin of the soul as he is with its judgment and damnation; in subsequent treatments of the theme, as already indicated, the focus tends to narrow to a concern with the later aspects of the soul's career.

Other features that appear unique to *SA* among "body and soul" poems also occur largely on ff. 63ᵛ and 66. On f. 63ᵛ are found the Signs of Death (A16–21) which recur in *Latemest Day* in a shorter form.[52] On f. 66ʳ is found an extended simile in which the body and its sins are compared to the hedgehog and its quills (F20–33); this does not occur in other "body and soul" poems. Near the bottom of f. 66ᵛ there appears a reference to the body "withsaking" the devil (G47), a clear indication that there was a time in the life of the body when it was not so thorough a sinner. This is unparalleled in English "body and soul" literature; as a rule, the soul depicts the body as wholly evil and no mention is made of a time before sin, a time of relative innocence.[53] The devil also plays a unique role in this poem; he actively participates in the corruption of the body (especially E17–29). In the other "body and soul" poems, the devil or devils torture the soul after death, as they do primarily in the prose versions; in *SA* references to the blandishments of the devil and the body's enslavement to him occur throughout. Also found in this work and not elsewhere in the English "body and soul" poems are references to the particular sins of the bodily organs. Primarily singled out are the ears (E17–35) and the tongue (G9–26); the eyes, surprisingly, are not mentioned.

Buchholz, the only editor of *SA* who examines the question of the order of the fragments, argues that the similarity in subject matter between the last lines on f. 64ᵛ and the opening lines on f. 65ʳ renders it likely that f. 65 does, in fact, follow f. 64.[54] In a poem in which repetition is a key stylistic attribute, one must exercise caution in ascribing structural significance to a given feature that may, in fact, recur at almost any point in the poem — almost, it seems, at random — but in this case Buchholz appears to be correct. The description of the worms ravaging the dead body at the bottom of f. 64ᵛ (C38–50) is very specific; it portrays them attacking various parts of the body:

> heo wulleþ gnawen þine bon,
> þeo orlease wur⟨mes⟩.   Heo windeþ on þin ærmes,
> heo brekeþ þine breoste   and borieþ þ(urh) ofer al,
> ⟨heo c⟩reopeþ in and ut: þet hord is hore owen.
> And so heo wulleþ waden   wide in þi⟨ne wom⟩be,
> todelen þine þermes   þeo þe deore weren,
> lifre and þine lihte   lod⟨liche⟩ torenden,
> and so scal formelten   mawe and þin milte.

                                                                C42-9

The same sort of specificity occurs at the top of f. 65ʳ (D5–6): *heo wulleþ wurchen hore hord   on þine heauedponne, / n⟨ulleþ⟩ heo bileafen   þine lippen unfreten.* This may be taken as the completion of the passage begun on f. 64ᵛ. Elsewhere in the poem (e.g., G4, B41, C28, D24) the references to the worms' voracity are more general. Also, on f. 65ʳ we find D3,

⟨*þu*⟩ *scalt nu herborwen   unhol wihte* (i.e., the worms), which is quite likely an ironic reverberation of C23, ⟨*nol*⟩*dest þu on þine huse   herborwen þeo wrecchen,* on f. 64ᵛ, and would, therefore, probably occur after it. If we can accept, then, that f. 65 does, indeed, follow f. 64, we are able to eliminate three possible orders of the final three fragments (65–64–66, 65–66–64, 66–65–64) as well as 64–66–65 in which the separation of the two leaves would significantly disturb the continuity Buchholz noticed. Two alternatives remain: the current order and 63–66–64–65.

No one has come forward in print to offer an explanation of the current order of *SA*. Ricciardi assumes the correctness of the fragments' manuscript order, but she does not undertake a thorough examination of the poem from the point of view of structure; neither does she test the validity of this order.⁵⁵ In fact, commentary on the literary qualities of the work has been sparse. This is not very surprising, however, because no underlying structural principle is readily apparent in the current order of the fragments. To move right to the heart of the matter, there seems little justification after the material on ff. 64 and 65 — the *ubi sunt* passage, the recurring condemnation of the body's activity in life, the grisly description of the worms at work in the grave, the lengthy consideration of the consequences of sin, that is, the eternal damnation that the body and soul will receive on Judgment Day — for the poet to begin an extended passage, interspersed with further accusations, on the soul's role in creation and on the birth and youth of this particular body. Yet this is what the current order presents in the movement from f. 65ᵛ to f. 66ʳ. A defense of the current order would have to rely on a belief in the poet's tendency toward prolixity and confusion. One might explain the material on creation, birth, and baptism as a digression from which the poet must have proceeded to yet another depiction of the Last Judgment before returning to the framing device of the work. One could point to the fact that both in the thirteenth-century *Desputisoun* and in the current order of *SA* the soul's speech begins with an *ubi sunt* passage; one might note that the few references to the soul's origin in the prose versions tend to come near the end of the "body and soul" passages.⁵⁶

Such a defense is problematical, however. The *ubi sunt* passage in the *Desputisoun* does occur at the beginning of the soul's first speech and early in other poems in general; however, such a passage does not occur at all in the Old English *Soul and Body,* nor is it the first thing the soul says in *Latemest Day;* the *ubi sunt* passage may have gradually moved to its initial or early position in "body and soul" poems and need not have occurred in such a position in *SA*. The statements on the origin of the soul in various prose versions of the "body and soul" theme are interesting for details they provide, but, as already stated, the prose versions cannot tell us much about the structure of this poem. These passages in the poem are greatly expanded in comparison with the analogous passages in the prose versions.

The alternative possible order — 63-66-64-65 — remains unexamined in any printed account, but it goes a long way, in fact, toward removing the problems presented by the current order. It brings *SA* more into line with other English "body and soul" poems in terms of structure, though it remains an idiosyncratic work. Further, it establishes more strongly within the poem a chronological, quasi-narrative structure which Ricciardi noticed.[57]

When f. 66 is placed in the second position, *SA* moves from its introductory lines with their general description of birth, death, and the time immediately following death to the voice of the soul lamenting its implantation in the body:

> *os meu(m) ap(e)rui   et attraxi sp(iritu)m,*
> þu[.... .]⟨dest þin muþ⟩   and drowe me to þe.
> Walawa and wa is me   þ(et) ic efre com to þe,
> for nold⟨est þu⟩ mid þine muþe   bimænen þine neode,
> ac efre diȝelliche   þu wold⟨est ham⟩ bidernan.
>
>   F2-5

Lines F34-50 on f. 66[r] describe the creation and the soul's particular place in it and f. 66[v] ends with a lengthy description of the body receiving the soul, their marriage, (that is, baptism), the body's apparent initial rejection of the devil, the subsequent capitulation, and the resultant loss of the *bearn* (that is, the good deeds the soul and body should have done together [G27-56]). Though the poem cannot be neatly summarized because of the recurrent castigation of the body and the general diffuseness of the poet's style, the primary line of development on f. 66 is chronological.

On ff. 64 and 65 the accusations continue; the emphasis shifts to the deserts of the body, moving first to its worldly possessions (the *ubi sunt* passage in B4-11, the acquisition of these goods by others in B12-16, C9-14, C33-36), then to the body itself, the culmination of that particular concern being the putrefaction in the grave (C38-50, D1-8). This key description of the putrefying body ends on f. 65[r], as we have seen, and the primary focus shifts on f. 65 to the damnation of the soul and body and the loss which that entails, culminating in the Last Judgment.

The former predominates on f. 65ʳ: *Forloren þu hauest þeo ece blisse,
binumen þu hauest þe paradis / bi⟨nu⟩men þe is þ(et) holi lond, þen deofle þu
bist isold on hond* (D37-38); the latter occupies much of f. 65ᵛ, E30-52:

> *ite maledicti in ignem eternu(m)*
> þonne sculen wit si⟨þien⟩ to alre seorüwe mest,
> faren mid feondes in þet eche fur,
> beornen ⟨þer e⟩fre, ende nis þer nefre,
> *et q(ui) bona eger(un)t ibu(n)t in uita(m) et(er)na(m),*
> þonne ⟨scule⟩n þeo goden mid gode siþian,
> echeliche wunien i(n) alre wuld⟨re mest⟩
>
> E46-52

In the alternative ordering of the leaves proposed here, then, the address of the soul begins with its creation and initial life in the body, describes in some detail, though not strictly chronologically, its torment in the body, and ends with its damnation on Judgment Day. The body is simultaneously seen moving from birth, old age, and death on f. 63ᵛ to putrefaction and eventual damnation on ff. 64-65.

From the point of view of structure, the placement of f. 66 (Fragments F and G in the current order) between f. 63 (Fragment A) and ff. 64 and 65 (Fragments B through E) serves to strengthen the poem considerably. Stylistically the results of this rearrangement are also salutary. For example, no mention is made on f. 66 of the decomposed body that has been described so vividly on ff. 64-65. The tongue is described as *ascorted*, G9, but this would follow from the Signs of Death on f. 63ᵛ, A19; it is not a Sign of Decomposition.[58] Whereas in other "body and soul" poems the horrific details — either of the putrefying body (especially in *Soul and Body*) or hell torment (especially in the debates) or both — occur near the end of each work, where they can achieve their optimum effect, in *SA* of the current order such descriptions are buried in the center of the poem. In the revised order, the passage describing the activity of the worms comes toward the end of the poem, the prelude to the consideration of Last Judgment and damnation. Also, variations on the line *ʒet sæiþ þeo soule   soriliche to hire licame,* which mark changes in the focus of the soul's address, occur only on ff. 64 and 65.[59] In the revised order they produce a cumulative, climactic effect and perhaps impel forward to its conclusion an already long work; in the current order there is no clear reason why variations of this line should occur in the middle of the poem (Fragments B-E) and not at all in Fragments G and F.

Further, if the rhyming and assonant lines, as suggested above, do function stylistically to break up the flow of the alliterative verse, arresting thereby the attention of the auditor, the passage of six consecutive such lines on f. 65^r, D37–42, can be seen as the emotional climax of the address, and of the poem itself:

> Forloren þu hauest þeo ece blisse,   binumen þu hauest þe
> paradis;
> bi⟨nu⟩men þe is þet holi lond,   þen deofle þu bist isold on hond,
> for noldest þu nefr⟨e hab⟩ben inouh   buten þu hefdest
> unifouh;
> nu is þ(et) swete al agon   þ(et) bittere þe bi⟨þ⟩ fornon;
> þ(et) bittere ilest þe efre, þet gode ne cumeþ þe nefre;
> þus ageþ nu þi⟨n siþ⟩   æfter þin wrecce lif.

No more than two rhyming or assonant lines occur in succession elsewhere in the poem. In the alternative order proposed here, these lines would come near the end of the work, followed on f. 65^v by the vision of the Last Judgment; in the current order, they, like the portrayal of the putrefying corpse, lie in the center of the poem, their effectiveness wholly undercut by the long discussion of the origin of the soul and its implantation in the body which follows on f. 66.

The proposal to move f. 66 to a position between ff. 63 and 64 brings us back to the manuscript and what it can tell us. The new order of the leaves proposed here violates the arrangement of leaves in gatherings according to hair side and flesh side outlined at the beginning of the Introduction. Folio 66 fits well with f. 63: 63^v and 66^r are both hair sides. However, the usual arrangement breaks down in the relation between ff. 66 and 64: 66^v is a flesh side; 64^r is a hair side. It is possible that at the end of the manuscript, the Ælfric material having been copied, the scribe took less care with these matters. Perhaps we are dealing with single leaves tacked on to the end of the work. However, Ker's conjectural collation (see p. 2 above), substantiated as it is by the arrangement of the leaves, compels us to think in terms of quaternion gatherings throughout: therefore, a haphazard addition of the final few leaves seems unlikely.

Nevertheless, we must bear in mind that the completeness suggested by the Ker collation seems illusory when we examine the contents of *SA*. Since in all "body and soul" poems of any length, there occurs a brief return to the framing device with which the work began, the lack of such a passage in *SA* would seem to indicate that something, at least one leaf, has been lost from the end of the manuscript. The likelihood of loss is only increased if one persists in retaining the current Phillipps order of the fragments, because not only is the return to the framing device still missing, but the poem also ends, very improbably, with an untranslated Latin line. The Latin lines that occur sporadically throughout the poem are almost always followed by an English translation or paraphrase.

Two explanations of the extant material can be made. One involves the loss of a leaf between repositioned f. 66 and f. 64. Loss at this point would account for the flesh side-hair side juxtaposition caused by the proposed reordering of the leaves. However, this explanation creates other difficulties. If we assume an original quaternion gathering, then both f. 65 and the leaf containing the end of the poem would fall outside of it. Also, loss of a leaf from between ff. 66 and 64 would mean approximately one hundred lines of text are missing from the middle of the poem. A neater and more probable explanation involves the folding of one additional leaf into the final gathering of the manuscript. The scribe, having finished the Ælfric material on f. 63ʳ (and filled up the rest of that page with the *"Sanctus Beda"* fragment), realized that he needed more than the seven sides left in his original gathering to complete the copying of *SA*. Therefore, he added one leaf, current f. 66, at a probable place for such an addition, between ff. 63 and 64. This explanation accounts for the violation of the arrangement of the leaves and restricts loss to the last leaf of the gathering, the leaf conjugate with f. 59, that would have contained the completion of the apocalyptic vision portrayed on f. 65ᵛ and a return to the framing device with which the work began.

The argument for reordering of the last three leaves of Worcester Cathedral MS F. 174 so that current f. 66 is placed between ff. 64 and 65 can only be hypothetical. The structural affinities with other "body and soul" poems, along with the fundamental structural and stylistic improvements which have emerged in the course of this investigation, all urge the superiority of the alternative order to the current one. No scholar since the publication of Buchholz's edition in 1890 has even questioned, let alone rejected, the order of the leaves established by Phillipps. The two most recent editors failed to investigate the possibility of an alternative order at all,[60] and scholars appear generally to have adopted the current order uncritically. However, the temptation to print the alternative order as the text of this edition must be resisted: without the indisputable evidence which a close source or analogue would provide, no final choice can be made; and, given both this fact and the need for ease of scholarly reference, it seems prudent to preserve the Phillipps order at this time.

In conclusion, it is necessary, and not purely a matter of speculation, to consider what might be missing from our version of *SA*. It is clear that some lines have been lost from the beginning of the poem. Heningham advances the opinion that the *"Sanctus Beda"* fragment on f. 63[r] serves as a prologue to *SA;* however, this view has gained no critical acceptance and there is nothing in the "body and soul" tradition to substantiate it. Ricciardi points out two French words in the fragment (as opposed to the very English vocabulary of *SA*) as well as some possible stylistic differences between the two works.[61] It is not inconceivable that the scribe of F. 174 viewed the poems in some sort of relation to one another, but, if there is anything artful in the positioning of the *"Sanctus Beda"* fragment before *SA,* it is almost certainly the art of the compiler of the manuscript and not the authors of the works. It has already been stated that a framing device of some sort is a feature common to all "body and soul" poems, that is, neither the beginning nor the end of the poem coincides exactly with the beginning or end of the soul's address. The failure to return to such a framing context after the speech of the soul would be unprecedented, but it seems unquestionable that the soul speaks throughout ff. 64–66. In all likelihood, then, a passage including the conclusion of the address and further comment by the poet is missing from the end of the work in the Worcester version.

Two remarkable features that occur in other "body and soul" poems must be considered only remotely possible parts of *SA* in its original form. The extended consideration of Last Judgment and of the torment awaiting the soul in hell, such as we find in *Latemest Day* and the later debates, could be lost from the end of the work as it now stands. However, the shorter, more general description of Last Judgment at the end of Fragment E does not give the impression that any fuller description will follow, perhaps particularly if this fragment is positioned last among the extant leaves as has just been suggested above. Another feature that must be considered unlikely for *SA* is a balancing portrayal of a righteous soul such as occurs in many prose versions and in the OE *Soul and Body I.* The poets of the theme, with the exception of the one OE version, seem to have been more interested in the damned than the blessed, and in the related *Latemest Day* there is no indication that a righteous soul was ever a factor in *SA*. Perhaps the best argument against the possible inclusion of a portrayal of a righteous soul in *SA* depends on the introductory material on f. 63[v]. It concentrates primarily on the painful nature of birth and death and the ingratitude of friends. It seems suitable only to introduce an address by a wicked soul (although there is no indication on f. 63ᵛ that the soul of the man who has just died is, in fact, wicked). Such a dreary introduction could hardly serve for the address of a righteous soul as well.

NOTES TO INTRODUCTION

1. The standard edition of this work is Ælfric, Abbot of Eynsham, *Ælfrics Grammatik und Glossar,* ed. Julius Zupitza (1880; rpt. Berlin: Weidmann, 1966).
2. Among the editions of this fragment are Joseph Hall, ed., *Selections from Early Middle English: 1130–1250,* 2 vols. (Oxford: Clarendon Press, 1920), pp. 1 (text) and 223–28 (notes); and Bruce Dickins and R. M. Wilson, eds., *Early Middle English Texts* (1951; rpt. London: Bowes and Bowes, 1965), pp. 1–2 (text) and 151–52 (notes).
3. Neil Riply Ker, *Catalogue of Manuscripts Containing Anglo-Saxon* (Oxford: Clarendon Press, 1957), p. 466 (item 398).
4. Ibid.
5. John K. Floyer, *Catalogue of Manuscripts Preserved in the Chapter Library of Worcester Cathedral,* ed. and rev. Sidney G. Hamilton (Oxford: James Parker, 1906), p. 101.
6. Ker, *Catalogue,* p. 466.
7. The "tremulous hand" is discussed briefly in a number of places: for example, Julius Zupitza, "Das Nicaeische Symbolum in englischen Aufzeichnung des 12 Jahrhunderts," *Anglia,* 1 (1878), 286–87; Wolfgang Keller, *Die litterarischen Bestrebungen von Worcester in angelsächsischer Zeit, Quellen und Forschungen zur Sprach- und Culturgeschichte der germanischen Völker,* 84 (Strassburg: Karl J. Trübner, 1900), p. 20; Margareta Ångström, *Studies in Old English MSS with Special Reference to the Delabialization of y (< u + i) to i,* Diss. Uppsala (Almquist and Wiksells, 1937), pp. 87–88. Facsimiles of his work can be seen in S. J. Crawford, "The Worcester Marks and Glosses of the Old English Manuscripts in the Bodleian, Together with the Worcester Version of the Nicene Creed," *Anglia,* 52 (1928), 1–25, and Neil Ripley Ker, "The Date of the 'Tremulous' Worcester Hand," *Leeds Studies in English,* 6 (1937), 28–29. A list of the MSS in which the "tremulous hand" occurs may be found in Neil Ripley Ker, *Medieval Libraries of Great Britain: A List of Surviving Books,* 2nd ed., Royal Historical Society Guides and Handbooks, no. 3 (London: Royal Historical Society, 1964), p. 206, fn. 3.
8. Ker, *Catalogue,* p. 467.
9. Neil Ripley Ker, *English Manuscripts in the Century after the Norman Conquest: The Lyell Lectures, 1952–53* (Oxford: Clarendon Press, 1960), p. 42.
10. Ker, *Catalogue,* p. lxii. A similar fate befell one of the most important manuscript products of medieval Worcester now also known, alas, as the "Worcester Fragments," "the largest extant repertory of English polyphonic music" of the thirteenth and early fourteenth centuries. See Dom Anselm Hughes,

Worcester Mediaeval Harmony of the Thirteenth and Fourteenth Centuries Transcribed with a General Introduction, Fifteen Facsimiles, and Notes (1928; rpt. Hildesheim: Georg Olms, 1971) and Luther A. Dittmer, *The Worcester Fragments: A Catalogue Raisonné and Transcription,* Musicological Studies and Documents, 2 (American Institute of Musicology, 1957).

11. On the history of the Chapter Library of Worcester Cathedral, see the Introduction by Atkins and Ker to Young, *Catalogus* (1622–23).

12. Sir Thomas Phillipps, ed., *A Fragment of Ælfric's* Grammar and Glossary *and a Poem on the Soul and Body* (London, 1838).

13. Dr. B. S. Benedikz offered this opinion in a letter of 29 November 1983. These class A muniments have been catalogued for the Royal Commission on Historical Manuscripts by B. S. Benedikz and S. L. Brock, 1977. The statement by Phillipps occurs on f. 53 of MS Phillipps-Robinson e. 374 (a letter book). The Phillipps correspondence has been catalogued for the Royal Commission on Historical Manuscripts by T. D. Rogers: *Catalogue of the Topographical Collections and of the Correspondence and Papers of Sir Thomas Phillipps, Bart. (1792–1872) given to the Bodleian Library, Oxford, by Lionel and Philip Robinson,* 2 vols., 1982. Phillipps' letters on his discovery also reveal that among the other fragments he found was Worcester Cathedral Additional MS 4 (Floyer and Hamilton Fragment IX), a bifolium from Paterius' *De Expositione Veteris et Novi Testamenti.*

14. Ernst Haufe, ed., *Die Fragmente der Rede der Seele an den Leichnam in der Handschrift der Cathedrale zu Worcester* (Greifswald, 1880), pp. 6–7.

15. E.g., Haufe, p. 7, and Hall, *Selections,* p. 223.

16. Richard Buchholz, ed., *Die Fragmente der Reden der Seele an den Leichnam in zwei Handschriften zu Worcester und Oxford* (Erlangen, 1890 ; rpt. Amsterdam: Rodopi, 1970), pp. vi–xlviii.

17. In my treatment of language I have relied most heavily on Buchholz (1890), Campbell (1959), d'Ardenne (1961), Hall (1920), Jordan-Crook (1974), and Mustanoja (1960).

18. Though I have not studied F. 174 with the rigour employed by the Middle English Dialect Project, I am indebted to Benskin and Laing (1981) for their discussion of scribal "translation" in ME manuscripts.

19. Hall, *Selections,* p. 232. See also J. P. Oakden, *Alliterative Poetry in Middle English,* I (Manchester, 1930; rpt. Archon Press, 1958), 43–44; Samuel Moore, S. B. Meech, and H. Whitehall, "Middle English Dialect Characteristics and Dialect Boundaries: Preliminary Report to an Investigation Based Exclusively on Localized Texts," in *Essays and Studies in English and Comparative Literature by Members of the English Department of the University of Michigan* (Ann Arbor: University of Michigan Press, 1935), p. 55; Hans Kurath and Sherman Kuhn, *Middle English Dictionary: Plan and Bibliography* (Ann Arbor: University of Michigan Press, 1954), p. 12.

20. See, e.g., Thorlac Turville-Petre, *The Alliterative Revival* (Cambridge: D. S. Brewer, 1977), pp. 6–14, and especially John C. Pope's discussion of Ælfric's rhythmical prose in *Homilies of Ælfric: Supplementary Collection,* I, E.E.T.S. (O.S.), no. 259 (London: Oxford University Press, 1967), pp. 105–36. The work of

McIntosh and Funke on Wulfstan will be referred to below. The most thorough effort I know of to locate Layamon's prosody in the OE tradition has been made by James Erwin Noble, "Layamon's *Brut* and the Continuity of the Alliterative Tradition," Diss. University of Western Ontario, 1981, pp. 55–121.

21. Angus McIntosh, "Early Middle English Alliterative Verse," in *Middle English Alliterative Poetry and its Literary Background: Seven Essays,* ed. David A. Lawton (Cambridge: D. S. Brewer, 1982), pp. 20–33.

22. Oakden, *Alliterative Poetry,* I, 139, offers the following breakdown for 165 lines (?) of the poem: seventy-nine lines alliterating xa:ay; forty-three alliterating aa:ax; thirty-seven alliterating ax:ay. It is a curious fact that, while Oakden acknowledges the authority of Buchholz, he quotes throughout from Singer's edition of *SA.*

23. Oakden, *Alliterative Poetry,* I, 139, claims that in *SA sc* does alliterate with *s* and *sk* but gives no examples. Lines such as F10, 29, and 34 provide possible, though not unequivocal, evidence to substantiate his view. In B34 *gr* alliterates with *g.* Of the two other initial clusters which Oakden mentions, *fl* occurs most clearly as an alliterating stave in D10, but no evidence supports his notion that *cl* functioned in this manner. Neither *sl* nor the traditional OE stave *sp* occur in alliterating position in this poem. *ȝ* alliterates with *g* in most OE poems, but they are distinct in the late *Battle of Maldon.*

24. Oakden, *Alliterative Poetry,* I, 140.

25. Pope's synopsis of Sievers in *Seven Old English Poems* (Indianapolis: Bobbs-Merrill, 1966), p. 108, makes this point clear:

> Among the very numerous verses with four syllables, Sievers found five principal stress patterns, which he designated, in order of frequency, by the first five letters of the alphabet. These are the basis of his five types. By counting resolved lifts and polysyllabic drops as single members, he found that most verses of more than four syllables can be said to have only four members and can be assimilated to the types established by those with four syllables.

Expanded verses, which are five-part, occur too infrequently to establish the rhythm of OE poetry in the way four-part verses do.

26. Otto Funke, "Some Remarks on Wulfstan's Prose Rhythm," *ES,* 43 (1962), 415, estimates only two or three percent of Wulfstan's "two-stress phrases" end with a monosyllabic main stress.

27. Ibid.

28. It could be reasonably argued that *licame* in A11b and elsewhere would be resolved and scanned / x, owing to the shortening of *i* in the first syllable of a trisyllabic word. Resolution is not a reasonable alternative in the other examples, however.

29. Line G41 may be corrupt; B6, a rhyming line.

30. In OE verse, certain words which were compounds in origin, e.g., *hlaford,* could be treated as simplexes.

31. Shortening may have brought about resolution in both *luþerliche,* B35a, and *soriliche,* D17b and E3b.

32. Funke, pp. 316–17.

33. The average number of syllables in all English verses of the poem, with or without anacrusis, is about 6.5; verses of six or seven syllables are the most common varieties though ones of five and eight syllables certainly are not rare. The figure of 6.5 is slightly lower than that given for the prose of Ælfric, 6.7, and lower still than the average length of a verse in Layamon's *Brut,* 7.26. It is significantly higher, however, than the figures for both *Beowulf* and the lOE *Exhortation to Christian Living,* "not quite five" and 5.3 respectively. See Pope, *Ælfric,* I, 119, and Sherman Kuhn, "Was Ælfric a Poet?" *PQ,* 52 (1973), 656.

34. Pope sees the line as an important rhythmical unit in Ælfric, one established more by syntax than rhythmical balancing of half-lines:

> A form so loosely governed as Ælfric's must depend upon syntax even more heavily than the traditional verse. As in the verse, the majority of Ælfric's half-lines are established by the syntactical phrasing even when no actual pause is in order. So far as half-lines go the syntactical indications are about the same for both forms; but syntax establishes the full line more firmly in Ælfric than in most of the poems. That is, Ælfric's lines are prevailingly endstopped, with only light stops or none at all in the middle. Full stops in mid-line do occur, but much less frequently than in most of the verse, and enjambment is correspondingly restrained. (*Ælfric,* I, 122)

(As a rule, the half-lines are more well defined in *SA* than in Ælfric.) Friedlander (1979) comments on the importance of the long line, and of the importance of syntax in establishing that line, in transitional verse. Pope and Friedlander both view the subject of rhythm from the perspective of "classical" OE verse.

35. R. M. Wilson, *Early Middle English Literature,* 3rd ed. (London: Methuen, 1968), p. 171, notes that, in its original form, the poem "must have been a powerful, if gloomy, work" and that in it "some of the descriptions are characterized by considerable vigour and power." Rosemary Woolf, *The English Religious Lyric in the Middle Ages* (Oxford: Clarendon Press, 1968), p. 94, comments in passing on the "force of the laconic straightforwardness" of descriptive passages in the poem.

36. Dorothy Everett, *Essays on Middle English Literature,* ed. Patrick Kean (1955; rev. Oxford: Clarendon Press, 1959), p. 39.

37. Cf. B8, *þin blisse is nu al agon   min seorwe is fornon.*

38. Rudolph Willard, "The Address of the Soul to the Body," *PMLA,* 50 (1935), 962.

39. Max Förster, ed., *Die Vercelli-Homilien: I–VIII Homilie, Bibliothek der angelsächsischen Prosa,* XII (1932; rpt. Darmstadt: Wissenschaftliche Buchgesellschaft, 1964), pp. 84–103. See especially the explanatory note for D31–36.

40. Woolf, *English Religious Lyric,* p. 93.

41. Oakden, *Alliterative Poetry,* II, 3-4.

42. Arnold Schroeer, ed., "The Grave," *Anglia,* 5 (1883), 289-90. The Buchholz and Ricciardi editions of *SA* also contain editions of this poem.

43. Buchholz advances the opinion that *The Grave* is a further fragment of *SA,* a view examined and rejected by Louise Dudley in *"The Grave," MP,* 11 (1914), 429-42. The opposite view, that *SA* derives from *The Grave,* seems equally improbable. It is put forward by Dudley and, most recently, by Turville-Petre in *The Alliterative Revival,* pp. 9-10.

44. Dudley, *"The Grave,"* pp. 436-38.

45. Carleton Brown, ed. *English Lyrics of the Thirteenth Century* (Oxford: Claren- don Press, 1932) contains two versions of *Latemest Day,* pp. 47-54.

46. Lists of correspondences and possible correspondences between the two works can be found in J. D. Bruce, "A Contribution to the Study of 'The Body and the Soul' Poems in English," *MLN,* 5 (1890), 197-99; Brown, *English Lyrics,* pp. 189-91; Heningham, "Old English Precursors," p. 293, fn. 7. A number of the correspondences listed by Heningham seem rather far fetched, while others are so short and mundane as to be of no significance. Close parallels to both *The Grave* and *The Latemest Day* in *SA* are given in the explanatory notes.

47. Heningham, "Old English Precursors," p. 293.

48. Brown, *English Lyrics,* pp. 42-46.

49. Bibliographical information on the standard editions of these works may be found in the Bibliography under the names of the editors: *Royal Debate* (Hen- ingham, 1939); *Un Samedi Par Nuit* (Varnhagen, 1889); *Desputisoun* (Linow, 1889); *In a thestri stude* (Reichl, 1973). No critical edition of the *Vision of St. Philibert* exists; see du Méril (1843) and Wright (1851) for versions of it.

50. No *ubi sunt* passage occurs in the Old English *Soul and Body,* and the descrip- tion of the grave and worms, found near the end of the work, is not part of the soul's address proper.

51. *Soul and Body I,* George Philip Krapp, ed., *The Vercelli Book* (New York: Columbia University Press, 1932), ll.27-28, and the *Vision of St. Philibert,* Wright, ed., ll.26-27.

52. *Latemest Day,* Brown, p. 47, ll.33-36. See Woolf, pp. 78-82 and 95, and Rossell Hope Robbins, "Signs of Death in Middle English," *MS,* 32 (1970), 282-98.

53. A similar passage does occur in the *Royal Debate.* See *An Early Latin Debate,* Heningham, ll.344-68.

54. Buchholz, pp. I-II. The last line of Fragment A, f. 63ᵛ, indicates that the address of the soul is about to begin: *þonne besihþ þeo soule   soriliche to þen lich⟨ame⟩.* In the rest of the fragments the soul is speaking. Had the address begun a little sooner in the poem, and especially if it had begun a little later, the order of the fragments could probably be established by the continuity of the subject matter.

55. Ricciardi, "Grave-bound Body," pp. 125-36.

56. See especially the "body and soul" passages from the two OE homilies edited by Willard (1935).

57. Ricciardi, "Grave-bound Body," pp. 127–28.

58. On the Signs of Death, see Woolf, *English Religious Lyric,* pp. 78–82, and Rossell Hope Robbins, "Signs of Death in Middle English," *MS,* 32 (1970), 282–98; on the Signs of Decomposition, see Woolf, p. 95.

59. Lines C2, D17, E3, and D36.

60. Hall and Ricciardi.

61. Heningham, "Precursors," p. 292; Ricciardi, "Grave-bound Body," pp. 208–10.

THE TEXT

The text is accompanied by two sets of notes: textual at the foot of the page and explanatory following after the text.

Manuscript spelling is reproduced, except in cases of emendation; *g* is distinguished from *ʒ* as it is in the manuscript; *ƿ* is printed *w;* word division is regularized. The abbreviations *7* and *&* for *and* are expanded without notice. The abbreviations *ꝥ* for *þet* and ˜ (tilde) for a following nasal are expanded with indication in the text. Other abbreviations, including all those in the Latin lines, are expanded in the text and marked in the textual notes. Capitalization and punctuation are the editor's own. Manuscript capitalization is recorded in the textual notes. Metrical pointing in the manuscript is indicated by the line division of the text; any eccentricities in this pointing are marked in the textual notes. Accent marks in the manuscript, which occur intermittently over *i,* have been ignored. The fragments are designated by letters, following the practice established by Haufe in his edition of the work. At the beginning of Fragment D, f. 65ʳ, and Fragment G, f. 66ᵛ, occur portions of lines that are designated 1a in order to preserve the established lineation of these fragments. All emendations are indicated in both the text and the textual notes and are discussed in the explanatory notes.

The critical symbols used in the text and the notes are, with some adaption, those recommended by M.L. West in *Textual Criticism and Editorial Technique* (Stuttgart: B.G. Teubner, 1973), pp. 80–82. They are as follows:

1. ( )   enclose expanded abbreviations as well as ordinary parentheses.

2. ⟨ ⟩   enclose letters, words, or passages added to the transmitted text by conjecture, including emendations.

3. { }   enclose editorial deletions.

4.   † †   mark passages judged to be corrupt. If only one word
              is involved, a single obelus is used.

5.   ạ ḅ ç   Dots under letters indicate that they are difficult to
              decipher or, more usually, that only a portion of them
              remains. When it occurs under a letter enclosed by
              angle brackets, a dot indicates that, though a por-
              tion of the letter remains, its identity has been sur-
              mised from the context. A dot under a letter not
              enclosed by angle brackets indicates that enough re-
              mains of the letter in the manuscript to allow proba-
              ble identification.

6.   [ ]   enclose sections of the text lost due to manuscript
              damage. Asterisks in square brackets indicate that the
              amount of text lost cannot be accurately determined;
              dots, on the other hand, indicate approximately the
              number of letters that are missing owing to the
              damage. Holes, cuts, and creases in the leaves are
              mentioned only if they hinder legibility.

The textual notes deal with the peculiarities of the manuscript and
emendations to it in the text. They also present a record of the many
reconstructions proposed by past editors for lost or damaged portions.
A number of these reconstructed passages are also dealt with in the explanatory notes. The abbreviations in the textual notes refer to the
following.

MS   Worcester Cathedral MS F. 174.

P   Sir Thomas Phillipps' work (1838) is a fairly accurate
      diplomatic edition with no attempts at reconstruction of
      damaged portions of the manuscript.

S   S. W. Singer (1845) attempted reconstructions on the basis
      of Phillipps' text, that is, he did not actually see the manuscript
      itself. His text is laid out in half-lines (rather than full-lines)
      with a facing translation; it is numbered continuously from
      the beginning of the first fragment to the end of the work.

H   Ernst Haufe (1880) based his knowledge of the manuscript
      on a collation of it made by Julius Zupitza and Hermann
      Varnhagan in 1879 while Zupitza was preparing his edition

of Ælfric's *Grammar and Glossary*. He also knew the Phillipps and Singer editions, though he acknowledges the latter only sporadically. Haufe provides a brief introduction touching on matters of language, prosody, and the state of the manuscript; he divides the text into fragments lettered A through G; he also provides explanatory notes to which he makes a few additions in an 1881 *Anglia* article. The Haufe edition was reviewed by Wissmann in 1881.

B   Richard Buchholz's edition (1890) contains the most thorough discussion of the poem's language to date as well as a complete description of the poem's prosody. Like Haufe, Buchholz relied on the Zupitza-Varnhagen collation for his knowledge of the manuscript, and further, it is only through Haufe's edition that he is aware of Singer's work. Important reviews of the Buchholz edition, which provide essential modifications of the work, were written by Zupitza (1891), Kaluza (1891), and Holthausen (1892). Buchholz, whose work includes an edition of *The Grave,* also provides a German prose translation of *SA*.

Ha   Joseph Hall (1920) apparently saw the manuscript, but he offers an edition of only Fragments A and B.

R   Gail D. D. Ricciardi's edition (1976), an unpublished dissertation, is a collection that includes the two versions of the OE *Soul and Body* and *The Grave* as well as the *SA*. She was the first editor of the complete poem since Phillipps actually to study the manuscript, and, consequently, her work includes a number of superior suggestions in regard to possible reconstructions of damaged portions. However, the effectiveness of Ricciardi's edition of the *SA* (and *Soul and Body*) is undermined by the vast scope of her project.

In the case of reconstruction, neither the manuscript nor, for the most part, Phillipps' diplomatic rendering of it is relevant. A reading from P is given only if S either has not followed it or has been misled by it. Suggestions for reconstruction or emendation made by non-editors have not been included in the textual notes; they are usually mentioned in the explanatory notes, however.

Fragment A, f. 63ᵛ

[* * * *] ⟨midd⟩enearde   1
and alle þeo isceæftan   þe him to sc̩ul̩en,
and mid much̩el̩e c̩r̩e̩⟨fte   þe⟩ne mon he idihte
and him on ileide   lif and soule.
     Softliche he heo isom⟨nede⟩,   ac þær biþ sor idol   5
þ(et) bodeþ þ(et) bearn   þonne hit iboren biþ.
Hit †⟨woan⟩eþ   †and mænet þeo weowe
and þene seoruhfule siþ   and þ(et) sori idol:
þ(et) soule sch̩al̩ ⟨of lic̩⟩ame   sorliche idælen.
Forþon hit cumeþ weopinde   and woniende iwiteþ,   10
⟨for d⟩eaþ mid his pricke   pineþ þene licame;
he walkeþ and wendeþ   and woneþ ⟨oftes⟩i̩þes;
he sæiþ on his bedde: "wo me þ(et) ic libbe,
þ(et) æffre mine lifdawes   þus ⟨lon⟩ge me ilesteþ";
for heui is his greoning   and seorhful is his woaning   15
and al⟨so biþ⟩ his siþ   mid seorwe biwunden.

---

1. ⟨midd⟩enearde R; ...enearde S, H, B, Ha. enearde *begins f.63ᵛ*.
2. sc̩ul̩en H, B, Ha, R; iculen P; *no reconst.* S. *The ascenders of long* s *and* l *have been cut away.*
3. c̩r̩e̩⟨fte þe⟩ne B, Ha, R; ...ne P; ⟨wisdome þon⟩ne S; cre⟨fte þon⟩ne H. *The ascenders of* h *and* l *in* muchele *as well as the tops of the first four letters in* c̩r̩e̩⟨fte⟩ *have been cut away.*
5. isom⟨nede⟩ H, B, Ha, R; isom⟨ne⟩ S
6. bearn þonne: MS bearn? þonne
7. ⟨woan⟩eþ S, Ha; ⟨won⟩eþ H; ⟨greoneþ ond woan⟩eþ B; ⟨weop⟩eþ R
9. sch̩al̩: al *very faded.* ⟨of lic̩⟩ame; ⟨hire li⟩came S; ⟨and li⟩came H, B; ⟨fro li⟩came Ha; ⟨wiþ li⟩came R
11. ⟨for d⟩eaþ; ⟨þonne D⟩eaþ S; ⟨D⟩eaþ H, B; ⟨for D⟩eaþ R. *Only a small portion of the* d *remains.*
12. *There is no point between* wendeþ *and* 7 (*the second one*). ⟨oftes⟩i̩þes H, B, Ha; ⟨his si⟩þes S; ⟨ofts⟩i̩þes R
16. al⟨so biþ⟩; ⟨reowliche⟩ S; ⟨is⟩ H, B; ⟨biþ⟩ Ha, R

†Him deaueþ þa æren,   him dimmeþ ⟨þa⟩ eiʒen,
him scerpeþ þe neose,   him scrinckeþ þa lippen,
him scorteþ ⟨þe⟩ ṭunge,
him trukeþ his iwit,   him teoreþ his miht,   20
him coldeþ his ⟨liche⟩:   ḷiggeþ þe ban stille.†
Þonne biþ þ(et) soulehus   seoruhliche bereaued
⟨at ạ⟩lso muchele wunne   þe þerinne wunede;
þus biþ þæs bearnes   ⟨boḍ⟩unge ifulled:
þeo moder greoneþ   and þ(et) bearn woaneþ.   25
So biþ þeo ⟨bu⟩ṛdtid   mid balewen imenged,
so biþ eft þe feorþsiþ   mid seoruwen al bewunden.
þonne þe licame and þe sowle   soriliche to⟨dæl⟩eþ:
þonne biþ þ(et) wræcche lif   iended al mid sori siþ.

    Þonne biþ þe ⟨fei⟩ʒe   iflut to þen flore;   30
he biþ eastward istreiht,   he biþ sone stif,
he ⟨col⟩deþ also clei—   hit is him ikunde.
Mon hine met mid one ʒerde   and þa mol⟨de⟩ ṣeoþþen,
ne mot he of þære molde   habben na(m)more
þonne þ(et) rihte imet   ⟨rih⟩ṭliche tæcheþ.   35
Þonne liþ þe cleiclot   colde on þen flore
and him sone from ⟨fleoþ⟩   þeo he ær freome dude;

---

17. æren: *the inkspot above and to the right of the* n, *but not aligned with the point, is probably accidental.* dimmeþ: *MS* dimmeþe. *The final* e, *slightly above the line, is offset.*

19-20. ṭunge / him S, H, B, R; ṭunge ⟨him starkeþ his skin⟩ / him Ha.

21. ⟨liche⟩;⟨heorte⟩ S; ⟨muþ⟩ H, B; ⟨siden⟩ Ha; ⟨liþe⟩ R. ḷiggeþ MS, P, H, B, Ha, R; leggeþ S.

23. ⟨at ạ⟩lso B, Ha, R; ⟨of a⟩lso S, H.

24. ⟨boḍ⟩unge H, B, Ha, R; ⟨pin⟩unge S. *Little of the* d *remains.*

26. ⟨bu⟩ṛdtid H, B, Ha, R; ⟨hear⟩dtid S. balewen: *MS* bawen *with* le *above the line over* aw.

27. feorþsiþ mid Ha, R; feorþsiþ sorhliche tod[...] mid MS, P; feorþsiþ sorhliche todæ⟨led⟩ mid S; feorþsiþ sorhliche to dæ⟨len⟩ mid H, B. H *prints one line.* B *prints* mid seoruwen al bewunden *as a separate line.*

28. to⟨dæl⟩eþ H, B, Ha, R; to ⟨dæl⟩eþ S.

30. ⟨fei⟩ʒe Ha, R; ⟨bodi⟩ʒe S, H; *no reconst.* B.

32. ⟨col⟩deþ Ha, R; ⟨hear⟩deþ S, H; *no reconst.* B.

nulleþ heo mid honden   his heafod riht wen⟨den⟩;
heom þuncheþ þ(et) hore honden   swuþe beoþ ifuled
ʒif heo hondleþ þe⟨ne⟩ d̦eade   seoþþen his deaʒes beoþ ạgon.40
Sone cumeþ þ(et) wrecche w̦i̦f̦   þe ⟨forh⟩oweþ þene earfeþsiþ,
forbindeþ þæs dædan muþ   and his dimme e̦ʒe̦n;
⟨þon⟩n̦e þet riche wif   forhoweþ þene earueþsiþ,
for ufel is þeo wrecche lufe   ⟨þo⟩n̦ne þeo unblisse cumaþ.
       Þonne besihþ þeo soule   sorliche to þen lich̦⟨ame⟩ 45

Fragment B, f. 64ʳ

                              [* * * *]
⟨w̦o̦a̦ w̦r̦o̦htest⟩ þu me   þeo hwule þet ic wunede inne þe, 1
for þu were leas and lutiʒ   and u̦⟨n⟩riht lufedest;
godnesse and riht   æfre þu onscunedest.
       Hwar is nu þe⟨o̦ mo⟩dinesse   (swo muchel þe þu lufedæst)?
Hwar beoþ nu þeo pundes   þurh ⟨pa⟩newes igædered? 5

---

40. ʒif: ʒ *is a small capital.* þe⟨ne⟩ B, Ha, R; þe S, H. d̦eade H, B, Ha, R; . .eade
P; ⟨d⟩æde S. ạgon; igon P, S, H, B, Ha, R. *The a is poorly formed and smudged.*
41. wif *is very faded.*
42. e̦ʒe̦n H, B, Ha, R; eiʒen P, S. *Very faded.*
43. ⟨þon⟩n̦e H, Ha, R; . . .ie P, S; ⟨ec⟩ B
44. ⟨þo⟩n̦ne S, R; ⟨in⟩ne H, B; ⟨þarin⟩ne Ha

1. ⟨w̦o̦a̦ w̦r̦o̦htest⟩; ⟨Hwui noldest beþenchen⟩ S, H, B; ⟨loþ were⟩ Ha; ⟨-o̦þ þu̦
w̦a̦ l̦i̦g̦g̦e̦ w̦o̦a̦ w̦r̦o̦htest⟩ R. þu *begins the first undamaged line of f. 64ʳ. The bottoms
of the letters in the preceding line are still visible.*
3. godnesse: g *is a small capital. Y*
4. þe⟨o̦⟩ H, B, Ha, R; þe P, S. *Part of the o is still visible.*
5. ⟨pa⟩newes Ha, R; *no reconst.* S, H, B

(Heo weren monifolde bi markes itolde.)
Hwar beoþ ⟨nu⟩ þeo goldfæten †þeo þe guldene comen to
           þine honden?†
(þin blisse iş ⟨nu⟩ al agon, min seoruwe is fornon.)
Hwar beoþ nu þine wæde þe þ⟨u⟩ wel lufedest?
Hwar beoþ þe [sibbe þe] seten sori ofer þe,   10
beden swuþe ʒeorne ⟨þet⟩ þe come bote?
Heom þuþte al to longe þ(et) þu were on liue,
for heo ⟨we⟩ren grædie to gripen þine æihte;
nu heo hi dæleþ heom imǫng, ⟨heo⟩ doþ þe wiþuten,
ac nu heo beoþ fuse to bringen þe ut of huse, 15
b⟨rin⟩gen þe ut æt þire dure: of weolen þu ęrṭ bedæled.
Hwui noldest þ⟨u be⟩þenchen me þeo hwile ic was innen þe,
ac semdest me mid sunne, fǫ⟨rþon⟩ ic seoruhful eam?
Weile, þ(et) ic souhte so seoruhfulne buc!
  Noldest þ⟨u ma⟩kien† lųfe wiþ ilærede men, 20
ʒiuen ham of þine gode þ(et) heo þe fǫ⟨re⟩ beden.
Heo mihten mid salmsonge þine sunne acwenchen,
mid ⟨ho⟩re messe þine misdeden fore biddæn;

7. goldfæten *and* guldene: g *is a small capital.* þeo þe guldene comen to MS, P, S, H, B, Ha; þe glyden to R
8. agon MS, P, H, B, Ha, R; igon S
10. þe [sibbe þe] seten R; þe seten MS, P, S, H, B; þe [sibbe] seten Ha
11. ⟨þet⟩ H, B, Ha, R; ⟨þat⟩ S
12. heom MS, S, H, B, Ha, R; heo in P
13. ⟨we⟩ren S, B, Ha, R; ⟨w⟩eren H
14. dæleþ MS, P, H, B, Ha, R; dæliþ S. imǫng H, B, Ha, R; imang P, S. *The o is poorly formed.*
16. b⟨rin⟩gen H, B, Ha, R; b⟨er⟩gen S. ęrṭ MS, P, H, B, Ha, R; art S. *Very faded.*
18. semdest MS, P, H, B, Ha, R; scendest S. fǫ⟨rþon⟩ B, Ha, R; fo⟨rþi⟩ S, H
19. MS *pointing*, seoruhfulne · buc · noldest
20. þ⟨u ma⟩kien H; þ⟨u lo⟩kien S, Ha, R; þ⟨u þe ma⟩kien B. lųfe: *the* u *is very faded.*
21. gode: g *is a small capital.* Y
23. ⟨ho⟩re messe H, B, Ha, R; …reịnesse P, S. biddæn; biddan P, S, H, B, Ha, R. *The second half of* æ *is indistinct.*

heo mihten offrian loc   leofli⟨che⟩ for þe,
swuþe deorwurþe lac,   licame cristes;   25
þurh þære þu were alese⟨d⟩   from hellewite,
and mid his reade blode   þ⟨et⟩ he ʒeat on rode.
Po þu we⟨re⟩ ifreoed   to farene i⟨n⟩to heouene,
ac þu fenge to þeowdome   þ⟨urh⟩ þæs ḑe⟨ofles⟩ lore.
    Bi þe hit is iseid   and soþ hit is on boken: 30
qui custodit diuitias   ser⟨uus⟩ est diuitiis.
Pu were þeow   þines weolan,
noldest þu nouht þærof d⟨on⟩   for drihtenes willæn,
ac æfre þu grædiliche   gæderedest þe more.
Lu⟨þer⟩liche eart þu forloren   from al þ⟨et⟩ þu lufedest,   35
and ic scal, wræcche soul⟨e,   weo⟩we nu driæn.
Eart þu nu loþ and unwurþ   alle þine freonden;
nu haṃ ⟨þun⟩cheþ al to long   þ⟨et⟩ þu ham neih list
ær þu beo ibrouht   þær þu be⟨on⟩ scalt,
on deope sæþe,   on durelease huse,   40
þær wurmes wældeþ   al ⟨þet þe⟩ wurþest was,
fules⟨t⟩ qualeholde   þe þu icwemdest ær
mid alre ⟨þære⟩ swetnesse   þeo þu swuþe lufedest;

---

24. leofli⟨che⟩ S, H, R; leofli⟨ch⟩ H; leofli⟨c⟩ B
25. swuþe deorwurþe MS, H, B, Ha, R; swuþe deor wurþe P; swuþ deor þurþe S
26. þære MS, P, S, H, B; þæ⟨n⟩e Ha, R. MS *pointing,* were · alese⟨d⟩ from
28. we⟨re⟩ H, B, Ha, R; we⟨ren⟩ S. *There is no point between* ifreoed *and* to.
29. þæṣ ḑe⟨ofles⟩: *there is a crease in the leaf at this point.*
30. bi: b *is a small capital.*
31. MS diuitias · ser⟨uus⟩
33. d⟨on⟩; d⟨ælen⟩ S, H, B, Ha, R. *The remains of the letter after* d *indicate that* o *or* e *is more likely than* æ.
36. soul⟨e weo⟩we H, B, Ha, R; soule ⟨ece⟩ we S
38. haṃ (*the first one*) S, H, B, Ha, R; har P. *The final minim in* m *has been cut away.*
39. be⟨on⟩ H, B, Ha, R; be⟨grafen⟩ S
40. on (*the first one*): o *is a small capital.*
41. al ⟨þet þe⟩ H, B, Ha, R; al⟨le þat⟩ S
42. fules⟨t⟩ qualeholde; fuweles quale holde MS, P, S; fuweles qualeholde H, B, Ha; fules⟨t alre⟩ holde R. icwemdest MS, P, S, B, Ha, R; icwendest H
43. ⟨þære⟩ Ha, R; ⟨kunde⟩ S, H, B. *Part of a descender is visible after* alre; *therefore,* þ *is possible while* k *is not.*

þeo swetnesse is nu al agon,   þ(et) b⟨ittere⟩ þe biþ fornon;
þ(et) bittere ilæsteþ æffre,   þet swete ne cumeþ þe ⟨næffre⟩45

Fragment C, f. 64ᵛ

[* * *] ⟨þunc⟩heþ   þ(et) þu hire bilefdest."   1
  ȝet sæiþ þeo sowle   soriliche to þen licame:
"Ne ⟨þea⟩rft þu on stirope   stonden mid fotan,
on nenne goldfohne bowe,   for þu ⟨scal⟩t faren al to howe
and þu scalt nu ruglunge   ridæn to þære eorþe,   5
ut⟨se⟩t æt þære dure   (ne þearft þu næffre onȝean cumæn),
reowliche riden   ⟨son⟩e beræfed
a⟨t⟩ þene eorþliche weole   þe þu iwold ohtest.
Nu mon mæi ⟨seg⟩gen bi þe: 'Þes mon is iwiten nu her,
weila, and his weolæn   beoþ her belæfed;   10
⟨nol⟩de he nefre þærof don   his drihtenes wille.'
Ac æfre þu gæderedest   gær⟨sume o⟩n þine feonde;
nulleþ heo nimen gete   hwo hit biȝete;
nafst þu bute ⟨wei⟩lawei   þ(et) þu weole heuedest:
al is reowliche þin siþ   efter þin wrecche ⟨lif⟩.   15

---

1. c⟩heþ *begins f.64ᵛ. The tops of the letters in this line are missing.* bilefdest R;
bileiben P, S; b.ei.en H; ...ei.en B
2,4. *The* l *of* sowle *and the first* e *of* nenne *are obscured by a crease.*
3. ne ⟨þea⟩rft H, B, R; sæ..... P; sæ, ⟨ne þea⟩rft S
6. ut⟨se⟩t H, B, R; ut⟨sceot⟩ S. u *is a small capital.*
7. reowliche: r *is a small capital.* ⟨son⟩e R; ⟨nu all⟩e S; *no reconst.* H; ⟨seoruhlich⟩e
B. *The letter before* e *may have been an* h, n, *or* w, *but not* l.
8. a⟨t⟩ B, R; ac MS, P, S, H
10. *There is a point between* weila *and* 7, *but not between* weolæn *and* beoþ. weolæn
MS, P, S, H, B; weolan R
12. gær⟨sume o⟩n H, B; gær⟨sume⟩n S; gær⟨suma⟩n R. g *is a small capital.*
14. ⟨wei⟩lawei H, B, R; ⟨we⟩lawei S
15. reowliche MS, P, S, B, R; reowlich H

Þeo men beoþ þe bliþre,   þe arisen ær wiþ þe,
þ(et) þin muþ is betuned;   ⟨þu⟩ þeo teone ut lettest
þe heom sore grulde,   þet ham gros þe aȝan;
⟨dea⟩þ hine haueþ bituned   and þene teone aleid.
Soþ is iseid   on þen salme ⟨bo⟩c: 20
os tuu(m) habundauit malitia,
was on þine muþe   luþernesse ri⟨f⟩e.

⟨Nol⟩dest þu on þine huse   herborwen þeo wrecchen,
ne mihten heo under ⟨þin⟩e roue   none reste finden;
noldest þu nefre helpen   þam orlease wrec⟨che⟩n,   25
ac þu sete on þine benche   underleid mid þine bolstre,
þu wurpe ⟨cne⟩ow ofer cneow   ne icneowe þu þe sulfen
þ(et) þu scoldest mid wurmen   ⟨wu⟩nien in eorþan.
Nu þu hauest neowe hus,   inne beþrungen;
lowe beoþ ⟨þe⟩ helewewes,   unheiȝe beoþ þe sidwowes, 30
þin rof liiþ   on þine breoste ful ⟨nei⟩h;
colde is þe ibedded,   cloþes bideled,
nulleþ þine hinen   cloþes þe sen⟨den⟩,
for heom þuncheþ al to lut   þ(et) þu heom bilefdest;
þet þu hefdest onhor⟨ded,   h⟩eo hit wulleþ heldan.   35

---

17. ⟨þu⟩; ⟨þe⟩ S, H, R; ⟨þe þu⟩ B. lettest MS, P, S, H, B; lettet R
18. þe heom sore MS, H, B, R; þe he heom sorc P; þe he heom sore S. *There may be a point after* gros.
19. ⟨dea⟩þ H, B, R; ⟨dæ⟩þ S. þene *is badly faded; the ascender of* þ *is not visible, even under ultraviolet light.*
20. ⟨bo⟩c R; ⟨be⟩c S, B; ⟨e⟩c H
22. ri⟨f⟩e R; ripe MS, P, S, H, B
25. *There is no point dividing this line.*
28. ⟨wu⟩nien H, B, R; ⟨husnien⟩ S
30. helewewes MS, P, S; helewowes H, B, R. *A crease obscures the sixth letter in the word, but it is more likely an* e *than an* o.
31. *There is no point dividing this line.* ⟨nei⟩h H, B; ...i P; ⟨nei⟩ S; ⟨lo⟩h R
32. colde *is very distorted by a crease. There is a small hole in the* i *of* is. bideled MS, H, B, R; bidcled P, S
33. sen⟨den⟩ H, B, R; *no reconst.* S
34. to: o *is very indistinct, even under ultraviolet light.* þ(et) *appears to be* þ *followed by an unerased, false stroke (or, perhaps, offset) giving the appearance of* þt
35. onhor⟨ded h⟩eo R; on hor.... þeo P; on hor⟨de⟩ þeo S; onhor⟨d⟩ed H, B. *An indistinct mark over the* e *of* heo *gives the impression of an ascender of a* d.

þus is iwitan þin weole,   wendest þet hit þin were:
þus ⟨ageþ⟩ nu þin siþ   efter þin wrecche lif.
    Þe sculen nu waxen   wurmes besiden,
⟨þeo⟩ hungrie feond   þeo þe freten wulleþ;
heo wulleþ þe frecliche freten   for ⟨heom⟩ þin flæsc likeþ; 40
heo wulleþ freten þin fule hold   þeo hwule heo hit fin⟨deþ⟩;
þonne hit al biþ agon   heo wulleþ gnawen þine bon,
þeo orlease wur⟨mes⟩.   Heo windeþ on þin ærmes,
heo brekeþ þine breoste   and borieþ þ(urh) ofer al,
⟨heo c⟩reopeþ in and ut: þet hord is hore owen.   45
And so heo wulleþ waden   wide in þi⟨ne wom⟩be,
todelen þine þermes   þeo þe deore weren,
lifre and þine lihte   lod⟨liche⟩ torenden,
and so scal formelten   mawe and þin milte,
and so scal þin i(n) [....]   50

---

36. iwitan MS, P, S, B, R; iwiten H
37. ⟨ageþ⟩ R; ⟨reowliche⟩ S; ⟨is⟩ H, B. *The remains of the letter before* nu *cannot belong to an* s.
38. besiden P, S, R; be siden H, B
39. ⟨þeo⟩ B, R; ⟨þene⟩ S; *no reconst.* H
40. ⟨heom⟩ H, B, R; ⟨heo⟩ S
41. heo (*the first one*) MS, S, H, B, R; he P
42. þine MS, H, B, R; þin P, S
43. ærmes R; armes P, S, H, B. *The* æ *and* r *are crowded closely together.*
44. þ(urh) H, B, R; þe P, S. MS ꝥ
45. ⟨heo c⟩reopeþ R; ⟨heo⟩ reoweþ P, S, H, B
46. þi⟨ne wom⟩be H, B, R; þi ⟨wom⟩be S
48,50. *A crease obscures the* i *in both* lihte *and* þin.
50. þin i(n); win P, S; þin H, B; þin i(n) w R

Fragment D, f. 65ʳ

[* * * *]w ẹfṛẹ þịṇ[.. .....]   1a
þụ ṣc̣ạḷṭ ṇụ [.......] ⟨wur⟩mes of þine flæsce;   1
þu scalt fostren þine feond   þet þu beo al ifreten;
⟨þu⟩ scalt nu herborwen   unhol wihte;
noldest þu ær gode men   for lufe gọ⟨de dæ⟩lan;
heo wulleþ wurchen hore hord   on þine heauedponne, 5
n⟨ulleþ⟩ heo bileafen   þine lippen unfreten
ac þu scalt grisliche   grennien ọ⟨n men⟩,
hwo so hit iseiȝe   he mihte beon offered:
reowliche biþ so þin siþ   efte⟨r þin⟩ wrecche lif.
    Nu me wule swopen þine flor   and þet flet clensien, 10
for hit is h⟨ẹom þe⟩ loþre   þe þu þeron leiȝe;
heo wulleþ mid holiwatere   beworpen ec þeo w⟨ọwes⟩,
ble⟨t⟩sien ham ȝeorne   to burewen ham wiþ þe,
beren ut þin bedstrau,   b⟨eornen⟩ hit mid fure;
þus þu ert nu ilufed   seoþþen þu me forlure: 15
al hit is re⟨ọwliche⟩ þin siþ   efter þin wrecche lif."
    Ȝet sæiþ þe soule   soriliche to hire licame:

1a. ẉ ẹfṛẹ þịṇ; *no reconst.* S, H, B; was...ond.....efre þinra R. *The first line that remains of f.65ʳ is cut through the middle.*
1. þụ ṣc̣ạḷṭ ṇụ R; *no reconst.* S, H, B
3. *There is no point between* herborwen *and* unhol.
4. gọ⟨de dæ⟩lan; gọ⟨d dæ⟩lan B, R; gọ⟨d sel⟩lan S, H
5. wulleþ: MS wulleþ wulleþ. *Dittography.*
6. n⟨ulleþ⟩ H, B, R; m.... P; m⟨oton⟩ S
7. ọ⟨n men⟩; ⟨þat⟩ S. a⟨nd gristbitien⟩ H, B; ọ[....] R. *The letter after* grennien *is probably an* o; a *is possible.*
9. reowliche MS, P, S, B, R; reowlich H. r *is a small capital.* wrecche: S's wercche *is likely a misprint.*
11. h⟨ẹom þe⟩ R; h⟨ẹom⟩ S; h⟨am⟩ H, B
12. holiwatere; holi watere P, S, H, B, R. w⟨ọwes⟩ R; p..... P; p⟨ædas⟩ S; w⟨ede⟩ H; w⟨æde⟩ B. *The second letter may be an* e.
13. ble⟨t⟩sien B, R; blecsien MS, P, S, H
14. b⟨eornen⟩ H, B, R; b⟨rennen⟩ S
16. re⟨ọwliche⟩ S, B, R; re⟨ọwlich⟩ H

"⟨Wen⟩dest þu, la, erming,   her o to wunienne.
Nes hit þe nowiht icunde   þet þu icore⟨n hit⟩ hefdest;
nes hit icunde þe more   þen þine cunne biuoren þe.   20
Ne heold ic þin⟨e ei3en⟩ opene   þeo hwule ic þe inne was?
Hwi noldest þu lefen   þa þu hi isei3e,
hu þine fordſ⟨æderes⟩   ferden biforen þe?
Nu heo wunieþ on eorþe,   wurmes ham habbeþ todæled,
isc⟨end hore⟩ sorhfulle bones   þe þeo sunne wrohten." 25
    Þa 3et seiþ þeo soule   soriliche to hire l⟨i̯came⟩:
"Æfre þu were luþer   þeo hwile þu lif hæfdest;
þu were leas and luti   and unriht lufede⟨st;
mid þine⟩ luþere deden   deredest cristene men
and mid worde and mid werke   so þu wurst mihte⟨ṣt. 30
Ic was⟩ from gode   clene to þe isend,
ac þu hauest unc fordon   mid þine luþere deden;
⟨æfre⟩ þu were gredi   and mid gromen þe onfulled;
unneaþe ic on þe   eni wununge ha̧⟨fde⟩
for hearde niþe   and ofermete fulle,   35
for þin wombe was þin god   and þin wulder ⟨waṣ⟩ iscend.

18. ⟨wen⟩dest H, B, R; ⟨nol⟩dest S. MS *pointing,* erming · her · o · to
19. *There is a small cut through the middle of* nes hit. icore⟨n hit⟩; icore⟨n me⟩ S;
    icore⟨n⟩ H, B, R
20. MS *pointing,* þe · more þen
21. ic MS, H, B, R; is P, S. ⟨ei3en⟩ B; ⟨æi3e⟩ S; *no reconst.* H; ⟨e3en⟩ R
22. hi MS, P, S, H, R; hi⟨t⟩ B
23. fordſ⟨æderes⟩ ; fordſ⟨eren⟩ S; for⟨e⟩ſ⟨æderes⟩ H, B, R. MS þineſ *with* ford
    written above it.
25. isc⟨end hore⟩ B, R; isc⟨eorſ⟩ S; isc⟨end⟩ H
26. 3et: 3 *is a small capital.* l⟨i̯came⟩ H, B, R; l⟨ichame⟩ S
28-29. lufede⟨st / mid þine⟩ B, R; lufede⟨st / and⟩ S; lufede⟨st / þurh þine⟩ H
30. wurst mihte⟨ṣt⟩: *What appears to be an* i *between the two words is probably the faul-*
    ty first stroke of an m.
30-31. mihte⟨ṣt / Ic was⟩ H, R; mihte / ⟨Ic was⟩ S; mihte⟨ṣt / Ic com⟩ B
31. gode: g *is a small capital.* MS *pointing,* gode clene · to
34. unneaþe: u *may be a small capital.* ha̧⟨fde⟩; ha.... P; ha⟨uede⟩ S; hæ⟨fde⟩ H,
    B, R. *The second half of an* æ *does not seem to be present.*
36. god: g *is a small capital. There is a small hole in the* w *of* wulder. ⟨waṣ⟩ H, B,
    R; ⟨þu⟩ S. *The remains of the letter after* wulder *appear to belong to* w, *not* þ.

Forloren þu hauest þeo ece blisse,   binumen þu hauest þe
                                                                      paradis;
bi⟨nu⟩men þe is þ(et) holi lond,   þen deofle þu bist isold
                                                                      on hond,
for noldest þu nefr⟨e hab⟩ben inouh   buten þu hefdest
                                                                      unifouh;
nu is þ(et) swete al agon,   þ(et) bittere þe bi⟨þ⟩ fornon;   40
þ(et) bittere ilest þe efre,   þet gode ne cumeþ þe nefre;
þus ageþ nu þ⟨in siþ⟩   æfter þin wrecce lif.

     Þu wendest þ(et) þin ende   nefre ne cuman scolde;
to long⟨e þo⟩lede deaþ þe   þ(et) he nolde nimen þe,
for efre þu arerdest sake   and unseihte ⟨were⟩,   45
and ic was wiþi(n)nen þe   biclused swuþe fule.
Þu were wedlowe and monsware   and [....] hund inouh,
for þu were mid sunne   ifulled al wiþinne,
for þe deofel ⟨leide his h⟩ord   ful neih þine heorte;
efre þu woldest fullen   al þ(et) was his wille   50
iç

---

38. bi⟨nu⟩men S, H, B, R; bu... P. b *is a small capital.*
44. long⟨e þo⟩lede R; *no reconst.* S; long⟨e maþe⟩lede H, B
45. ⟨were⟩; *no reconst.* S; ⟨makedest⟩ H, B; ⟨scerp⟩ R
47. MS *pointing,* wedlowe ·7 monsware ·7. hund P, S; huned H, B, R. *The ap-
    parent loop of an* e *between the* n *and* d *is probably an errant penstroke.*
49. ⟨leide his h⟩ord R;]..... / ...l.ord P; l⟨ored þe al⟩l / ord S; l⟨æi la⟩ford H;
    l.....ord B. *The left-hand corner of the leaf is missing. There is no point before* ful.
51. iç H, B, R; *no reconst.* S

Fragment E, f. 65ᵛ

[* * * *]
⟨nold⟩est þu nefre wurchen drihtenes ⟨wille⟩　　　　1
　　　　[* * * *] ⟨iwo⟩ld ahte."
Þe ʒet seiþ þeo soule　　　soriliche to hire licame:
"Clene biþ þeo eor⟨þe　　ær⟩ þu to hire tocume,
ac þu heo afulest　　mid þine fule holde;　　　　5
þet is þ(et) fu⟨le hol⟩d　　afursed from monnen.
Nu þu bist bihuded　　on alre horde fulest,
on ⟨deope⟩ seaþe,　　on durelease huse.
Þu scalt rotien and brostnian,　　þine bon beoþ bedæled
⟨of þ⟩ære wæde　　þe heo weren to iwunede;　　10
brekeþ liþ from liþe,　　liggeþ þe bon stil⟨le,
oþ⟩ ure drihten eft　　of deaþe heo aræreþ,
so he alle men deþ　　þonne domesdai ⟨cum⟩eþ.
Þonne scalt þu, erming,　　up arisen,
imeten þine morþdeden,　　þeo þe murie ⟨were⟩n,　　15
seoruhful and sorimod　　so þin lif wrouhte.
　　Nu beoþ þine earen fordutte　　⟨ne drea⟩me ihereþ;
þeo leorneden þeo listen　　þa luþere weren,
wowe domes　　and gultes ⟨feole⟩;

---

1. ⟨nold⟩est B, R; *no reconst.* S, H. wurchen H, B, R; þurchen P; þ... S. ⟨wille⟩ R; *no reconst.* S; wille H, B. *The last half of the first line on f.65ᵛ is almost totally lost.*

4. tocume H, B, R; to cume P, S

6. fu⟨le hol⟩d H, B, R; fu.... P; fu⟨lnesse⟩ S

7. *This line is not divided by a point.*

9. MS *pointing,* þu scalt rotien ·7 brostnian · þine

11. brekeþ: b *is a small capital.*

11-12. stil⟨le / oþ⟩ H, R; stil / ⟨þa⟩ S; stil⟨le / ac⟩ B

13. domesdai R; domes dai P, H, B; domes dæie S

15. imeten: i *is a small capital.*

17. ⟨ne drea⟩me; ⟨non drea⟩me S; *no reconst.* H, R; ⟨heo none herunge⟩ ne B. *The letter before* e *is clearly* m, *not* n.

19. wowe domes MS, P, B, R; ⟨mid⟩ wowe domes S; wowedomes H. ⟨feole⟩ H, B, R; ⟨feole / þu⟩ S

oþre beræfedest   rihtes istreones   20
þ(urh) þæs deofles lore   þeo þe likede wel.
Þe ⟨wel⟩ tuhte his hearpe   and tuhte þe to him;
þu iherdest þene dream;   he was drih⟨ten f⟩ul loþ;
he swefede þe mid þen sweiʒe;   swote þu sleptest
longe on þine bedde   [. . .]is þe to chirche;   25
ne mostes þu iheren   þeo holie dræmes,
þeo bellen rungen   ⟨þet u⟩nker becnunge wæs,
ne holie lore   þe unker help wære;
ac efre he tuhte þe   ⟨þet lut⟩ þeo þe iwold ahte.
Ac nu beoþ fordutte   þine dreamþurles,   30
ne ihereþ heo ⟨nefr⟩ę more   none herunge of þe
ær þeo bemen blowen   þe unc becnien scu⟨len
f⟩rom deaþes dimnesse   to drihtenes dome.
Þonne þu scalt iheren   þene ⟨hea⟩rde dom
þe þu on þisse life   luþerliche ofeodest."   35
      Þe ʒet seiþ þe sowle   ⟨soril⟩iche to hire licame:
"Nu þu bist afursed   from alle þine freonden;
⟨nu⟩ is þiin muþ forscutted   for deaþ hine haueþ fordutted,

---

20. rihtes: r *is a small capital.*
22. ⟨wel⟩ B, R; ⟨deafle⟩ S; ⟨deofel⟩ H. *The final letter cannot be an* e.
23. he MS, P, S, H, B; ⟨þ⟩e R. drih⟨ten f⟩ul loþ B, R; . .ulloþ P; drih⟨tene f⟩ulloþ
      S; drih⟨tene fu⟩l loþ H
24. MS *pointing,* he swefede þe · mid þen sweiʒe · swote. sweiʒe MS, P, H, B,
      R; sweize S
25. [. . .]is þe H, R; ⟨n⟩is þe S; ⟨loþ wa⟩s B. *The letter before* s *cannot be an* a.
27. ⟨þet u⟩nker B, R; . .iker P; ⟨þat s⟩iker S; ⟨þe un⟩ker H
29. ⟨þet lut⟩ þeo R; . .beo P; ⟨and nu⟩ beo S; ⟨oþ⟩ heo H; ⟨to him, ne⟩ heo B.
      The letter before e *is more likely* þ *than* h.
31. ⟨nefr⟩ę; ⟨n⟩e S, B; ⟨næffr⟩e H; ⟨nu n⟩e R
32-33. scu⟨len / f⟩rom H, B; scu⟨llen / f⟩rom S, R. *What appears to be the top por-
      tion of two* l's *after* u *is probably offset.*
34. ⟨hea⟩rde H, B, R; ⟨lauer⟩de S
35. ofeodest H, B, R; of eodest P, S
36. þe ʒet MS, H, B, R; þet et P, S. *Since the scribe would probably not have written
      a single letter at the end of a line, the* s *following* soule *must be considered offset.*
38. þiin MS, B, R; þim P; þine S; þin H

ne biþ he ne ⟨nam⟩mare undon   ær cume þæs heiʒe
                                    kinges dom.
Þonne hit biþ isene   ⟨so hi⟩t on psalme seiþ: 40
reddit(ur)i su(n)t de factis p(ro)p(ri)is rat(i)one(m),
Þonne sculen þeo ⟨so⟩ule   seggen hore deden
wisliche þurh wisdome,   for drihten hit wot;
⟨þon⟩ne heo onfoþ hore dom   of drihtenes muþe,
Also hit is awriten   †of ⟨drih⟩tenes muþe:†   45
ite maledicti in ignem eternu(m).
Þonne sculen wit si⟨þien⟩   to alre seoruwe mest,
faren mid feondes   in þet eche fur,
beornen ⟨þer e⟩fre,   ende nis þer nefre,
et q(ui) bona eger(un)t ibu(n)t i(n) uita(m) et(er)na(m),   50
þonne ⟨scule⟩n þeo goden   mid gode siþian,
echeliche wunien   i(n) alre wuld⟨re mest⟩
[* * * *]

---

39. ⟨nam⟩mare R; ..nare P; mare S, H, B. *The letter before* a *is* m, *not* n.
40. ⟨so hi⟩t R; ⟨þe⟩t S, H; ⟨so he hi⟩t B
41. MS redditī sut de factis ppis ratōnē
42. ⟨so⟩ule B, R; ..eile P; ⟨w⟩eile S; ⟨f⟩ule H
45. ⟨drih⟩tenes S, H, B, R; ..te tenes P. muþe MS, P, S, H, B; ⟨writ⟩e R
46. ite: i *is a small capital.* eternu(m): MS eternū
49. beornen: b *is a small capital.* ⟨þer e⟩fre B, R; ⟨æ⟩fre S; ⟨e⟩fre H
50. MS Et q̇ bona egert ibut ī uitā ėtnā
51. ⟨scule⟩n H, B, R; ⟨go⟩n S. goden *and* gode: g *is a small capital.*
52. ⟨mest⟩ H, B, R; *no reconst.* S

Fragment F, f. 66ʳ

[* * * *]   "me suke þe: 1
os meu(m) ap(e)rui   et attraxi sp(iritu)m,
þu[.....]⟨dest þin muþ⟩   and drowe me to þe.
Walawa and wa is me   þ(et) ic efre com to þe,
for nold⟨est þu⟩ mid þine muþe   bimænen þine neode,   5
ac efre diȝelliche   þu wold⟨est ham⟩ bidernan.
Noldest þu ham siggen   biforen none preosten
þer ⟨sunfu⟩le men   secheþ ha(m) ore,
bimæneþ hore misdeden   and seoþþen milts⟨e on⟩foþ,
þurh soþne scrift   siþieþ to criste,   10
seggeþ hore sunnen   and hor⟨e soule⟩ helpeþ.
Þurh soþe bireousunge   þeo soule reste onfoþ,
ac ne þe⟨arf ic⟩ nefre resten   þurh þine bireousunge,
ac altogædere ic am forlor⟨en⟩   þurh⟩ þine luþere deden:
noldest þu mid muþe   bidden me none milts⟨unge⟩.   15
Nu þu ert adu(m)bed   and deaþ haueþ þeo keiȝe;
mid clutes þu ert for⟨bun⟩den   and loþ alle freonden
efre ma eft   on to lokienne.

---

1. me suke to þe *begins f. 66ʳ.*
2. MS os meu ạprui & attraxi spm. *The ascenders of* s *in* os *and* spm, *as well as those of* tt *in* attraxi, *have been cut away along with some abbreviation marks.* sp(iritu)m; ipsum P, S, H, B, R
3. *The ascender of* þ *in* þu *has been cut away along with tops of the following letters.* [.....]⟨dest þin muþ⟩ R; *no reconst.* S, H; ⟨opnedest þin bon⟩ B
5. nold⟨est þu⟩ S, B, R; nold⟨est⟩ H. MS noln *with a small* d *above the second* n. *There is a small hole in the* m *of* muþe.
6. wold⟨est ham⟩ S, B, R; wold⟨est⟩ H
8. ⟨sunfu⟩le B, R; ⟨al⟩le S, H
9. milts⟨e on⟩foþ H, B, R; milts⟨unge⟩ foþ S
11. hor⟨e soule⟩ H, B, R; hor ⟨soules⟩ S
13. þe⟨arf ic⟩ B, R; þe ⟨scalt⟩ S; þe ⟨þearf⟩ H
15. milts⟨unge⟩ S; milts⟨e⟩ H, B, R
17. for⟨bun⟩den H, B, R; forl.... / den P; forl⟨ig⟩den S. *An* l *or* b *is possible after* r.
18. efre ma P, S, H, B; efrema R

Þus is reoulic ⟨þin⟩ siþ   efter þin wrecche lif,
for þu were biset   þicke mid sunne⟨n⟩   20
and alle ⟨heo⟩ weren prikiende   so piles on ile.
He biþ þicke mid piles   ne p(ri)kieþ he⟨o hine⟩ nowiht,
for al biþ þ(et) softe   iwend to him sulfen
þ(et) ne mawen his pil⟨es   pri⟩kien hine sore,
for al biþ þ(et) scearpe   him iwend fromward: 25
so þu we⟨re⟩ mid sunne   iset al wiþine.
Þeo sunfule pikes   p(ri)kieþ me ful sore,
ac ⟨al þet⟩ softe   was iwend to þe suluen
and efre þet scerpe   scorede me touwar⟨d,
for⟩ heo weren iwend   so me wurst was: 30
ic was mid þine p(ri)ckunge   ipin⟨ed ful⟩ sore.
Ac nu me wulleþ prikien   þeo pikes inne helle,
pinien me ful so⟨re   all⟩ for þine sunne.

    Ic was on heihnesse isceapen   and soule ihoten;
ic was þe se⟨oueþe⟩ isceaft,   so þeo bec seggeþ,   35
þe þe almihti god   mildeliche iwrouhte

---

19. reoulic ⟨þin⟩ H, R; reoulic⟨he þin⟩ S, B. þin (*the second one*) MS, H, B, R; þine P, S.

20. sunne⟨n⟩ R; sunne MS, P, S, H, B

21. ⟨heo⟩ H, R; ⟨þeo⟩ S; ⟨sunnen⟩ B. *The letter after* alle *may have been an* h *or* þ, *but* s *is unlikely.*

22. piles MS, H, B, R; wiles P, S. p(ri)kieþ: MS þkieþ. he⟨o hine⟩ H, B, R; he⟨om⟩ S

25. *The stroke between the* m *of* him *and the* i *of* iwend *is probably offset.*

26. so: s *is perhaps a small capital.* we⟨re⟩ H, B, R; we⟨ren⟩ S. wiþine MS, R; wiþ inne P, S; wiþi(n)ne H, B

27. p(ri)kieþ: MS þkieþ. ful sore H, B, R; fulsore P, S

28. ⟨al þet⟩ B, R; ⟨þu al þat⟩ S; ⟨þet⟩ H. MS *pointing,* softe was · iwend

29-30. touwar⟨d / for⟩; touwar⟨des⟩ S; touwar⟨d⟩ H, B, R

31. p(ri)ckunge: MS þckunge. ipin⟨ed ful⟩ sore B, R; ipin⟨ed ful⟩sore S; ipin⟨ed⟩ sore H

33. pinien MS, H, B, R; pinion P, S. so⟨re all⟩ B, R; so⟨re⟩ S, H. sunne; synne P, S, H, B, R. *The unusual pointed form of the* u *and a discoloration below it give the appearance of a* y.

34. heihnesse MS, P, H, B, R; heihnes S

35. ic: i *is a small capital.* se⟨oueþe⟩ B, R; se⟨ofoþe⟩ S; se⟨oveþe⟩ H

wisli⟨che⟩ mid worde;   so hit al iwearþ—
heouene and eorþe,   luft and engles,
wind and watę⟨r,   and⟩ þæs monnes soule—
þis beoþ þeo seouene   þe ic ær foreseide.   40
Þis was ma⟨kunge⟩   þæs almihties fæder,
of þissen andweorke   alle þing he iwrouhte
and þ⟨us⟩ hit is iwriten   on holie wisdome:
fiat et f(a)c(t)a sunt om(n)ia,
he seide, 'iwu⟨rþe'   and⟩ alle þing iworþen.   45
Þus mid one worde   al hit was iwurþen;
he iscop þ⟨urh⟩† þene sune   alle isceafte
wisliche þurh wisdome,   and efre he hit wiseþ;
[....]⟨i⟩maginem *et similitudinem,*
and ic deorewurþe   drihtenes onlicn⟨esse⟩   50

---

38. MS *pointing,* heouene · & eorþe · luft · 7 engles
39. MS *pointing,* wind · & watę⟨r⟩. watę⟨r and⟩; wate⟨re⟩ S; wate⟨r⟩ H, B, R
40. foreseide P, S, H; fore seide B, R
41. ma⟨kunge⟩ H, B, R; ma⟨kede⟩ S
42. of: o *is a small capital.*
44. MS fiat et fcā sunt omīa
45. iwu⟨rþe⟩: i *is a small capital.*
47. þ⟨urh⟩ þene; þ..... þene P; þ⟨onne⟩ þene S; þ⟨urh⟩ ⟨hit⟩ þene H, B; þ⟨urh⟩ [...] þene R. þ⟨urh⟩: MS þ
49. [....] ⟨i⟩maginem R; imaginem P, S; ⟨ad i⟩maginem H, B

Fragment G, f. 66ᵛ

[* * * *] ⟨god⟩   1a

and ic þe [..]æ[.]e   mid loþre lufe   1
and ic þin wale iwearþ   hu so ⟨þu wol⟩dest.
weila, þine fule iwill,   wo haueþ hit me idon.
Þu fule maþe⟨me⟩te,   hwi hauest þu me biswiken?
For þine fule sunne   ic scal nu ⟨to hell⟩e,   5
dreizen þer wrecche siþ   all for þine fule lif.

    Zet ic wulle þe ætwi⟨ten   mi⟩ne weasiþes
nu ic scal soriliche   siþien from þe.
Nu beoþ þine teþ atru⟨ked;   þin⟩ tunge is ascorted
þeo þe facen was   and þen feonde icwem⟨d⟩e   10
mid wowe ⟨domes⟩   and mid gultes feole;
oþre birefedest   rihtes istreones,
gæderedest to ⟨gærsu⟩me.   Ac hit is nu all agon
þurh þæs deofles lore   þe þe licode wel.
Nu liþ þin ⟨tung⟩e stille   on ful colde denne;   15
nafest þu gærsume þe mo   þe heo was spekinde ⟨so,
for⟩ heo was faken biforen   and atterne bihinden;

1a. ⟨god⟩ H, R; of god P, S; *no reconst.* B. *At least one letter is still partially visible before this word.*

1. [..]æ[.]e R; imæne P, S, H, B

2. ⟨þu wol⟩dest H, B, R; ⟨þu nol⟩dest

4. maþe⟨me⟩te H, B, R; maþe⟨mæ⟩te S

5. ⟨to hell⟩e R; ⟨in hell⟩e S; ⟨inne hell⟩e H, B

7. ætwi⟨ten mi⟩ne R; ætwi⟨nne and þin⟩e S; ætwi⟨ten þe⟩ H, B

9. atru⟨ked þin⟩ R; atru⟨þin⟩ S; atru⟨kied þi⟩ H; atru⟨kied þin⟩ B. *There is a small hole in the g of* tunge.

10. icwem⟨d⟩e; icweme MS, P, S, H, B, R

11. ⟨domes⟩ H, B, R; ⟨dræmes⟩ S. gultes: g *is a small capital.*

12. oþre MS, P, H, B, R; ⟨þu⟩ oþre S

13. gæderedest: g *is a small capital.* ⟨gærsu⟩me H, B, R; ..ime P; *no reconst.* S

15. ⟨tung⟩e H, B, R; ⟨bodig⟩e S

16. þe mo H, B, R; þemo P, S

16-17. ⟨so / for⟩; ⟨for⟩ S; ⟨of⟩ H; ⟨so⟩ B, R

heo demde feole domes   þe drihten ⟨weren⟩ loþe;
isæid hit is on psalme   and ful soþ hit is bi hire:
lingua tua concinnabat ⟨dolos⟩,   20
heo ȝeo⟨dde⟩de fakenliche   and þen feonde icwemde.
Heo heou mid hearde worde   and ⟨huned⟩e þa wrecches;
scearp heo was and kene   and cwemde þen deofle
mid †alle þen sun⟨ne†   so⟩ efre was his wille —
a wurþe hire wa   þ(et) heo spekinde was so —   25
heo hauef unc ⟨þus ide⟩med   to deoppere helle.

    Nis hit non sellic   þauh ic segge of boken,
þauh ic ⟨sorilich⟩e   þ(et) soþe repie,
for ic was ilered   of mine leoue fæder
feire on frumþe   ær ⟨ic to⟩ferde.   30
Ic was godes douhter,   ac þu amerdest þ(et) foster;
ic sceolde lif holden   ⟨nouht u⟩nleþe he wolde;
sone þu were lifleas   seoþþen ic þe forleas;
ic was þin imake   ⟨so þeo⟩ bec siggeþ:
uxor tua sicut uitis habundans.   35

---

18. ⟨weren⟩ H, B, R; ⟨was⟩ S
19. isæid: i *is a small capital.* bi hire H, B, R; bihire P, S
20. ⟨dolos⟩ S, H, B; ⟨dolum⟩ R
21. ȝeo⟨dde⟩de H, B, R; ȝeoððde P; ȝeoþode S. MS ȝeoddde: ȝ *is a small capital.*
22. ⟨huned⟩e R; ⟨icwem⟩de S; *no reconst.* H; ⟨chid⟩de B
24. sun⟨ne so⟩ R; sun⟨ne þat⟩ S; sun⟨ne þe⟩ H; sun⟨nen so⟩ B
25. a *(the word) is a small capital.*
26. hauef MS, P, B, R; haue⟨þ⟩ S, H. ⟨þus ide⟩med; . . .ned P; ⟨dom⟩ned S; ⟨de⟩med H, B; ⟨so dem⟩ed R
27. non P, S, B, R; nou H. *The second n is quite indistinct.*
28. ⟨sorilich⟩e ⟨þonne⟩ S; ⟨wrecch⟩e H; ⟨wræcche soul⟩e B; ⟨þin soul⟩e R. *The letter before e is more likely an h or d than l or r.*
29. leoue S, H, B, R; leone P. n *is poorly formed.*
30. ⟨ic to⟩ferde R; ⟨ic ford⟩ferde S; ⟨ic for⟩ferde H, B. *The letter before f is likely an o and clearly not an r.*
31. godes: g *is a small capital.*
32. ⟨nouht u⟩nleþe B, R; . . .uleþe P; ⟨me sell⟩eþe S; ⟨noht u⟩nleþe H. *The n before the l is poorly formed. There is a small hole in the e of he.*
34. ic: i *is a small capital.* ⟨so þeo⟩ H, B, R; ⟨so so⟩ S

Ic was þe biwedded   wurþliche ⟨so winbow⟩e
et þen fontstone   þ⟨et⟩ þu hauest ifuled;
mid þine fule oþes   þu hafest þin ful⟨luht⟩ forloren;
bihinden and biuoren   feire þu were imerked
heie on þine heafde   ⟨mid þ⟩en holie ele;   40
þu hauest †kinemerke.†
Þu sceoldest beon on heouene   heih ⟨arerd⟩ under gode
ȝif þu hit ne forlure   þuruh þæs deofles lore.
Þine godfæderes ⟨behet⟩en   ær heo þe forleten
þ⟨et⟩ þu me scoldest holden   þuruh holie lufe cristes   45
and ⟨mid r⟩ihtere lawe   leden me to criste.
Þu wiþsoke þene deofel   efter drihtenes cwi⟨de,
his⟩ modes and his wrænches   and his wieles þærto;
seoþþen þu hine lufedest   and for[....]ịnne drihten,
for þu lufedest þeo lawen   þe drihten weren loþe.   50
Unker team ⟨is for⟩loren   þe wit scolden teman
so ic was þe bitæiht   †þ⟨et⟩ wit scolden teman;†
þu ⟨scolde⟩st beon bearne fæder   and ic hore moder;
wit scolden fostrien bearn   and bring⟨en ham ṭ⟩o criste.
Þet beoþ þeos bearn,   so so bec mæneþ: 55
filii tui sicut nouel̤l̤⟨ạ oliuarum⟩[.........]

---

36. ic: i *is a small capital.* ⟨so winbow⟩e; *no reconst.* S; ⟨þonn⟩e H; ⟨in wedd⟩e B; ⟨on wedd⟩e R

41. *There may be a point after* hauest. kinemerke H, B, R; kine merke P, S

42. ọn: *left-hand stroke of the* o *is faded.* heih ⟨arerd⟩; *no reconst.* S; heih⟨mod⟩ H, B; heih ⟨hefde⟩ R. gode: g *is a small capital.*

44. godfæderes: g *is a small capital.* ⟨behet⟩en B, R; ⟨ihat⟩en S; ⟨tauht⟩en H

46. ⟨mid r⟩ihtere H, B, R; ..ihtere P; ⟨drig⟩htene S

47-48. cwi⟨de / his⟩ H, B, R; cw⟨iþe / his⟩ S

49. for [....] ịnne R; for⟨wi⟩nne S; for⟨lu⟩nne H, B. *The acute accent over the minim before the first* n *reveals that the letter must have been an* i.

51. unker: u *is a small capital.* ⟨is for⟩loren H, B, R; ⟨for⟩loren S

52. so: s *may be a small capital.*

53. ⟨scolde⟩st H, B, R; ⟨haue⟩st S

54. bring⟨en ham ṭ⟩o R; bring ⟨ham⟩ to S; bring⟨en heom ṭ⟩o H, B

56. nouel̤l̤⟨ạ oliuarum⟩ ; *no reconst.* S; nouel⟨læ oliarum in circuita mensæ suæ⟩ H, B; nouella⟨e olivarum⟩ R

EXPLANATORY NOTES

An effort has been made in the explanatory notes to make the text accessible to the reader at a linguistic level; discussions of a more speculative nature have been kept to a minimum, though attempts have been made to illuminate especially murky passages and to guide the reader to secondary sources that should be of use in coming to terms with the work. Commentary of a more interpretative nature may be found in the introductory discussions of Style and of Sources and Structure. The previous editions are referred to by the names of their editors; reviews of these editions are referred to by the names of the reviewers. Other works are referred to by author or editor; full bibliographical information can be found in the bibliography. A list of abbreviations occurs at the front of the volume.

Fragment A, f. 63ᵛ

1. Hall thinks it likely that *enearde* are the last seven letters of *middenearde* since the usual uncompounded form for "earth" in the poem is *eorþ*.
2. Phillipps and Hall retain the abbreviation 7 for "and"; Buchholz and Ricciardi expand to *ond;* Singer and Haufe expand to *and.* While OE ă before nasals becomes ŏ, written *o*, when accented, *a* prevails in unaccented position, e.g., *licame*, A9, 11. Haufe's suggestion is that *sculen* is used here as an auxiliary with an elided verb of motion, a view accepted by Buchholz; alternatively, Hall suggests *sculen* is an independent verb with the meaning "to pertain to, to be proper to" and translates the line "and all created things which pertain to it" (see Visser 176). Without the context that would be provided by the lines missing from the top of the leaf, the meaning of *sculen* cannot be precisely determined.
3. Hall and Ricciardi accept *þene,* Buchholz's reconstruction, though the former believes *þonne* to be a plausible alternative, which it is.
4. *him on ileide:* In poetry, prepositions sometimes follow the personal pronouns they govern, particularly if this allows them to stand before a finite verb (Mossé 169.1). Hall is of the opinion that *ileide on* has a meaning "apparently without a parallel" in this line: "put into" or perhaps "entrusted to"; however, as Ric-

ciardi points out, "to lay on" meaning "to bestow," OED *lay,* 55, is acceptable in this context; cf. MED *leien,* 12a, "to put in place, set."

5. *isom⟨nede⟩:* Ricciardi believes part of the final *-e* of this word is visible, but the mark on the MS is probably the point dividing the verses.

6. *ꝥ* is expanded to *þet,* the form that consistently appears when the word is unabbreviated.

7. The line has only three stresses. Singer reconstructs the text ⟨*woan*⟩*eþ* without comment; Haufe prints ⟨*won*⟩*eþ,* noting that a stress is missing from the on-verse. Buchholz prints *greoneþ ond woaneþ* by analogy with A15 and 25; Hall points out that this reconstruction is too long for the gap in the MS and he returns to Singer's suggestion while noting that *weopeþ and woaneþ* might have been the original construction; Ricciardi reconstructs *weopeþ* by analogy with A10, another possibility. As there is no point in the MS before *and mænet,* homoeoteleuton may be suspected, at least, with the omission occurring in the on-verse. Regarding the two conjectures that have been made about the original line, one can note that in this poem lines with the alliterative pattern xa : ya are roughly twice as common as lines with the pattern aa : ax. It might be allowed, therefore, that Buchholz's suggestion is the more probable of the two. Regarding *mænet,* see Language, no. 15.

9. Hall argues that *idælen* here is transitive so that a preposition is probably required; *and,* which occurs in the apparently similar A28, would be unusual in this position, and furthermore, *todæleþ* in that line is intransitive. Hall provides one example for the use of *fro* in this situation, Morris, p. 61, l. 32, but the form does not occur elsewhere in *SA; from/fram* is consistently used but would probably be too long for the space missing from the MS. Hall also provides an example for the use of *wiþ* from Assmann, p. 167, l. 17, "*wið þone lichaman seo sawle ӡedælan*". The latter is not an impossible reconstruction here, but *of* with its clear sense of separation seems preferable.

10. *hit,* i.e., the *bearn* of l. 6.

11. ⟨*for d*⟩*eaþ: swo* or *for* seem equally possible. There is no MS justification for the other editors' capitalization of *deaþ:* only a very small portion of the *d* remains.

12. ⟨*oftes*⟩*iþes:* Singer reconstructs the text ⟨*his si*⟩*þes,* but, as Ricciardi points out, this would be the only occurrence in the poem of *siþ* in the plural. Haufe reconstructs ⟨*oftes*⟩*iþes* and is followed by both Buchholz and Hall, though the former, in a list of corrections to his edition, reveals a later preference for *weasiþes* by analogy with G7. However, *wonien* is intransitive in this poem, as a rule, and further, *weasiþes* would create a line with the alliterative pattern aa : aa, a much less common type than aa : ax. Ricciardi prefers the usual OE spelling, *oftsiþes,* for reasons of length, but if *fleoþ* can be accepted in l. 37, as it is by all editors including Ricciardi, the common ME spelling, *oftesiþes,* cannot be considered excessively long. *he,* i.e., the *licame* of l. 11.

16. *al⟨so biþ⟩:* Singer's reconstruction, ⟨*reowliche*⟩, is very long, but ⟨*is*⟩, printed by Haufe and Buchholz, and even ⟨*biþ*⟩, preferred by Hall and Ricciardi, seem rather short. Perhaps preferable is *and al⟨so biþ⟩ his siþ,* i.e., "and thus is his death ..." See OED, *also,* A1.

17-21. One verse is missing from this passage. Singer apparently did not notice the omission. Haufe and Buchholz believe the missing verse is in l. 21, and for l. 20 they print *him teoreþ his miht   him coldeþ his ⟨muþ⟩.* Hall, following an analogous passage in Furnivall, p. 253, ll. 3-6, reconstructs ll. 19-21:

him scorteþ ⟨þe⟩ tunge   ⟨him starkeþ his skin⟩
him trukeþ his iwit   him teoreþ his miht
him coldeþ his ⟨siden⟩   liggeþ þe ban stille.

Hall admits the alliteration of *siden/stille* is imperfect but claims that a more general term than *heorte* or *muþ* is wanted here. Robbins, p. 291, and Woolf, p. 80, both suggest *fet.* Ricciardi locates the missing verse in l. 20 and replaces Hall's *siden* with the stronger *liþe* "limbs" by analogy with E11; *liche* "body" renders 21a similar to a number of OE verses: e.g., *lic acolod bið, Soul and Body* I 123a and *lic colode, Guthlac* 1307b as well as *hraw colian, Rune Poem* 92a, *hræw colode, Dream of the Rood* 72b, etc. Two of the features which create the sense of balance in ll. 17 and 18 are alliteration of the verbs in each verse and prosodical repetition of the on-verse in the off-verse. Though *him teoreþ his miht* does not precisely repeat *him trukeþ his iwit* from the point of view of rhythm, the alliteration and probable rhyme urge that these two verses should form one line and that a verse is missing from l. 19, as Hall suggests. Given the *him ... him ...* repetitive pattern, homoeoteleuton is the likely cause of omission. In this passage, the various parts of the body may be construed as the causative objects of impersonal verbs (Visser 31); one might expect *deauîeþ* in l. 17 if the plural *æren* were the subject (however cf. *hondleþ,* l. A40, which is plural but lacks the *-i-* of Class II weak verbs). On the Signs of Death in ME literature see Woolf, pp. 78-82, 95, 102, 330-2, 341, 373, 376, Robbins, pp. 282-98, and Wenzel, pp. 197-99.

23. ⟨*at*⟩*:* Singer and Haufe have ⟨*of*⟩. The two prepositions are often interchanged (Mustanoja, pp. 350-51); however, *bereven* is followed by *at* in C7-8 (by emendation).

24. ⟨*boð*⟩*unge:* cf. *bodeþ,* A6.

27-28. Haufe prints *So biþ eft þe feorþsiþ sorhliche to dæ⟨len⟩ mid seoruwen al bewunden* as a single line, which it clearly is not; Buchholz prints *mid seoruwen al bewunden* as a separate half line making his lineation one number greater than the other editions from this point to the end of the fragment; Hall omits *sorhliche todælen* as does Ricciardi. It would appear that, at some point in the MS history of the poem, 28b, *soriliche todæleþ,* was miscopied into a position between 27a and b. *feorþsiþ* is perhaps a back spelling owing to a confusion of ŏ and ĕo (see Language, no. 10). However, OE ŏ spelled *eo* does occur elsewhere in twelfth- and thirteenth-century Southern and WML mss (see Schlemilch, p. 15). Elsewhere in the MS, but not in *SA, þeonne* frequently appears for *þonne.*

29. Cf. C15, 37, D9, 16, 42, F19, G6.

30. ⟨*fei*⟩*ʒe:* Singer reconstructs the word ⟨*bod*⟩*iʒe,* which Haufe accepts despite the lack of alliteration. Haufe rejects his own alternative suggestion, *felaʒe,* and Buchholz also rejects *bodiʒe,* which does not agree with the masculine pronouns of the following lines. Zupitza (1891), p. 79, and Holthausen both suggest *feiʒe* and this has been adopted by both Hall and Ricciardi. *iflut:* past participle of *flitten* "to move, convey (something)" from ON *flytja.* The movement of the body to a position on the floor just prior to death was an Anglo-Saxon custom that continued into Norman times (Rock, II, 246). Cf. the death lyric printed by Siegfried Wenzel in "Unrecorded Middle English Lyrics," *Anglia,* 92 (1974), 76 (no. 85), and Alan J. Fletcher, "A Death Lyric from the *Summa Praedicantium,* MS Oriel College 10," *Notes and Queries,* 222 (1977), 11-12.

31. In the church the body was laid with its feet toward the high altar, i.e., the east; it lay in the same direction in the grave (Rock, II, 380).

32. ⟨*col*⟩*deþ:* Zupitza (1891), p. 79, and Holthausen (1892) both suggest *coldeþ,* and both Hall and Ricciardi accept this suggestion. Cf. A36.

33-35. Cf. *The Grave,* l. 6, *"Nu me sceæl þe meten and þa molde seoðða."* The priest marks the length and breadth of the grave with the sign of the cross, using a spade (Rock, II, 383-4). *ʒerde* would appear to mean "staff" here.

36. Cf. *Latemest Day,* A, l. 21, *"þenne liit þe cleyclot cold alse an ston."*

37. Haufe suggests that a relative pronoun is missing after *fleoþ;* however, *þeo* may be a relative and the subject of *fleoþ,* unexpressed.

38. *riht:* Apparently an adverb, but one would expect *rihte* or *rihtliche.*

40. *agon.* Previous editors print *igon:* the *a* is poorly formed and smudged.

41. In OE, *earfoþsiþ* occurs only in verse.

43. The similarity of this line to A41 has prompted all editors since Singer to suggest that *riche* is a mistake for *wrecche,* though no one emends. Repetition of *wrecche* might serve to intensify the feeling of the passage: however, if the image of death presented in Fragment A is meant to be general, i.e., not limited to a specific individual, the poet may have been trying to achieve an antithetical balance between the verses: *riche* meaning "great, powerful"; *wrecche* meaning "weak, insignificant." Hall is also of the opinion that A41b is A43b misplaced through scribal error and that A41b should actually be something like *þe woneþ þe feorþsiþ.* While this is not inconceivable, it also must be remembered that repetition of verses, even within a small number of lines, is characteristic of the style of this poem; cf. A5b and A8b.

44. The number of *unblisse cumaþ* is ambiguous, but probably plural: feminine o-stems occasionally show plural in *-e,* e.g. B9, F47; *-aþ* occurs only here in *SA.*

45. Singer translates *besihþ* as "saith" while Buchholz translates it as *"seufzt,"* i.e., "sighs." Neither rendering is phonologically justified: according to Zupitza, p. 79, the development of the *c* in OE *besican* into *h* would be unparalleled; the development of *æ* in 3rd sg. *sæʒþ* into *i* is also unlikely. Zupitza (1891) believes that *besihþ* is, in fact, derived from OE *beseon,* and the MED confirms that it is a common early form of *bisen,* 2b, "to give heed, pay attention." Cf. *Besyhð þonne sio sawl swiðe bliðum eaʒum to hire lichoman* from the fourth Vercelli homily (Förster, p. 85, ll. 148-49) in reference to a blessed soul.

Fragment B, f. 64^r

1. The first line of f. 64^r is almost wholly cut away. On the left-hand side of the leaf only descenders remain; on the right-hand side bottoms of letters can be made out as well. The second MS line begins with *þu me*. By analogy with B17, Singer, Haufe, and Buchholz offer the reconstruction ⟨*Hwui noldest beþenchen*⟩ *þu me* for the on-verse of the first line, but this is paleographically unjustified. Haufe proposes *þ þu ligge woa w* in his note. Ricciardi's reconstruction of the damaged first line, ... ⟨*– oþ þu wa ligge · woa wro*⟩ ... appears to be possible and her suggestion for the on-verse of l. 1, ⟨*woa wrohtest*⟩ *þu me*, also seems reasonable. Hall's alternative suggestion, *loþ were*, is unlikely; the letter in *woa* that Ricciardi takes to be a *þ*, i.e., *w* — its descender is partially obscured — is almost certainly not an *l*.

2. Cf. D28. *lutiʒ* marks the only occurrence of final *ʒ* in *SA*.

4-11. On the *ubi sunt* theme in OE, see J. E. Cross, "*Ubi Sunt* Passages in Old English — Sources and Relationships." Though he refers to Heningham's "Old English Precursors to the *Worcester Fragments*," Cross does not deal with this passage from *SA*. The concern with earthly riches, ll. 5–9, may ultimately derive from the latter portion of the passage in Isidore's "*Synonyma de lamentatione animae peccatoris*," which Cross shows to be the primary source for most OE versions of the theme; however, the relationship is not particularly close. A similar focus is evident in a homily edited by Assmann (1889) from MS Corpus Christi 302 and MS Cotton Faustina A9 (see Heningham, pp. 302–303, and Cross, pp. 38–39); there are no close verbal parallels to *SA*, however. Woolf, p. 96, is of the opinion that *quid profuit* would be a more accurate designation of this type of passage than *ubi sunt*.

4. The best translation of this line would appear to be "Where is your pride now, which you loved so much?" The position of the antecedent *þe* is odd, however. Another possibility is that the off-verse should be rendered "you loved yourself so much," which may, in fact, be preferable given the reconstruction *modinesse*. However, with reflexive pronouns, *sulfen* is the rule. In either case, *muchel* appears to be an uninflected adverb.

5. ⟨*þa*⟩*newes:* This reconstruction is suggested by Holthausen (1892) and adopted by both Hall and Ricciardi. Cf. *Latemest Day*, A, l. 45, "*Wer boit þine þonewes.*" Another possible spelling is ⟨*þe*⟩*newes*.

7. Though he himself prints the MS version, Hall states that *guldene* "golden" is a corruption of *glyden* "glided" and that *comen* is a gloss on *guldene/glyden*. He suggests emending the off-verse to *þe glyden to þine honden* by analogy with *Latemest Day*, B, l. 54, "*Hwer beoð þine nappes þat þe glideþ to honde?*" This change is adopted by Ricciardi. There is clearly corruption here, but while Hall's suggestion makes fine sense, it is not without difficulties. One must wonder why *comen* should be written after, rather than over, the word to which it is a gloss, and why it should be separated by a point from that word. Indeed, the points after *goldfæten*, *guldene*, and *honden*, dividing the line into three verses, may indicate the omission of words — at least one verse — as has happened elsewhere in the poem. *goldfæt* may mean "golden," rendering the troublesome *guldene* redundant; however, it could also be a survival of the OE *goldfæt* meaning "golden vessel."

8. Haufe believes *fornon* derives from OE *fornean* "near"; Hall says it is a contraction of *foran an* meaning "before, to come." See OED *forne,* 3b, "before, in front of." Cf. B44, D40.

10. Hall adds *sibbe* to the on-verse which is otherwise deficient. Ricciardi expands this to *þe sibbe* as the omission is probably an example of homoeoteleuton, i.e., the scribe omitted *sibbe* due to the repetition of *þe* in the line.

12. Regarding *þupte,* see Language, no. 15. The variation between *longe* here and *long* in a nearly identical verse in B38 is probably owing to the common nature of the phrase "all too long."

14. In his corrections Buchholz proposes to change the reconstruction ⟨*heo*⟩ to ⟨*heo hit*⟩, but *don* here has the meaning "to put, bring" as it did in OE; see BT Supp. *don,* 4. *þe* is the direct object and *wiþuten* is an adverb: "they put you without." Furthermore, *heo hit* is too long for the gap in the MS. The earliest instance of *do without,* i.e., "to get on without, dispense with," is 1713, according to the OED. *hi,* which occurs only here and D22, would appear to be accusative plural, its antecedent being the collective *æihte* from l. 13.

18. *semdest* from OE *siman* "to load, place a burden on."

20. Singer, Hall, and Ricciardi reconstruct *þ*⟨*u lo*⟩*kien* here and would have the verse translated "you would not look to, that is, take heed of, love." Haufe has *þu* ⟨*ma*⟩*kien,* though he himself finds it unsatisfactory; Buchholz expands Haufe's suggestion to *þu*⟨*þe ma*⟩*kien,* which is rather long. *Makien lufe* "to make love" is unattested in English before the sixteenth century—it is for this reason that Hall rejects it—but *lokien lufe* is itself rather obscure in this context. The phrase intended in all probability is *makien lof* "to praise," a common eME construction, e.g., *Brut* 8376 (E.E.T.S. 4176), *scullen alle mine Bruttes … liðen to Lundene, & þer lof makien ure lauerd Appollin.* See MED *maken,* 8a(c). It is conceivable that the spelling *lufe* has been caused by confusion with "love," i.e., OE *lufu,* as indicated in the MED *lof.* The body's lack of *lufe,* whether of its fellow men or God, seems to be a preoccupation of the soul (see the numerous citations for *lufe* and *lufien* in the Glossary); for this reason, and for the fact that *makien* is a reconstruction, emendation to *lof* has been resisted here. On rhetorical patterning in ll. 20–29, see Style, pp. 34–35. Cf. *Latemest Day,* B, ll. 61–62, "*Hwi noldest þu mid crist maken us isahte / Masse leten singe of þat he þe bi-tahte?*"

23. *biddæn* likely means "to pray" in this context; see BT Supp. 2b and MED, 2. According to the MED citation, *fore,* as opposed to *for,* is used as a preposition only in regard to spatial relations; according to Mustanoja, pp. 377–78, however, the distinction was not so pronounced in either the OE or ME periods. Therefore, *fore* in both ll. 21 and 23 can be construed as a preposition meaning "in the place, instead of," i.e., that the "learned men" might pray for the body. *messe* is the only possible French loanword in *SA;* however, it could very well derive from OE *mæsse.*

24. leofli⟨che⟩: The OE adjectival suffix *-lic* is written *liche* in all instances in the poem but two — *sellic*, G27, and probably *reoulic*, F19. However, *-che* may be a little long for the gap in the MS.

26. *þære:* Haufe and Buchholz accept *þære*, the MS reading, but for different reasons. Haufe believes it is a masculine genitive plural form referring to *men*, l. 20; Buchholz believes it is a feminine genitive singular form referring to *messe*, l. 23. As Hall points out, *þurh* + genitive is very rare in ME, and the antecedent in this case is rather far removed from the pronoun if either Haufe or Buchholz is correct. Zupitza (1891), p. 79, suggests the antecedent is *cristes* in the previous line and recommends emendation to the masculine *þæne*, a change accepted by both Hall and Ricciardi. If one were to accept this emendation, it is more probable that *licame*, not *cristes*, would be the antecedent in question: if it were *cristes*, one would expect *him*, not *þæne*. The MS reading need not be abandoned, however. *þære*, as Hall concedes, can be dative as well as genitive, and its antecedent, as Hall does not notice, can be the feminine singular *lac* of the previous line. Also militating against the change proposed by Zupitza is the fact that *þæne* does not occur elsewhere in the poem: the masculine dative singular demonstrative pronoun is always *þen*, the accusative form is always *þene*. The mood of *were* is probably subjunctive.

There is a point in the MS after *were,* and both Singer and Hall accept this division of the line. However, as in F28, this division causes an auxiliary to be separated from the participle that follows it — an unlikely situation. In OE poetry, the auxiliary *wæs* in the final position of a verse is almost invariably preceded by the participle. On the few occasions when the participle follows in the next verse, it is separated from the auxiliary by a direct or indirect object, e.g. *Andreas*, l. 1307, *and se halga wæs   to hofe læded, Guthlac*, l. 1317, *swa ðe burgstede wæs   blyssum gefylled.* Including *alesed* in the on-verse renders it stronger metrically and does not cause the off-verse to be deficient.

28. The mood of *were* is probably subjunctive.

29. Regarding *fenge to,* see MED *fon*, 2, "to succeed to, inherit." Cf. G14.

31. Remotely similar biblical passages occur at Prov. 11, 28 and Eccl. 5, 9, but Hall suggests the line is an "imperfect reminiscence" of "*Qui enim divitiarum servus est, divitias custodit ut servus,*" *Bedae Opera* (1612), v. col. 378. "He who is the slave of riches, guards riches as a slave." The notion of a sinner being a slave to his sin is a patristic commonplace.

32. This eight-syllable line is the shortest in the poem. *weolan* is one of very few genitive nouns in the work which do not stand before the nouns they describe (cf. *feonde*, C12); it may be either plural or a survival of the OE weak genitive singular (cf. *dædan*, A42).

33. Singer divides this line into three verses: *noldest þu nouht / þærof d⟨ælen⟩ / for Drihtenes willæn.* The point in the MS has been lost. *d⟨on⟩:* All editors print *d⟨ælen⟩*, but what remains of the letter following *d* would indicate that it was more likely an *e* or *o*, than an *æ*. For reasons of length and the similarity to C11, *don* seems preferable. See MED, *don*, 7(a), "to give alms, charity."

35. *forloren from,* i.e., "removed from"; see MED *from*, 5a, "in prepositional phrases construed with verbs ... denoting separation, removal, etc."

39. Cf. l. 5 of *The Grave: "Nu me þe bringæð þer ðu beon scealt."*

40. Regarding the off-verse, cf. l. 13 of *The Grave: "Dureleas is þ(et) hus."* Cf. E8.

42. *fules⟨t⟩ qualeholde:* This is a puzzling verse. Singer prints *fuweles quale holde* and translates "of the foul dead carcase." Haufe and Buchholz both print *qualeholde,* a compound, and Buchholz offers the translation "dem Tode holde Vögel," i.e., "birds friendly to death" which Hall rejects as "a flight of imagination beyond our writer's power." Though he himself prints the MS version, Hall suggests, by analogy with C41, E5, and E7, that *fulest alre holde,* "foulest of all bodies," is the correct reading. His suggestion is adopted by Ricciardi. However, while *fuweles* would indeed appear to be a corruption of *fulest,* the unique *qualeholde* need not be rejected. A similar compound, *qualehus* "torture house," occurs twice in *Brut,* ll. 727 and 3770 (E.E.T.S. 365 and 1882), and it seems conceivable that what to the body was *wurþest* "most honorable" would be to the soul "the foulest torture-body." This is less prosaic than Hall's suggestion and admittedly a little unusual for this poet, but there is some evidence in the poem, e.g., *dreamþurles,* E30, for unusual and, perhaps, original compounds of which this could very well be one.

44-45. Cf. D40–41, and also B8. ⟨næffre⟩ by analogy with *æffre* in the on-verse; *nefre* is the more usual form.

Fragment C, f. 64ᵛ

1-3. All the editors offer *þunchep· þet þu hire* as the reconstruction of the first four words. Phillipps reconstructs the next word as *bileiben* and Singer accepts this, translating "remain." Haufe prints *b.ei.en* in his text but *..ei.en* in both his note and his *Anglia* article; Buchholz prints *...e..en.* Ricciardi offers *bilefdest* which seems somewhat more probable than *bileiben* paleographically. Certainty cannot be achieved here, but cf. C34.

3-8. On the significance of the horse-and-rider image in the later ME "body and soul" poem, the *Desputisoun,* see Sister Mary Ursula Vogel's *Some Aspects of the Horse and Rider Analogy in "The Debate between the Body and the Soul".* She does not mention this passage in the *SA.* Ruth Mellinkoff, in "Riding Backwards: Theme of Humiliation and Symbol of Evil," explores the backwards ride as an icon of evil, ridicule, and mockery. The degradation associated with the image may come into play here, but Mellinkoff deals only with rides of the living, not the dead.

This passage is remarkable for its density of archaic linguistic features: *stirope* and *goldfohne* both show retention of *o* in a position of reduced stress; *fotan* marks the only occurrence in the poem of a dative plural in *-an;* *ruglunge* contains the only instance of OE j spelled *g* and is also the only adverb with the suffix *-lunge; onჳean* occurs beside the more modern *aჳan,* C18. Also worthy of note, though not unique to this passage, are covered *æ* in *cumæn* and *ridæn* and the maintenance of gender and case distinction in verses 4a, 5b, and 6a.

The attempt at stylistic variation, especially in 4a and 7a, though feeble by the standards of "classical" OE verse, might also be construed as an archaic feature of these lines.

5. *ruglunge,* i.e., "backwards," from OE *hrycg* "back."
6. Buchholz prints the off-verse of this line in parentheses as does Ricciardi: *riden,* l. 7, appears to be parallel with *ridæn,* l. 5, and not *cumæn,* l. 6.
7. ⟨*son*⟩*e:* Ricciardi prints ⟨*so*⟩*ne* in her text but suggests *niwe* as another possibility; another alternative is * þonne* meaning "when," though it might be considered too long for the gap in the MS.
8. *a*⟨*t*⟩*:* MS *ac.* Singer and Haufe retain the MS reading, which does not give good sense. Buchholz emends to *at* and is followed by Ricciardi; the MED indicates *bireven of (at)* is a common ME construction. Perhaps *c* was accidentally written for *t* in this case; see Jordan 17 rem. 1 and cf. *bletsien,* D13.
10. In the MS there are points after *her,* l. 9, and *weila,* l. 10, but no point after *weolæn,* which would seem to be the last word in the on-verse of l. 10. Singer includes *nu her* from l. 9 in a verse with *weila* and prints *and his weolæn beoþ her belæfed* as a single verse. Ricciardi conjectures that an omission has occurred after *weila,* but she, along with the other editors, prints that word with *and his weolæn* as the on-verse of l. 10, leaving *nu her* in l. 9. If there has been an omission, it has not damaged the sense of the passage: "this man has departed from here, alas, and his riches are left here, i.e., remain behind." It is possible that the point that should have been after *weolæn* has been misplaced after the somewhat similar *weila.*
11. Cf. B33.
12-13. Zupitza (1891), pp.79–80, argues that the antecedent of the plural *heo* in l. 13 is *þine feonde,* l. 12, and that *þine feonde* is not likely to be dative plural. Therefore, he rejects the reconstruction of Haufe and Buchholz for l. 12, *gær*⟨*sume o*⟩*n,* and prefers Singer's *gær*⟨*sumen*⟩. Zupitza does not make clear how this change would solve the problem of *heo's* antecedent: to construe *feonde* as either nominative or accusative plural would create convoluted syntax in l. 12. Perhaps he means *feonde* to be taken as genitive plural, "the treasures of your foes." Ricciardi believes a preposition might well be expected here — *fra* rather than *on* — but rejects one on the basis of length. She prints *gærsuman,* though the weakened *-en* ending would be more probable. Plural *gærsumen* creates a new syntactical problem, however, since it must be the plural antecedent of the singular *hit* in l. 13. It seems preferable, therefore, to return to Haufe's reconstruction, since it preserves the *gærsume/hit* relation, and also because, contrary to Zupitza's view, *feonde* of l. 12 does not have to be the antecedent of *heo* in l. 13. Someone will fall heir to the possessions which the body gathered from his foe (probably a singular implying common number), but the foe himself need not be the beneficiary. For *on* meaning "from" used with verbs of "winning, gaining, taking (by force)," see OED, *on,* 23. *nimen gete* means "to take care"; see MED *gete.* Zupitza also argues that *biȝete* meaning "acquire," l. 13, is a preterite form; Buchholz and Ricciardi believe it is present subjunctive, a reading which does seem preferable in the context.

14. ⟨*wei*⟩*lawei:* Cf. B19, C10, and G3.

15. *reowliche:* The appearance of an inflected adjective, or, for that matter, an adverb, in this position is unusual. Cf. D9 and F19. Phillipps prints a colon between the two verses of this line.

17. ⟨*þu*⟩*:* All the previous editors view the off-verse of this line as a relative clause dependent on the on-verse. Singer and Haufe reconstruct ⟨*þe*⟩ therefore, and Buchholz expands this to ⟨*þe þu*⟩ in order to provide the second singular *lettest* with a subject. Ricciardi returns to the reconstruction ⟨*þe*⟩ but emends *lettest* to third singular *lettet:* "...your mouth is closed which let out injury." Emendation can be avoided by reconstructing *þu* for the damaged portion of the MS and by viewing the off-verse of the line as a nondependent clause: "the men are blither, who struggled with you before, that your mouth is closed: you let out injury that sorely offended them, that made them frightened of you." *ut lettest* may be, in fact, one, compound word. *teone* appears to have moved from the masculine to the feminine gender at this point: in l. 19 it is masculine.

20. ⟨*bo*⟩*c:* The singular ⟨*bo*⟩*c* supplied by Ricciardi is required for agreement with *þen,* unless the OE ablaut dative has survived, in which case Buchholz's *bec* would be acceptable.

21. "Your mouth was overflowing with wickedness." Ps. 49(50), 19: *Os tuum abundavit malitia.*

22. *ri*⟨*f*⟩*e:* MS. *ripe.* Zupitza (1891), p. 80, and Holthausen (1892) both suggest emending the MS *ripe* "ripe" to *rife* "abundant." *rife,* a more prosaic word, provides a closer translation of the Latin and the emendation can be defended on that ground. An ironic use of the MS *ripe,* in the sense of "mature, full," (see OED, *ripe,* 4a) is not out of the question, however. The corresponding word in the OE psalters is usually a form of the verb *nyhtsumian* "to suffice, abound."

25. Dative plural *þam* occurs only here in the poem. In OE, *helpen* takes objects expressed in the dative.

26. Cf. *Latemest Day,* B, l. 45, "*Ne schaltu neauer sitten on bolstre ne on benche.*"

27. Buchholz translates *þe sulfen* as an accusative, "*Nicht erkanntest du dich selbst*"; Zupitza (1891), p. 80, and Ricciardi claim it is more likely dative, i.e., "you did not acknowledge to yourself." Woolf, obviously taking it as an accusative, views the line as a strikingly early punning reference to the *nosce teipsum* theme, p. 87, fn. 4.

28. Cf. *Latemest Day,* B, l. 79, *Nu þe sculen wormes wunien wið-inne.*"

29. *beþrungen* occurs only in verse in OE. "Now you have a new house, (you are) encircled within."

30. There is a crease in the leaf that has caused some letters to be obscured. One of these is the sixth letter of *helewewes* "endwalls." Phillipps prints *helewewes* and is followed by Singer; Haufe, Buchholz, and Ricciardi print *helewowes;* cf. *sidwowes* in the off-verse. The letter seems more likely to be an *e* than an *o,* however. Cf. *The Grave,* l. 9, "*Ðe helewaȝes beoð laȝe, sidwaȝes unheȝe.*"

31. ⟨*nei*⟩*h:* Cf. l. 10 of *The Grave,* "*þe rof bið ibyld   þire broste ful neh.*" Ricciardi prefers the alternative reconstruction, *loh,* that Buchholz suggests in his note, as it gives the line the alliteration it otherwise lacks. The similar *þu schald nu in eorþe liggen ful lohe, Latemest Day,* B, l. 83, seems to support this reconstruction. However, as in the *Latemest Day* line, adverbial "low" almost always ends with *-e* (see MED, *loue,* adv.). Adverbial "near," on the other hand, frequently occurs without *-e* and with intensifying *ful* (see MED *neigh,* adv. 2, and D49). Given these facts, and the closeness of both this line and the preceding one to *The Grave,* it seems preferable to choose *neih,* despite the lack of alliteration. Cf. also *Latemest Day,* B, ll. 73, 77–78.

35. *onhor⟨ded h⟩eo:* One would expect the personal pronoun *heo,* especially since its antecedent is animate, i.e., *hinen,* l. 33.

36. Haufe has a question mark after this line. Use of the independent possessive, i.e., *þin,* in this line is very rare in this poem.

37. Ricciardi prints *ageþ* by analogy with D42 but acknowledges that *biþ,* by analogy with D9, would also be acceptable.

38–50. Cf. *Latemest Day,* B, ll. 85–86, "*Nu schal for–rotien þine teð & þi tunge / þi mahe & þi milte, þi livre & þi lunge.*" Cf. also *Soul and Body I,* ll. 112–25.

38. *besiden* is ambiguous. It could mean "in the sides": Buchholz translates the line "*Dir sollen nun wachsen Würmer in den Seiten.*" It could also be an early occurrence of the preposition "beside" (Mustanoja, p. 369) but it is far removed from *þe,* the word it likely governs.

39. *⟨þeo⟩:* Singer reconstructs *⟨þene⟩,* but *feond* is nominative, not accusative; Haufe believes no reconstruction is necessary, but it is certain the gap in the MS would have been filled.

40. *⟨heom⟩:* Singer has *⟨heo⟩,* but a dative is required with *likien. Ham* is a conceivable alternative.

42. Haufe places a full stop after *agon,* but this does not seem probable syntactically, i.e., the on-verse depends on the off-verse.

45. *⟨heo c⟩reopeþ:* Singer, following Phillipps, reconstructs *⟨heo⟩ reoweþ in and ut* and translates it "they rove in and out." His suggestion is accepted by both Haufe and Buchholz, though the latter translates *reoweþ* as "*rudern,*" i.e., "row." However, Zupitza (1891), p. 80, argues that "rowing" would be a very unusual term to apply to the movement of worms: he suggests that the *w* (i.e., *ƿ*) of *reoweþ* is, in fact, a *þ* and that the correct reconstruction is *heo creopeþ.* Ricciardi accepts this suggestion. The MS is quite unambiguous: the letter in question is a *þ.*

48. *lihte,* i.e., "lungs."

49. *milte* probably means "spleen" in this instance since lungs have already been mentioned in l. 48.

Fragment D, f. 65ʳ

1a-1 Only the bottom portion of letters in the first line on f. 65ʳ remains. Ricciardi prints *was...ond.....efre þinra .... / þu scalt nu. ....wurmes of þine flæsce* for the first two lines of the fragment, and, therefore, her lineation in this fragment is one number greater than in the other editions. In line 1a she appears to be correct regarding the words *efre þinra* (more of the letters remain from those words than others in the line), but her estimation of the other words and the number of letters in the line is more conjectural. *þinra* seems a very archaic form for this poem; *þinres* seems equally possible. Her construction for the on-verse of l. 1 is not only acceptable paleographically but also strengthened by the repetitions of *þu scalt* in ll. 2 and 3. The word missing from this verse likely begins with an *f* to establish alliteration with *flæsce;* it does not begin with a *w* to establish alliteration with ⟨*wur*⟩*mes* as there is no descender from it. There are eight to ten letters at the beginning of the first MS line, some or all of which must belong to another line or poetry. They cannot be distinguished, however. The second MS line begins with *-mes* of *wurmes,* l. 1.

2. The mood of *beo* is subjunctive.

3. *unhol* offers difficulties of both form and meaning. If *wihte* is feminine accusative plural, as its form would indicate, then *unhole* should be written. If *wihte* is, in fact, neuter (but why the *-e?*), then *unhol* may be a survival of the OE uninflected accusative plural form.

   Buchholz translates the word "*unrein,*" but Zupitza (1891), p. 80, contends that "*krank*" is the only legitimate translation available; he recommends accepting Haufe's suggested emendation of *unhol* "sick" to *unholde* "hostile." Ricciardi defends the MS reading on the basis of a rare meaning for *unhol* "causing sickness" that occurs in the *Ancrene Riwle.* Alternatively, the verse may be related to *Beowulf* 120b, *wihte unhælo,* which Klaeber translates "creature of evil." Phonologically, the development æ ⟩ ō would not appear defensible, but the primary meaning of OE *unhælu* "sickness, unsoundness" may have caused it to become confused with *unhal* "sick, ill, weak" from which the form in l. 3 would appear to derive. Certainly the translation of *unhol* as "evil" is preferable in this context to either "sick" or "causing sickness."

4. *go⟨de dæ⟩lan:* Singer's completion, *go⟨de sel⟩lan,* "give goods," is not an impossibility, but *dælan* (or *delen*) occurs elsewhere in the poem, e.g., B14, and is frequently found in OE verse in combination with articles of value, e.g., *frætwa dælan, Genesis* 2830b, and *hringas dælon, Beowulf* 1970a. The form *god* might be considered preferable from the point of view of length, but singular *gode* does appear in D41. The translation of the reconstructed line would appear to be "Before you would not give goods for love to good men;" however, dative plural *monnen* occurs in E6. Possible, though not probable, is that *men* is a survival of the OE ablaut dative singular. The problems with the line are compounded by its context. Ricciardi treats it as parenthetical, oddly placed within the description of the worms' activity; however, she notes correctly the ironic parallel between the "hoard" of the body, which it would not share, and the *hord* of the worms in the following line, which is vigorously worked.

7. *grennien o⟨n men⟩*: Singer prints *ac þu scalt grisliche grennien / ⟨þat⟩ hwo so hit iseiȝe.* However, there is a point in the MS after *grisliche* and no point after *grennien* so that what is missing in all likelihood belongs to the off-verse of l. 7 of which *grennien* is the first word. Haufe, who says the letter following *grennien* must be an *a,* offers *grennien and gristbitien* by analogy with *Juliana,* l. 596; Buchholz accepts this reconstruction, but it is clearly too long for the space available. Zupitza's alternative suggestion, *mid teþ,* p. 80 (1891), is appropriate in length, despite Ricciardi's view to the contrary, but must be ruled out on the basis of paleography along with the more usual ME construction, *wiþ teþ:* the letter after *grennien* — which almost wholly remains — is in all probability an *o* though *a* is possible, and certainly not either an *m* or a *w.* MED, *grennen,* 1(a), makes clear that *grennen on* "to snarl at" plus substantive is a very common phrase. It must be considered probable, therefore, that a reconstruction such as Ricciardi's suggestion, *on al,* or *on men,* is wanted.

10. Cf. *Latemest Day,* A, l. 27, "*Me wole suopen þin hus & bernen þi bout.*"

11. *h⟨eom þe⟩:* Zupitza (1891), p. 80, suggests *h⟨am þe⟩ loþre* by analogy with C16, *þeo men biþ þe bliþre;* Ricciardi prefers *heom* for paleographical reasons: the remains of the letter following *h* are unlikely to belong to an *a.*

12. *w⟨owes⟩:* Zupitza (1891), pp. 80-1, concludes from the context that *w⟨ealles⟩* is the probable reconstruction, and Ricciardi accepts this proposal but alters the spelling to *wowes* by analogy with C30, i.e., *sidwowes.* However, in the same line *helewewes* occurs. If "holy water" in the on-verse was, in fact, two separate words (they are so printed by the previous editors), it is probable that *holi* would end in *-e* to mark the dative case; cf. ll. F43 and G40. Apparently "holy water" was still considered a compound in this work as it was in OE.

13. *ble⟨t⟩sien:* MS. *ble{c}sien.* Buchholz and Ricciardi emend *blecsien* to the usual OE form, *bletsien;* often, as Ricciardi points out, the orthographically similar *c* and *t* were confused in ME (Jordan 17 rem. 1); cf. C8. However, the MS form is not indefensible; as the MED citations for *blessen* show, early thirteenth-century forms of the word frequently are written with a *c:* e.g., *Heo hef up hire hond & blecede al hire bodi wið þe taken þe holi rode,* Mack, p. 18, l. 22. It would appear that the phoneme s could be graphemically represented by *c* at this time and *ss* by *sc,* e.g., *iblesced, Vices and V*(i), Holthausen (1888), p. 51, l. 18. *blecsien,* then, could be a representation of OE *bletsien* after the assimilation of *ts* to *ss.* It does not seem likely that *cs* could represent a transitional phonological stage in the assimilation process. *burewen ham,* i.e., "to guard themselves against," from OE *beorgan* with a reflexive dative.

16. *re⟨owliche⟩:* The shorter *reowlic* may be preferable here; cf. F19.

18-23. This passage is ambiguous syntactically. Buchholz treats it as a series of five questions. Zupitza, p. 81, concedes that l. 18 may be a question (but cf. D43); he doubts, however, that either ll. 19 or 20 should be so viewed. Ricciardi places question marks after ll. 21 and 22-23 only. Nevertheless, given the fact that l. 18 might be a question and that ll. 21 and 22–23 are, the possibility must be entertained that ll. 19 and 20 are questions as well: the finite verb in both cases is in initial position, the usual situation for inter-rogative statements, and the initial negative of l. 21 is quite possibly to be seen as parallel to the initial negative forms in the preceding two lines.

18. It would appear that pointing has been used in the MS here to draw atten-tion to the adverb *o* "ever, always," perhaps in an effort to distinguish it from adjacent words. The MS reads *erming· la· her· o· to wunienne.*

19. *icore⟨n hit⟩:* *icoren,* the preterite participle of OE *ceosan* "to choose" would ap-pear to require an object that is not supplied in what remains of l. 19. Ric-ciardi, following Zupitza (1891), p. 81, takes this object to be 18b *her o to wu-nienne,* i.e., "... you had not chosen always to be living here." Buchholz's translation, "*War es dir nicht natürlich, was du erwählt hattest?*" only obscures the identity of this object. Haufe admits difficulty with this line and suggests that something more than the *n* of *icoren* might be missing from the text, a sugges-tion no doubt inspired by Singer's reconstruction, *icore⟨n me⟩,* which Haufe neglects to mention in his note. Singer translates the line "it was no whit known to thee that thou hadst chosen me." The problem with this translation is the misinterpretation of *icunde* as the preterite participle of *cunnan* "to know"; it is almost certainly related to OE *cynde.* Bucholz translates the word "*natürlich,*" a meaning rejected by both Zupitza and Ricciardi. The latter translates the word "innate," which is not obviously better. It is possible that the word, as in A32, has a moral connotation, i.e., "fitting, proper," along with the more neutral "natural, innate," and this possibility is strengthened by the statement in 19b that the body has "chosen" something or other. The Zupitza sugges-tion, that this object of selection is represented by the phrase in 18b, seems the best available, but it would appear, nevertheless, that something more than the *n* or *icoren* is required to fill the gap in the MS.

20. A line with rhyme, *þe/þe,* and a rather long off-verse is created if one follows the MS pointing here. Alternatively, *more* could be placed in the on-verse in order to create balance between the verses.

21. Wissmann, p. 92, proposes ⟨eiȝen⟩, which is accepted by subsequent editors.

22. *hi:* Buchholz emends the MS *hi* to *hit. Hi* does occur as an accusative plural, however, in B14 and it may refer here to the *cunne* of l. 20 who are also the *fordfæderes* of l. 23.

23. *fordf⟨æderes⟩:* The MS appears to read *þinef ford*; Phillipps prints *ford f...*; Singer reconstructs *fordf⟨eren⟩* which he translates "forefathers"; Haufe offers *forefæderes* and is followed by both Buchholz and Ricciardi. The adverb *forþ* is occasionally spelled *ford,* however, and does occur so spelled as a loosely connected prefix in the word *forddæȝes,* see MED *forþdæȝ.* It does not seem necessary to reject the MS reading, therefore.

24. Cf. *The Grave,* l. 16, "*Ðer þu scealt wunien and wurmes þe todeleð.*"

25. In her note to this line, Ricciardi finds it odd that the worms would be described as having "wrought sin." However, Buchholz is clearly correct in seeing *bones* of the on-verse, probably a metonym for the bodies of the ancestors, as the referent of *þe* in the off-verse and *þeo* as the definite article, i.e., "the worms have dismembered them, confounded their sorrowful bones which wrought sin."

28. Cf. B2.

28-29. *lufede⟨st / mid þine⟩:* Haufe has *lufede⟨st / þurh þine⟩* by analogy with F14; Buchholz and Ricciardi, *lufedest / mid þine* by analogy with the following line, i.e., because of the repetition of *mid*.

30-31. *mihte⟨st / ic was⟩:* Buchholz changes Haufe's *was* to *com* for the sake of alliteration but Ricciardi prefers *was* in order to provide *isend* with an auxiliary. (In C29, however, the preterite participle *biþrungen* occurs, apparently without an auxiliary.) The MS pointing indicates that *clene* should be placed in the on-verse, but it seems preferable that it be moved to initial position in the off-verse, a change that provides a more even distribution of the stressed words in the line.

31-36. There appears to be a close relation to the fourth Vercelli homily in these lines, the closest in the poem: *"Ponne clypað sum sawl to hire lichoman. . : 'Ic wæs gast fram gode on þe sended"* (Förster, pp. 92–93, ll. 224–26); *"ac he fylde his wambe mid searu–mettum ond mid ofer–fillo sua ungemetlice, þæt ic un–eaðe meahte ræste findan. Næs me næfre gyt in him ieðe to wunianne"* (Förster, p. 95, ll. 250–53); *"He wende . . . þaet his wamb wære his Drihten God"* (Förster , p. 96, ll. 276–78).

37-42. For commentary on the significance of this passage, see Style, p. 35, and Sources and Structure, p. 48.

38. *isold on hond,* i.e., "given into the possession of."

40. *bi⟨þ⟩:* This reconstruction is very short. It is possible that a short word such as *nu* or *þus* has also been lost, but cf. B45.

44. *long⟨e þo⟩lode:* Singer offers no reconstruction here; Haufe and Buchholz print *long⟨e maþe⟩lede* which does not make particularly good sense. Zupitza (1891), p. 81, suggests *long⟨e dwe⟩lede* but acknowledges that it too is unlikely. Kaluza's suggestion, *longe sparede,* p. 16, does not take account of the *-lede* that remains in the MS. Holthausen's suggestions (1892), *longe þolede* and *long⟨e gi⟩lede,* are both superior to the others made. Ricciardi prefers *þolede* from OE *þolian* "to suffer (a person), bear with, tolerate" (see BT *þolian,* 2) which does provide adequate sense if death is here personified, as it is in A11, E38, and F16. *gilede* "beguiled" is a possibility, but it perhaps makes its way into the English language too late to be considered for this poem; its earliest recorded occurrence is in the *Ancrene Riwle.*

45. *⟨were⟩:* Haufe's proposal, *⟨makedest⟩,* is accepted by Buchholz by analogy with *Brut* l. 11457, (EETS, l. 5715), but Ricciardi is almost certainly correct in thinking it too long for the space available. Her alternative reconstruction is *⟨scerp⟩,* which is possible. *unseihte* need not be a substantive meaning "hostility," however; it could be an adjective meaning "hostile" and the missing word could simply be *were.*

47. *hund:* Phillipps prints *hund* as does Singer who offers no reconstruction here and no translation for *hund.* In the MS it appears that an *e* may have been squeezed in between the *n* and *d* and all editors since Haufe print *huned,* the past participle of OE *hienan,* meaning, in this case, "to accuse, condemn." However, the lack of a prefix for this past participle is disturbing, as is the fact that what has been construed as an *e* bears no resemblance to the scribe's usual form. The apparent loop of the *e* is more probably an errant pen stroke (or, perhaps, offset) and the MS form is, in fact, *hund* "hound," a term of abuse which could fit here. See MED *hound,* 2b. A compound, the initial term beginning with *w* or *m,* would supply the line with the alliteration it otherwise lacks.

49. The damage to this line is more extensive than elsewhere on f. 65ʳ because the left-hand corner of the leaf is missing and, with it, the beginning of the last line of the fragment. Ricciardi's reconstruction, *l⟨eide hi⟩ș hǫrd,* provides both adequate sense and alliteration but is not without problems. One would have expected a point in the MS after *hord;* also, this reconstruction places three stresses in the on-verse of the line. Further, in its other occurrence in the poem, A4, "laid," i.e., "placed," is prefixed with an *i-.*

Fragment E, f. 65ᵛ

1-2. The first line of f. 65ᵛ is partially cut away and the letters toward the right-hand side of the leaf — the on-verse of l. 2 and probably some of the off-verse as well — are almost wholly missing. The words *þu nefre wurchen drihtenes* in l. 1 are quite distinct, though Phillipps has *þurchen* for *wurchen;* the word *wille* is probably correct. In his *Anglia* article, Haufe suggests ⟨*nold*⟩*est* as a reconstruction for the first word of the line, most of whose letters remain, and this suggestion is adopted by both Buchholz and Ricciardi. Singer reconstructs ⟨*iwo*⟩*ld ahte* for what remains of l. 2 and is followed by the later editors; cf. C8 and E29.

6. Ricciardi remarks in her note that *þet,* presumably the first one, may be a corruption of another short word such as *þus.* This is possible, but there is no reason to assume that *þet* is a relative pronoun as Ricciardi does; it can be simply a demonstrative pronoun used as a pronoun rather than a definite article: "but you befouled it with your foul body: that is that foul body (now) removed from men."

8. Cf. B40.

9-11. On the Signs of Decomposition in ME lyrics, see Woolf, pp. 94-5.

10. ⟨*of þ*⟩*ære:* See B16, where *of* is used with *bedælen. iwunede* is the past participle of OE *wunian* and probably has the meaning "to be accustomed to, used to" in this passage. The position of *to,* as Ricciardi points out, is unusual; it probably should be taken with the relative *þe,* i.e., "to which."

11-12. *stil⟨le / oþ⟩:* Either *oþ* or *ac* is possible. Cf. A21.

12-31. Ricciardi indicates by her punctuation that these lines are to be treated as parenthetical. They are not so obviously parenthetical in the alternative order of the fragments argued for in the discussion of Sources and Structure. Heningham, "Old English Precursors," p. 300, points out two homiletic passages which bear some similarity to this part of *SA: "Deofel us læreð slæpnesse*

and sent us on slæwðe, þæt we ne magon þone beorhtan beacn þære bellan gehyran"
(Assmann, p. 168, ll. 104ff.); "*Forþan domesdæg is wel neah, þe þu arisan scealt,
and ic þonne cume to þe, and þu þonne onfehst min, mid þinum yfelum dædum þe þu
æer geworhtest on þisum middanearde* (Willard, "Address of the Soul," p. 959).

15. *imeten* is ambiguous: it could be either the strong, class V verb meaning "to
repay, require" or the weak, class I verb meaning "to meet, encounter."

17. ⟨*ne drea*⟩*me:* Singer reconstructs the off-verse ⟨*non drea*⟩*me iherep* and translates
"no pleasant sounds they hear"; Buchholz reconstructs the verse ⟨*heo none herunge*⟩
ne iherep by analogy with l. 31. Ricciardi, however, follows Haufe's example
and offers no reconstruction. She rejects Buchholz's proposal as too long, which
it is, and Singer's for the same reason, which it might be. Singer's suggestion
has some merit, however, since in both l. 23 and l. 26 *dream* occurs as the
object of *heren*, and in l. 30 the ears are called *dreamþurles*. With an -*e* ending
dream would be dative singular, but if *heren* has the meaning "to listen to" in
this instance, it would take an object in the dative; the preposition *to* would
not be necessary (see BT Supp. *hiran*, 4a, and MED *heren*, 4a(a)). *dream* also
provides the line with alliteration, and the reconstruction ⟨*ne drea*⟩*me* is similar
in length to ⟨*deope*⟩, the reconstruction accepted by all editors for l. 8 of this
fragment.

19-20. Cf. G11-2.

22. *Þe,* which begins the line, is most likely a dative personal pronoun rather
than a relative pronoun, i.e., "for you (he) plucked his harp well and drew
you to him."

23. *drih*⟨*ten f*⟩*ul loþ:* *drihten* is probably dative referring to God; cf. G50. Ricciardi emends *he* to *þe*, a relative pronoun whose antecedent is *dream* in the on-
verse. This change does render the line more typical syntactically of others
in the poem, but it is not strictly necessary. If one places a full stop after *dream*
(Buchholz has a colon), the MS *he* can be retained as a personal pronoun referring to the devil mentioned in the previous two lines. One might also construe *he* as referring to the masculine *dream,* i.e., "you heard the joy—it was
to the lord wholly loathsome—"; this is a less probable alternative, but see
Language no. 19.1 on the maintenance of gender distinction in the poem.

24. There are points in the MS after *þe, sweize,* and *sleptest;* Singer divides the
line into three verses accordingly. However, though the on-verse is rather
long, it is not overburdened metrically by the standards of this poem.

25. [. . .]*is þe:* Singer's completion, ⟨*n*⟩*is,* changes the tense of the passage abruptly
and is also rather short; Wissmann's suggestion, p. 92, ⟨*loþ wa*⟩*s,* is adopted
by Buchholz but is paleographically unlikely: the letter that remains or partially remains before *s* is not an *a;* Ricciardi and Haufe both offer no reconstruction and print ...*is þe.* Ricciardi suggests *læt þis þe* in her note to this line,
but without much conviction. It is possible that what remains before the *s*
is the right side of an *n*, less possibly, a *u*, instead of an *i*.

27. *rungen* is the only possible occurrence of an unprefixed past participle of an
OE strong verb in the poem.

28. Ricciardi questions the agreement of the singular *lore* with the plural *wære,* but Buchholz is certainly correct in viewing *wære* as singular subjunctive in this instance.

29. ⟨*þet lut*⟩ *þeo:* The remains of the letter before *e* look more like *þ* than *h;* the bottom of the letter is missing but the right-hand side of the top portion which remains has the shape and the distance from the ascender more characteristic of the bow of a *þ* than the second leg of an *h*. Ricciardi's reconstruction, *þet lut þeo iwold ahte,* "so that little they had power over you," does not provide the line with alliteration, and it seems a little awkward, even for this poet; however, it does give adequate sense: *þeo* refers to the holy alternatives to the devil's blandishments.

30. *dreampurles,* i.e., "soundholes, ears," is a *hapax legomenon.*

31. ⟨*nefr*⟩*ę: nefre* is the usual spelling of the word in this poem; *næffre,* printed by Haufe, occurs only once certainly, C6. Haufe has a period after this line.

38. *þiin: ii,* a graphic representation of ī, also occurs in *liiþ,* C31.

40. ⟨*so hi*⟩*t:* Buchholz has ⟨*so he hi*⟩*t,* which Zupitza (1891), p. 81, suggests be shortened to *so hit* since the pronoun *he* is superfluous. Ricciardi's complaint that Buchholz's reconstruction is too long is not necessarily just; she follows Zupitza. Cf. G55, B30, and E45.

41. "They will give an account of their own deeds." Athanasian Creed, clause 40: *ad cuius adventum omnes homines resurgere habent cum corporis suis et reddituri sunt de factis propriis rationem.* See John Johansen, "The Sources and Translations of some Latin Quotations in *The Worcester Fragments,*" *Notes and Queries* 32 (1985), 445–47. Cf. E50.

43. As Ricciardi indicates, *hit* does not agree in number with *deden,* the word to which it would appear to refer. It is perhaps possible that *hit* refers to *wisdome,* though OE *wisdom* is masculine in gender, i.e., "wisely through wisdom for the Lord knows it (their knowledge, wisdom, i.e., what they are going to say)." Cf. the identical phrase at F48 where *wisdom* may have some theological connotation (OED *wisdom,* 1c).

44-45. The repetition of the off-verse in these two lines leads one to suspect dittography in l. 45 where there is no alliteration. Ricciardi emends *muþe* in l. 45 to *write;* a stronger alternative is *word* which alliterates with *awriten* and also retains the oral quality of *muþ.* Nevertheless, the MS reading can be defended syntactically, semantically, even stylistically. However, though repetition is a key stylistic feature in this poem, identical verses are almost always separated from each other by at least one line.

46. "Go, you cursed ones, into the eternal fire." Cf. Mat. 25, 41: "*Discedite a me maledicti in ignem aeternum.*"

50. "And those who did good works will go into eternal life." Athanasian Creed, clause 41: *et qui bona egerunt ibunt in vitam aeternam, qui mala in ignem aeternam.* Cf. E41.

52. ⟨*mest*⟩*:* Haufe reconstructs *mest* by analogy with l. 47 and is followed by both Buchholz and Ricciardi.

Fragment F, f. 66ʳ

2. "I opened my mouth and drew in the spirit." *sp(iritu)m:* MS is either *ipm* or *spm* with the ascender of the long *s* cut away. All editors since Phillipps have printed *ipsum,* though this does not give good sense. Kaluza, p. 16, notes, however, that the Vulgate reads *spiritum* at this point and suggests that the abbreviation of this word was confused with that of *ipsum* by the scribe. In fact, the damage to the MS here makes it impossible to tell whether the first letter of the word in question is an *i* or a long *s,* and, since *spiritum* is the desired reading and *ipsum* makes little sense, it seems preferable to accept the former as the MS reading. Any abbreviation marks that may have been above the letters have been lost in the trimming of the leaf. Cf. Ps. 118 (119), 131: *"Os meum aperui, et attraxi spiritum."*

3. Buchholz, following the Latin of the previous line, reconstructs *opnedest þin bon* for the damaged portion of the verse. Zupitza (1891), p. 82, Kaluza, p. 16, and Holthausen (1892) all point out that *os* in this case is to be translated "mouth," not "bone." Ricciardi prints *þu . . . . dest þin muþ,* claiming correctly that *opnedest* is paleographically unjustified: the word following *þu* contains no letter with a descender; therefore *þ* is an impossibility. In the OE psalters *aperui* is usually translated with a form of *ontynan* "to open, reveal, display," but this word—even with *y* written as *u*—does not seem to fit the remains of the letters either. It is interesting that *&* occurs much more frequently in the English lines on f. 66, especially near the top of f. 66ʳ, than elsewhere in the poem. 7 is the usual symbol for "and."

5. MED *bimenen,* 1b, means "to complain about one's troubles," or in this case, "needs"—not necessarily "sins" as Buchholz suggests; certainly not "pleasures" as Ricciardi suggests.

8. *þer,* i.e., "where."

9. *milts⟨e on⟩foþ:* Singer's reconstruction is *milts⟨unge⟩ foþ.* It is likely, given the presence of *onfoþ* in F12, that *onfoþ* is correct here; moreover, *miltsunge onfoþ* would be too long for the gap in the MS.

10. In this line, *þurh* governs the accusative case; in l. 12, the dative case.

13. It is probable that the soul is the subject of this clause; Haufe believes it is an impersonal construction.

15. *milts⟨unge⟩:* Singer reconstructs *miltsunge;* all subsequent editors print *milts⟨e⟩,* probably by analogy with F9. However, *miltse* would leave a rather large space in the MS, certainly enough space for a point and the first word on the next MS line, *nu.* Singer's *miltsunge* plus a point would likely have filled up the space in the MS right to the edge of the leaf. It must, therefore, be given consideration.

16. Ricciardi capitalizes *deaþ.* Cf. *The Grave,* l. 14, *"Ðær þu bist feste bidytt and dæð hefð þa cæʒe."*

17. *for⟨þun⟩den:* The reconstruction here poses difficulties. OE *lecgan,* as in l. 17 of *The Grave,* *"Ðus ðu bist ileʒd and ladæst þine fronden,"* must be rejected because past participles of OE weak verbs do not end in *-den* in this poem (Singer's

reconstruction *forligden,* must be ruled out for the same reason). OE *forleten,* as in l. 51 of *The Latemest Day,* A, "*Hwer beoð alle þine frond þat faire þe bihete .... Nu heo wulleð, wrecche, alle þe for-lete,*" is also unlikely: OE *t* does not occur as *d* elsewhere in the poem. Paleographically, however, it seems more probable that the vertical stroke after the *r* is a partially visible *l,* not the back of a *b,* and a reconstruction in *l* would provide the line with the alliteration it otherwise lacks. *forbunden* is accepted here because it is possible paleographically and provides the line with adequate sense.

19. Singer and Buchholz reconstruct *reoulic⟨he þin⟩;* Haufe and Ricciardi, *reoulic ⟨þin⟩.* As Ricciardi points out, the space between the *c* of *reoulic* and the remains of the letter which followed it is closer in length to a space separating two words than two letters of the same word. *reowliche* occurs in the similar C15 and D9, but *-lic* appears in *sellic,* G27.

20-21. *⟨heo⟩:* The referent of the plural *heo* clearly should be *sunne,* l. 20, which is singular, and both the plural verb in 21a and the comparison to the plural *piles* in 21b reinforce Ricciardi's decision to emend *sunne* to *sunnen,* a change that has been adopted in this edition as well. It is possible that a tilde representing the final *n* was lost in transmission. Lines 20–33 comprise a rather labored simile in which the body is compared to a hedgehog (*ile,* l. 21), the quills of the hedgehog (*piles,* l. 21) being likened to the body's sins. What renders the image ineffectual, quite apart from matters of expression, is the position external to the body which the soul must occupy if it is to be pricked by the quills, i.e., the sins (l. 27). An inside-out hedgehog would solve this problem! The lines do not justify such a reading, however, nor does the poet give much evidence elsewhere of an imaginative tendency toward the bizarre. No source for this simile has come to light.

25. Ricciardi's view is that the unusual word order and lack of alliteration indicate that this line is corrupt. If *fromward* is construed as an adverb, its position is defensible; however, if, as is more likely, it is a preposition with *him* as its object, its position is unusual. Lack of alliteration, however, does not necessarily imply corruption in this poem. Ricciardi also believes that the *i* of *iwend* is probably a later addition to the MS as it is squeezed in between the *w* and *m* of *him* and written in a different ink than the words around it. The letter is squeezed in, but variations in ink color occur throughout the MS, often on the same leaf.

26. *wiþine:* Phillipps prints *wiþ inne* as does Singer; Haufe and Buchholz both have *wiþi(n)ne;* Ricciardi prints *wiþine.* Double *n* is the usual spelling in OE forms of the word and it is possible that a tilde over the second *i* has been lost in transmission. Forms with a single *n* do occur in ME, however. This compound could be two separate words. See OED, *within.* Cf. D48, basically the same line with the form *wiþinne.*

28. *⟨al þet⟩:* Cf. F23, 25. The pointing in the MS indicates that *was* in this line is in the on-verse, and in the on-verse is where it is placed by both Singer and Ricciardi. (Neither Haufe nor Buchholz shows half-line divisions in his text.) Ricciardi notes, however, that the point after *was* is probably misplaced

since it creates syntactical confusion by separating the auxiliary from the participle and disrupts the balance between F28a and F29a. Cf. B26.

29-30. *touwar⟨d/for⟩:* The proposal of Haufe, Buchholz, and Ricciardi, *touwar⟨d⟩,* would have left sufficient space after the point to write the next word, *heo,* without beginning a new MS line. A short word, such as *for* or *þus,* may have been wholly lost when the leaf was trimmed. Cf. F23.

31. *ipin⟨ed ful⟩ sore:* Cf. F27, 33.

33. *so⟨re all⟩. al* is the usual spelling in the poem; *all* occurs twice, G6 and 13. Buchholz uses the *-ll* form here because the word is in stressed position. *synne* is printed by the previous editors; the unusual pointed form of the *u* and a discoloration below the letter account for the error. *y* does not occur elsewhere in the poem.

37. Haufe has only a comma after *worde.*

40. *foreseide:* Phillipps, Singer, and Haufe print one word, *foreseide.* However, OE *forsecgan,* as Ricciardi points out, means "to accuse, slander"; Buchholz and Ricciardi print two words, *fore seide,* i.e., "said before," ignoring the tautology of *ær fore* created by this word division. The verb *foreseggen* "to say something beforehand" does not eliminate the repetition altogether, but it is superior to *ær fore seide.* See MED, *foresaien,* as well as *foresaid.*

41. *ma⟨kunge⟩:* Ricciardi believes the MS may say *mæ* and she also thinks *makunge* is too long a reconstruction. The addition of *-kunge* to what appears to be *ma* would take the writing on this MS line to the edge of the leaf, but it is not too long for the space available. *almihties:* one might expect a weak form of the adjective following the definite article, but, even in early ME, strong and weak forms were often confused (Mustanoja, pp. 276-7). *fæder* is an uninflected genitive here, as in OE. The problem with *almihties* may have arisen because a later copyist, not detecting the genitive case of the noun, added a clarifying pronoun, *þæs,* to the line, without adjusting the form of the adjective. Ricciardi capitalizes *fæder.*

44. "Let there be, and all things were"; cf. Gen. 1, 3. *Fiat lux. Et facta est lux,* though a closer source probably exists.

45-47. Despite their difference in form, *iworþen/iwurþen* are both preterite participles. The MS reads þ [....] / *þene sune.* Phillipps, however, prints þ.... *þene sune* causing Singer to reconstruct the passage *þ⟨onne⟩ þene sune* and translate the verse "he made then the sun." Haufe and Buchholz print *þ(urh) ⟨hit⟩ þene sune,* and Buchholz translates the verse *"Er schuf durch dasselbe den Sohn..."*: *sune* is an improbable spelling for "sun"; it would seem to mean "son." Zupitza (1891), p. 82, and Holthausen (1892) strenuously object to this reading on theological grounds, i.e., that the Son was created by the word of the Father would never have been written. They recommend the elimination of *hit,* arguing that nothing is missing from the MS at this point. And, in fact, if the reconstructions in F45 and 50 are correct, at least nine millimeters of space were available after þ, sufficient for a short word such as *hit,* though perhaps not sufficient for *þene,* the next word in the text that still remains. Ricciardi prints *þ(urh)... þene Sune* but suggests that *sune* may, in fact, refer to the sun, as Singer suggests, and the reconstruction *hit* to the "word" of the previous line. Given the tendency toward repetition in the poem and given the subject under discussion, the creation, this latter view must be considered; possibly a tilde representing the second *n* of *sunne* has been lost in transmission. However, *þene* is unambiguously masculine in the *SA* while in OE *sunne* is feminine. Unless gender distinction has broken down here (which is not probable) or MS corruption has caused the scribe to alter the form of the article, the view of Zupitza and Holthausen seems preferable. And it is supported by two similar OE prose passages: *He / wæs æfre of ðam fæder acenned. for ðan þe hé is þæs fæder wisdom. þurh ðone he geworhte. and gescop ealle gesceafta; .... se fæder ðurh hine gesceop ús. and eft ða ða we forwyrhte wæron* (Godden, p. 3, ll. 6 ff.); *Ne méჳ nan iscefte fulfremedlice smeaჳen ne understonden embe god. heo ჳescop ჳesceafte þaða he wolde. þurh his wisdom (se sune) heo ჳeworhte alle þing* (Morris, p. 219). On the probable meaning of *wisdom*, l. 48, see OED, *wisdom*, l(c) "one of the manifestations of the divine nature in Jesus Christ (cf. I Cor. 1, 24, 30, etc.); hence used as a title of the second person of the Trinity."

49. Ricciardi thinks it possible that the remains of the letter following *wiseþ*, F48, is an *f*, perhaps the first letter in an abbreviation of *faciamus*. Cf. Gen. 1, 26–7, *faciamus hominem ad imaginem et similitudinem nostram:* "let us make man in our image and likeness."

50. Ricciardi capitalizes *drihtenes*. This word is very faded in the MS, but it does not have a capital.

Fragment G, f. 66ᵛ

1a–1. Most has been lost of the first few letters of the first line that remains on f. 66ᵛ, and at least part of any ascender in the other letters of the line is missing as well. Preceding *ic*, l. 1, are three letters, the first of which is almost certainly a *g*, followed by what appears to be · 7 *(and)*. The remains of perhaps two letters before the *g* offer no clue to their original form. Phillipps prints *(of God)* · 7 *ic;* Haufe prints ⟨*god*⟩ as part of his first line, i.e., l. 1; Buchholz notes the possibility of this word being present but does not include it in his text: Ricciardi prints *God* and calls that word l. 1, thereby causing all her numbers in this fragment to be one greater than in all the other editions. It is possible that Phillipps could make out *of* when he examined the MS, and that further damage has obliterated it; *god* is a very feasible reconstruction of what remains in the MS.

All editors, with the exception of Ricciardi, follow Phillipps and print *and ic þe imæne* as G2a. Buchholz translates *imæne* as "*Genosse*," i.e., "comrade," though "slave" might be a better translation; cf. *wale* in the following line. The first meaning given for *mene* (1) in the MED, however, is "sexual intercourse," which would go well with the phrase in the off-verse, "with loathsome love." Zupitza (1891), p. 82, notes that the word could also be an adjective, i.e., "false, wicked," or an adverb. Damage to the MS here makes precision impossible; Ricciardi prints *ond ic þe .... æ.e mid loþre lufe.* She thinks it unlikely that *imæne* is the correct reconstruction, but admits that it is paleographically possible. If *imæne* is accepted, the line has neither strong alliteration nor rhyme. Ricciardi suggests, with reservation, *lufæste,* a reconstruction that would provide the line with alliteration, though not much sense.

4. *maþe⟨me⟩te:* Ricciardi quite correctly questions the shortness of this completion. It does not seem at all sufficient.

5. *⟨to hell⟩e:* Singer's reconstruction is *⟨in hell⟩e;* Haufe and Buchholz print *⟨inne hell⟩e* by analogy with F32. Ricciardi rejects *inne* because of its length and prints *to* instead, suggesting that an alliterating verb such as *sechen* might be lost. However, in eME *in* as well as *to* can be used with a verb of motion (Mustanoja, pp. 388–89), in this case an elliptical verb of motion with "shall." Singer's completion, therefore, is also acceptable.

6. *þer* is likely an adverb, i.e., "there," not a demonstrative pronoun.

7. *weasiþ,* "woetime" or "journey," is probably related, at least in connotation, to OE *weagesiþ* "companion in woe" often used for the inhabitants of hell.

9. *atru⟨ked þin⟩:* Although Buchholz prints *atrukied þin* in his text, he changes this to *atruked þin* in his list of corrections. Cf. A19.

10. *icwem⟨d⟩e:* The subject of MS *icweme* is almost certainly *tunge,* l. 9, and the sense of the passage requires a preterite indicative form, i.e., *icwemde;* cf. the identical G21b and the similar G23b where the tongue is also the subject. All previous editors print *icweme.* Haufe has no punctuation after this line; however, the subject changes from the third to the second singular, i.e., from the tongue to the body.

11. *⟨domes⟩:* Cf. E19.

12. Cf. E20.

13. *to* may be an adverb meaning "too, also" (this is Haufe's opinion), but it could also be construed as a preposition used in a final sense (Mustanoja, p. 410), i.e., G13a may be translated either "you gathered also treasure" or "you gathered (them) as treasure." Zupitza (1891), p. 82, believes the offverse of this line is parenthetical, and Ricciardi treats it as such. However, perhaps what is implied is that the *gærsume* was not only gathered by means of the *deofles lore,* but also lost by means of it as well: G13b need not be parenthetical.

14. Cf. E21.

15. *⟨tung⟩e:* Singer has *⟨bodig⟩e,* which agrees neither with the feminine pronouns nor with the context of the following lines. The line neither rhymes nor alliterates with either reconstruction, however.

16. Singer's reconstruction of the damaged passage is *⟨for⟩,* l. 17. Haufe has *of,* l. 16, which Buchholz changes to *so,* a reconstruction that gives the line rhyme and renders it analogous to G25. Ricciardi follows Buchholz. All these reconstructions seem too short, however; a combination of Singer's and Buchholz's suggestions seems preferable.

18. *⟨weren⟩:* Cf. G50.

20. "Your tongue framed deceit." *⟨dolos⟩:* Ricciardi reconstructs *⟨dolum⟩.* In the

Vespasian Psalter, Ps. 49(50), 19 reads *concinnavit dolum;* in the *Salisbury Psalter* it reads *concinnabat dolos.*

21. *ʒeo⟨dde⟩de:* MS.*ʒeoddde.* Phillipps prints *ʒeoððde* and Singer simplifies this to *ʒeoþode,* which he translates "poured." Haufe, Buchholz, and Ricciardi all adopt Stratmann's emendation to *ʒeoddede* "sang, recited" from OE *ʒieddian;* in the BT entry for *giddian,* the form *geoddede* does occur. Ricciardi believes the MS form actually signifies *ʒeodedede;* *d* with a loop to the right-hand side of its ascender is a scribal abbreviation for *de,* but it does not occur elsewhere in the work. She thinks it possible that the scribe was confused by a word unusual in a homiletic context. In the OE psalters, *concinnabat/concinnavit* is translated either by *singan* or *hleoðrian;* it would appear that the word was taken to be a form of *concinere,* "to sing in a chorus, harmonize," rather than of *concinnare* "to put or fit together carefully."

22. *⟨huned⟩e:* Haufe, in his edition, offers no reconstruction, but later, in his *Anglia* article, suggests *⟨chid⟩de,* a reconstruction adopted by Buchholz. Ricciardi suggests *hunede.* Either *chidde* or *hunede* would be acceptable (both can mean "abused, insulted"), but we might expect the dative case after *chidden* (Mustanoja, p. 101), and *hunede* provides the line with alliteration. Regarding *heou,* see MED *heuen* (1), 1f, "to be cutting." *worde* is apparently singular.

24. *sun⟨ne so⟩:* The number of *sunne(n)* is unclear. *Þen* invariably denotes masculine dative singular nouns in this poem, while *alle* is invariably plural. The reconstructions of both Haufe and Ricciardi may be too short for the gap in the MS; Singer's is comparable to Buchholz's in length. Buchholz argues that *þen* is derived from masculine dative plural *þam,* but this word occurs in an unweakened form in C25. For the plural form of *sunne* in *-n,* see F11. The problem here can be solved by emending *þen* to *þin* which, though usually singular, occurs as a plural form in C43.

26. *hauef:* Singer and Haufe, in his edition, emend to *haueþ.* In his *Anglia* article, however, Haufe reverts to the MS reading which is also accepted by both Buchholz and Ricciardi. (See Language, no. 15). Haufe and Buchholz print *⟨de⟩med,* which is too short; Ricciardi expands this to *⟨so de⟩med. þus* yields a slightly longer completion. Also, past participles in this work usually take the verbal prefix *i-* if another prefix is not already present. *deoppere* is in all likelihood a feminine dative singular form, not comparative.

27. *non sellic:* The second *n* of *non* is very indistinct now and was apparently unclear when Zupitza and Varnhagen made the collation of the MS on which Haufe depended. He prints *nou* claiming that *non,* printed by Phillipps and accepted by Singer, makes no sense in the context. Wissmann, p. 92, rejects *nou* on the grounds that it is a late thirteenth-century form, i.e., too late for this MS. Buchholz prints *non* but translates the verse *"Nicht ist est ... seltsam,"* apparently believing the substantive described by the adjective *sellic* to be missing. However, Zupitza (1891), p. 82, points out that OE *sellic* could be used as a substantive in ME. See also Mustanoja, pp. 646–47.

28. The adverb *soriliche,* which occurs elsewhere in the poem, fits both the context and the space available while providing the line with alliteration.

29. Heningham points out the similarity between ll. 29–30 and Riddle XL, l. 34, of *The Exeter Book, swa me leof fæder lærde æt frymþe,* where the speaker is Creation.

31. MED *foster,* 1b, gives the meaning "care, keeping, protection," but quite possibly the meaning of the word here is closer to "bringing up, fostering" given in BT Supp. *foster,* 3. Cf. *"Ic wæs Godes dohter, and ængla swistor gescapen, and þu me hafæst forworht, þæt ic eam deofles bearn, and deoflum gelic."* (Willard, "The Address of the Soul," p. 959).

32. ⟨*nouht u*⟩*nleþe:* The two somewhat indistinct vertical strokes that precede the *l* are rather close together. They could very well form an *n,* though they could also be a *u,* the form Phillipps prints. At less well preserved places in the MS — and less carefully written places as well — these two letters are hard to distinguish from one another. *unleþe,* if that is the correct form, would appear to be from OE *unlæde* "misery, suffering."

34-56. In this passage, baptism is seen as a wedding of the soul and body. The *fontston* in l. 37 is obviously the baptismal font; ll. 39–40 refer to chrismation, the anointing of the initiate with chrism, i.e., *mid þen holie ele;* the *kinemerke* of l. 41 is probably a reference to the post-baptismal consignation of the initiate with the cross, i.e., the seal of the cross; the *godfæderes* of l. 44 are those who sponsor the initiate. G. W. H. Lampe in *The Seal of the Spirit* gives no indication that such a view of baptism was ever held, nor has any source for this passage come to light. Lines 35 and 56 are both from Ps. 127(128), 3, and frame a passage, see especially l. 51 ff., which refers to the children of the body and soul who should be the result of this marriage, i.e., baptism. Probably these "children" are to be understood as the body and soul's good deeds in life (see the note for l. 56).

34. ⟨*so þeo*⟩*:* Singer has ⟨*so so*⟩ by analogy with G55. The other editors have *so þeo,* which seems preferable from the point of view of length.

35. "Your wife will be like a fruitful vine"; Ps. 127(128), 3. See the note for G34–56, above.

36. ⟨*so winbow*⟩*e:* Haufe offers the reconstruction ⟨*þonn*⟩*e;* Buchholz, ⟨*in wedd*⟩*e;* Ricciardi, ⟨*on wedd*⟩*e.* Buchholz argues that the neuter *wed* is required as an antecedent for *þet* in the next line since *þet* cannot agree with the masculine *fontston.* However, neither *se* nor *seo,* the OE masculine and feminine forms, are found in this text; and, elsewhere, *þet* is used as a relative pronoun with a masculine antecedent in an oblique case, e.g., A5–6 and B21. Even in OE the neuter *þæt* occurs as the relative pronoun for masculine and feminine forms (Mustanoja, pp. 188–89).

The previous suggestions would leave the Latin *vitis* untranslated, and, given the poet's treatment of the other Latin lines in the poem, this omission would be unusual. In the OE psalters, *vitis* is translated by either *wintreow* or *winʒeard;* in the OE Gospels, *vitis* in John 15, 5 is translated *wintreow* while in the ME "Genesis and Exodus," the accusative *vitem* in Gen. 40, 9 is translated *win-tre.* It is unlikely that either *wintreow* or *winʒeard* can fit here as the word required must end in *-e* and is probably nominative in case: *win-tre* is a later thirteenth-century form. However, the synonymous *winbowe* from OE *winboh* would fit. *So* is probably preferable to *also*, given the length of *winbowe*. For ME use of *so* in this sense, see Mustanoja, p. 336. The line could be translated: "I was to you wedded as a worthy vine." See note for G34–56, above.

41. One verse is missing at this point, or, at least, the equivalent of one verse. There appears to be a point after *hauest*, and, for this reason, Ricciardi suggests the words omitted lay between *hauest* and *kinemerke*.

42. ⟨*arerd*⟩: Singer attempts no reconstruction here; Haufe and Buchholz have *heih*⟨*mod*⟩, though *-mod* would certainly fit on the MS line after *heih*. Ricciardi's suggestion, ⟨*hefde*⟩, is possible; *arerd* might be preferable by analogy with E12 where the context is similar. Both these suggestions give the off-verse three stresses, however.

43. ⟨*behet*⟩*en*: Haufe's reconstruction, ⟨*tauht*⟩*en*, is rejected by Wissmann, p. 92, as unlikely, but Wissmann's own suggestion, *loveden* with a meaning of "promised," cannot be justified either. Singer has ⟨*ihat*⟩*en* (Zupitza, [1891], p. 79, believes this is a misprint for *iheten*); Buchholz and Ricciardi have *beheten*, though the former acknowledges that *iheten* would be equally suitable. Buchholz did not have access to Singer's edition, of course, and if Haufe neglects to note Singer's reading of a particular passage — as he does in this case — Buchholz makes no mention of it.

46. *rihtere* is in all probability a feminine dative singular form here, not comparative.

48. Ricciardi points out that this is a very early occurrence of the plural form, *modes*. MED *mod*, 1a, records one twelfth-century occurrence. On the body's initial rejection of the devil, cf. *Royal Debate*, Heningham, ed., ll. 344–68.

51–52. It does seem likely that the repetition of the off-verses in these two lines is an example of dittography, as Ricciardi believes. However, one cannot be certain, because the passage does not fall apart semantically and repetition is one of the essential features of the poem's style.

54. *bring*⟨*en ham*⟩: Haufe and Buchholz have *bringen heom*, which Ricciardi rejects on the basis of length. *Ham* is the usual accusative plural form in the poem; *heom* occurs exclusively as a dative plural.

56. *nouella oliuarum:* Haufe and Buchholz misspell *oliuarum* as *oliarum* (Zupitza, 1891, p. 83). The *Vespasian Psalter* has *novella*, not *novellæ*, so that *a* and not *æ* may be the correct reading. In the lower right-hand corner of f. 66ᵛ, the words are very blurred and indistinct. Ps. 127(128), 3: "Your children will be like olive shoots." Cf. Hrabanus Maurus, *P.L.* vol. 112, col. 927: "*Per filios, bona opera, ut in Paulo: 'Salvabitur mulier per filiorum generationem'* (1 Tim. 2, 15) *id est, anima fidelis per bonorum operum multitudinem; item juxta illud: 'Et videas filios tuos'* (Ps. 127(128), 6), *id est, praemia bonorum operum.*" (By children we should understand good works, as in Paul: "A woman will be saved by bearing children," i.e., the faithful soul by many good works; likewise: "And you may see your children," i.e., the rewards of these good works.) This interpretation of Ps. 127(128) is quite common. See the note for G34–56, above.

GLOSSARY

With the exception of a handful of very common words, the glossary is a complete presentation of the English forms in the poem. Not included are the Latin words of B31, C21, E41, E46, E50, F2, F44, F49, G20, G35, G56. Each of the entries in the glossary consists of four main parts: HEADWORD, GRAMMATICAL CATEGORY, DEFINITION, CITATION.

1. The Headwords are arranged alphabetically; *æ, ʒ,* and *þ* are treated as separate letters after *a, g,* and *t,* respectively. (However, words beginning with *bi-* or *be-* are all grouped under *bi-*; the prefix *i-* has been ignored in the alphabetical arrangement.) Unusual forms, i.e., ones orthographically remote from the chosen headword, are cross-referenced with that headword. Also, a number of similar words with separate entries are cross-referenced with one another, e.g., *FON* and *ONFON*.

2. If a single headword represents more than one Grammatical Category, these categories are marked by Roman numerals, e.g., I adj..... II adv..... Nouns are marked by their gender distinction, i.e., masculine (m.), feminine (f.), or neuter (n.). Verbs are indicated by the abbreviation v. followed by a designation of the verb class to which they belong. Clear abbreviations mark the other grammatical categories: adj. (adjective), pron. (pronoun), adv. (adverb), prep. (preposition), conj. (conjunction), num. (number), and interj. (interjection).

3. Some headwords have more than one Definition, and, if these definitions for a single headword are sufficiently distinct from one another, each is marked by an Arabic numeral and grouped with the citations representative of it, e.g., prep., 1. at: .... 2. of: ....

4. The Citations exemplifying a given definition or series of definitions form the final part of the entry. If no form appears before a line number, the headword is to be assumed. All reconstructed forms are marked as they are in the text; all emended forms are followed by the MS form in brackets; all forms for which further information can be found in the explanatory notes are preceded by an asterik (*). Many reconstructed forms are discussed in the explanatory notes.

A more detailed description of the style of entry for each grammatical category follows.

1. *Nouns.* The gender of a noun appears after the headword. Each citation is marked according to number, i.e., singular (s.) or plural (p.), and according to case, i.e., nominative (n.), accusative (a.), dative (d.), and genitive (g.).

All singular forms appear first so that the sequence of citations moves from nominative singular (ns.) to genitive plural (gp.).

2. *Adjectives.* Besides number and case, each citation of an adjective includes a designation of gender, i.e., m., f., and n. All singular forms are given first; masculine forms precede feminine forms with neuter forms last; the order of cases, as with the nouns, is n., a., d., and g. The sequence of citations proceeds from nsm. to gpn. Comparative forms (com.) and superlative forms (supl.) occur at the end of the entry.

3. *Pronouns.* Pronouns are described, by and large, in the same manner as adjectives. The dual number occurs occasionally in the personal pronouns.

4. *Verbs.* After the headword and the abbreviation v., one of the following indications of verb class appears: an Arabic numeral indicating a strong verb class; a Roman numeral indicating a weak verb class; PP indicating a Preterite-Present verb; AN indicating an Anomalous verb. The citations are in the indicative mood, unless otherwise indicated. Their sequence is: infinitive (inf.); present forms, singular, then plural, in all three persons (1s., 2s., 3s., 1p., 3p.; 2p. does not occur); preterite forms (pret. 1s., pret. 2s., etc.); subjunctive forms (subj. pres. and subj. pret.); imperative (imp.); present participle (prp.); past participle (pp.); negative forms (neg.).

5. Other forms—*Adverbs, Prepositions, Conjunctions, Numbers,* and *Interjections*—require no special attention.

Precision has been aimed for in the glossary, but some imprecision is inevitable. The spellings of some reconstructed words for lost portions of the text are conjectural and should be treated as probable alternatives rather than absolute certainties. In some cases, definitions or syntactical designations are ambiguous and the alternative possibilities have been given. Regarding definitions, one must, of course, be alive to the possibility of shades of meaning. Regarding syntax, it is clear that a form cannot be, for example, both singular and plural; however, if ambiguity exists, it is preferable to reveal the difficulty to the reader rather than to hazard a guess on one option or another. Question marks precede questionable definitions or syntactical designations.

A   *adv.,* always: G25, O D18.

AC   *conj,* 1. but: A5, F13, F28, etc. 2. on the contrary, but rather: F14, B18, etc. 3. moreover, and, also: F32, B15, etc.

ACWENCHEN   *v.I,* to subdue, overcome: *inf.* B22.

ADUMBED   *v.II,* to become dumb: *pp.* F16.

AFULEST   *v.I,* to defile, corrupt: *2s.* E5. Cf. IFULED.

AFURSED   *v.II,* to remove, expel: *pp.* E6, E37.

AGON   *v.AN,* 1. (with BEON) to be gone: *pp.* C42.   2.(with BEON) to be lost, vanished: *pp.* A40, B8, B44, D40, G13.   3. to come to pass: *3s.* AGEÞ D42, ⟨AGEÞ⟩ C37. Cf. OFEODEST.

AЗAN   *prep.,* before, in the presence of: C18. See ONЗEAN.

AHTE   *v. ,* see OHTEST.

AL   I *adj.,* all: *ns ?n.* ⟨AL⟩ F28; *dsf.* ALRE

B43, ALLE *G24; *gpf.* ALRE E47; *gpn.*
ALRE E7, E52; *npf.* ALLE A2; *apmn.*
ALLE E13, F42, F45; *apf.* ALLE F47;
dpm. ALLE B37, E37, F17. II *pron.* all:
nsn. AL B41, D50, F46; *?dsn.* AL B35,
C44; *npf.* ALLE F21. III *adv.*, utterly,
entirely, completely: AL A27, A29, etc.
ALL G6, G13, ⟨ALL⟩ F33.

ALEID *v.I*, to quell, stop: *pp.* C19. Cf.
ILEIDE, UNDERLEID.

ALESE⟨D⟩ *v.I*, to deliver, redeem: *pp.*
B26.

ALMIHTI *adj.* almighty: *nsm.* F36; *gsm.*
ALMIHTIES *F41.

ALSO *adv.*, 1. like: A32. 2. ? likewise,
in this manner: AL⟨SO⟩ *A16, ⟨A⟩LSO
A23. 3. ? likewise, ? thus, moreover:
E45.

ALTOGÆDERE *adv.*, completely, entirely: F14.

AMERDEST *v.I*, to mar, destroy: *pret.*
2s. G31.

AND *conj.*, and: *A2, A3, A4, A7, etc.
(written in the MS as 7 and *&*).

ANDWEORKE *n.*, handiwork, creation: *ds.* F42.

ARÆREÞ *v.I*, 1. to raise, resurrect: *3p.*
E12; *pp.* ⟨ARERD⟩ G42. 2. to cause
discord, strife: *pret. 2s.* ARERDEST
D45.

ARISEN *v.I*, 1. to rise: *inf.* E14. 2. to
rise in hostility: *pret. 3p.* C16.

ASCORTED *v.II*, to become short, to
fail: *pp.* G9. Cf. SCORTEÞ.

AT *prep.*, see ÆT.

ATRU⟨KED⟩ *v.II*, to fail, ? deceive: *pp.*
G9. Cf. TRUKEÞ.

ATTERNE *adj.*, poisonous: *nsf.* G17.

AWRITEN *v.I*, to write: *pp.* E45. Cf.
IWRITEN.

ÆFRE, ÆFFRE *adv.*, see EFRE.

ÆFTER *adv.*, see EFTER.

ÆIHTE *n.*, possessions collectively,
property: *a.* B13.

ÆR I *adv.*, before: A37, F40, G30, G44,
etc. II *prep.*, before: D4.

ÆRMES *m.*, arm: *adp.* *C43.

ÆREN *n.*, see EAREN.

ÆT *prep.*, 1. at: B16, C6, ET G37. 2.

of: ⟨AT⟩ *A23, A⟨T⟩ (MS.AC) *C8.

ÆTWI⟨TEN⟩ *v.6*, to attribute to, to
blame on: *inf.* G7.

BALEWEN *n.*, pain: *ds.* A26.

BAN *n.*, bone, skeleton (in p.): *np.* A21,
BON E9, E11; *ap.* BON C42, BONES
D25.

BE- see BI-.

BEARN *n.*, child: *ns.* A25; *as.* A6; *gs.*
BEARNES A24; *np.* G55; *ap.* G54; *gp.*
BEARNE G53.

BECNIEN *v.II*, to summon: *inf.* E32.

BECNUNGE *f.*, summons, order: *ns.*
E27.

BEDDE *n.*, bed: *ds.* A13, E25.

IBEDDED *v.II*, to put to bed: *pp.* C32.

BEDEN *v.*, see BIDDEN.

BESTRAU *n.*, straw for bedding: *as.*
D14.

BELLEN *f.*, bell: *ap.* E27.

BEMEN *f.*, trumpet: *np.* E32.

BENCHE *f.*, bench, seat: *ds.* C26.

BEON *v.AN*, 1. to be: *inf.* G42, G53,
BE⟨ON⟩ B39; *1s.* EAM B18; *2s.* EART
B37; *3s.* BIÞ A5, A31 (twice), F22, B44,
etc., IS A15 (twice), A44, F19, etc.; *3p.*
BEOÞ B5, B7, B9 etc.; *pret. 1s.* WAS
F35, G31, G34, B17, B41, etc.; *pret. 2s.*
WERE B2, B12, B32, etc.; *pret 3s.* WAS
F30, F41, G10, etc.; *pret. 3p.* WEREN
B6, C47, E18, F21, G50; *sub. pret. s.* *
WÆRE E28, ?WÆS E27; *neg.* NIS E49,
G27 NES D19, D20. 2. (as an aux-
iliary with a past participle): *inf.* D8; *1s.*
AM F14; *2s.* BIST D38, E7, E37, ÆRT
B16, ERT F16, F17, D15, EART B35;
3s. BIÞ A6, A22, A24, etc., IS A32, F43,
G9, etc.; *3p.* BEOÞ A39, A40, G9, etc.;
pret. 1s. WAS F31, F34, G29, etc.; *pret.*
2s. WERE B26, D48, F20, etc.; *pret. 3s.*
WAS,* F28, F46; *pret. 3p.* WEREN F30.

BEORNEN *v.3*, to burn: *inf.* E49,
B⟨EORNEN⟩ D14.

BEREN *v.4*, 1. to carry: *inf.* D14. 2.
to give birth to: *pp.* IBOREN A6.

BI *prep.* 1. with reference or respect to:
B30, C9, G19. 2. according to or by
a certain standard unit: B6.

BICLUSED *v.I*, to confine: *pp.* D46.

BIDDEN   *v.5,* to ask, entreat for: *inf.* F15, BIDDÆN *B23; *pp.* BEDEN B11, B21.

BIDELED   *pp.* deprived, bereft: C32, BEDÆLED B16, E9. Cf. IDÆLEN.

BIDERNAN   *v.I,* to conceal: *inf.* F6.

BIFOREN   *adv.,* 1. before (in terms of position): F7, G17.   2. (with BEHINDEN) front and back: BIUOREN G39.   3. before (in terms of time): D23, BIUOREN D20.

BIƷETE   *v.5,* to acquire: *subj. pres.* C13.

BIHETEN   *v.7,* to promise, pledge: ⟨BEHET⟩EN *pret. 3p.* G44. Cf. IHOTEN.

BIHINDEN   *adv.,* 1. in back, behind: G17.   2. (with BIFOREN) back and front: G39.

BIHUDED   *v.I,* to conceal, hide: *pp.* E7.

BILEAFEN   *v.I,* to leave (something): *inf.* D6; *pret. 2s.* BILEFDEST C34, ? C1; *pp.* BELÆFED C10.

BIMÆNEN   *v.I,* to bemoan: *inf.* *F5, *3p.* BIMÆNEÞ F9. Cf. MÆNEÞ.

BINUMEN   *v.5,* to take away, destroy: *pp.* D37, BI⟨NU⟩MEN D38. Cf. NIMEN.

BIREFEDEST   *v.II,* to deprive, rob: *pret. 2s.* G12, BERÆFEDEST E20; *pp.* BEREAUED A22, BERÆFED C7.

BIREOUSUNGE   *f.,* contrition: *ads.* F12, F13.

BISET   *v.I,* to beset, studded: *pp.* F20.

BISIDEN   *adv.,* at the side of, beside, ? in the side of: *C38.

BISIHÞ   *v.5,* to look to, pay attention to: 3s *A45. Cf. ISEIƷE.

BISWIKEN   *v.1,* to seduce, deceive: *pp.* G4.

BITÆIHT   *v.I,* to give, grant: *pp.* G52.

BITTERE   *n.,* grief, suffering: *ns.* B45, D40, D41, B⟨ITTERE⟩ B44.

BITUNED   *v.I,* to shut: *pp.* C19, BETUNED C17.

BIÞENCHEN   *v.I,* to think on, consider: *inf.* ⟨BE⟩ÞENCHEN B17.

BIÞRUNGEN   *pp.,* enclosed, hemmed in: BEÞRUNGEN *C29.

BIWEDDED   *v.I,* to give in marriage: *pp.* G36.

BIWORPEN   *v.3,* to sprinkle: *inf.* BEWORPEN D12.

BIWUNDEN   *v.3,* to wind, entwine: *pp.* A16, BEWUNDEN A27. Cf. WINDEÞ.

BLE⟨T⟩SIEN (MS. BLECSIEN)   *v.II,* to bless oneself: *inf.* *D13.

BLISSE   *f.,* bliss: *ns.* B8; *as.* D37.

BLIÞRE   *adj.,* joyful, glad: *comp.* BLIÞRE C16.

BLODE   *n.,* blood: *ds.* B27.

BLOWEN   *v.7,* to sound (a wind instrument): *3p.* E32.

BOC   *?mn,* book, authoritative source: *ds.* ⟨BO⟩C *C20; *np.* BEC F35, G34, G55; *dp.* BOKEN B30, G27.

BODEÞ   *v.II,* to announce, ?to threaten: *3s.* A6.

⟨BOD⟩UNGE   *f.,* announcement, declaration, ?omen, ?portent: *ns.* A24.

BOLSTRE   *mn.,* a cushion or pad for leaning or sitting on: *ds.* C26.

BORIEÞ   *v.II,* to bore a hole, make a perforation: *3p.* C44.

BOTE   *f.,* relief: *ns.* B11.

BOWE   *m.,* saddlebow: *as.* C4.

BREKEÞ   *v.4,* to break or carve into pieces: *3s.,* E11; *3p.* C44.

BREOSTE   *?f.,* breast, chest: *as.* C44; *ds.* C31.

BRINGEN   *v.3,* to bring, convey: *inf.* B15 (with TO), B⟨RIN⟩GEN B16, BRING⟨EN⟩ G54; *pp.* IBROUHT B39.

BROSTNIAN   *v.II,* to decay, rot: *inf.* E9.

BUC   *m.,* body, carcass: *as.* B19.

⟨BU⟩RDTID   *f.,* time of birth: *ns.* A26.

BUREWEN   *v.3,* to protect (with d.): *inf.* *D13.

BUTEN   *conj.,* 1. unless: D39.   2. (with adv. force) nothing but, only: BUTE C14.

CHIRCHE   *f.,* church: *ads.* E25.

CLEI   *m.,* clay: *ns.* A32.

CLEICLOT   *n.,* a lump of dirt, a corpse: *ns.* A36.

CLENE   *adj.,* pure, unpolluted: ? *nsn.* D31; *nsf.* E4.

CLENSIEN   *v.II,* to cleanse: *inf.* D10.

CLOÞES   *m.,* clothes, garment: *ap.* C32, C33.

CLUTES   *m.,* rags, sheets: *dp.* F17.

CNEOW   *n.,* knee: *as.* C27, ⟨CNE⟩OW C27.

ICNEOWE   *v.7,* to acknowledge to oneself, ?to know: *pret. 2s.* C27.

COLDE   I *adj.,* cold: *dsn.* G15. II *adv.,* coldly A36, C32.

COLDEÞ   *v.II,* to lose warmth, feel cold: *3s.* A21, ⟨COL⟩DEÞ A32.

ICORE⟨N⟩   *v.2,* to choose, select: *pp.* *D19.

CRE⟨FTE⟩   *m.,* skill, might: *ds.* A3.

⟨C⟩REOPEN   *v.I,* to crawl, creep: *3p.* *C45.

CRISTE   *m.,* Christ: *ds.* F10, G46, G54; *gs.* CRISTES B25, G45.

CRISTENE   *adj.,* Christian: *apm.* D29.

CUMEN   *v.4,* to come, approach: *inf.* D43, CUMÆN *C6; *3s.* CUMEÞ A10, A41, B45, D41, ⟨CUM⟩EÞ E13; *3p. ?s.* *CUMAÞ A44; *pret. 1s.* CŌM F4; *pret. 3p.* COMEN *B7; *subj. pres. 3s.* CUME E39; *subj. pret. 3s.* COME B11. Cf. TOCUME.

ICUNDE   *adj.,* natural, ?instinctive, ?fitting, ?proper: *nsn.* *D19, D20, IKŪNDE A32.

CUNNE   *n.,* kin: *ds.* D20.

ICWEMDEST   *v.I,* to please (with d.): *pret. 2s.* B42; *pret. 3s.* CWEMDE G23, ICWEMDE G21, *ICWEM⟨D⟩E G10.

CWI⟨DE⟩   *m.,* speech, statement: *ds.* G47.

IDÆLEN *v.I,* 1. to separate, divide: *inf.* *A9. 2. to divide up, distribute: *3p.* DÆLEÞ B14. 3. to give away, share: *inf.* *⟨DÆ⟩LAN D4. Cf. BIDELED.

DEADE   *m.,* a dead person or thing: *as.* A40; *gs.* (? adj.) DÆDAN A42.

DEAȝES   *m.,* day: *np.* A40.

DEAÞ   *m.,* death, death personified: *ns.* D44, E38, F16, ⟨D⟩EAÞ A11, ⟨DEA⟩Þ C19; *ds.* DEAÞE E12; *gs.* DEAÞES E33.

DEAUEÞ   *v.II,* to destroy the hearing, make deaf: *3s.* A17.

DEDEN   *f.,* deed, action: *ap.* E42; *dp.* D29, D32, F14.

DEMDE   *v.I,* 1. to pass judgement: *pret. 3s.* G18. 2. to sentence, condemn: *pp.* ⟨IDE⟩MED *G26.

DENNE   *n.,* grave, ?chamber: *ds.* G15.

DEOFEL   *m.,* the devil: *?ns.* D49; *as.* G47; *ds.* DEOFLE D38, G23; *gs.* DEOFLES E21, G14, G43, DE⟨OFLES⟩ B29.

DEOPE   *adj.* deep: *dsm.* B40, ⟨DEOPE⟩ E8; *dsf.* DEOPPERE G26.

DEREDEST   *v.II,* to hurt, injure: *pret. 2s.* D29.

DEORE   *adj.,* dear, beloved: *npm.* C47.

DEORWURÞE   *adj.,* excellent, precious: *?nsm.* F50, *asn.* B25.

DIȝELLICHE   *adv.,* secretly: F6.

IDIHTE   *v.I,* to make, fashion: *pp.* A3.

DIMME   *adj.,* dim, lacking clear vision: *apn.* A42.

DIMMEÞ   *v.I,* to become dim, i.e., the eyes: *3s.* A17.

DIMNESSE   *f.,* dimness, darkness: *ds.* E33.

IDOL   *n.,* parting, separation: *ns.* A5; *as.* A8.

DOM   *m.,* judgement, decision, choice: *as.* E34, E39, E44; *ds.* DOME E33; *ap.* DOMES E19, G18; *dp.* ⟨DOMES⟩ G11.

DOMESDAI   *m.,* Doomsday, Judgement Day: *ns.* E13.

DON   *v.AN.,* 1. to perform (an action), to do: *inf.* C11; *3s.* DEÞ E13; *pret. 3s.* DUDE A37; *pp.* IDON G3. 2. to put, bring: *3p.* DOÞ *B14. 3. to give alms, charity: *inf.* B33. Cf. FORDON, UNDON.

DOUHTER   *f.,* daughter: *ns.* G31.

DREAM   *m.,* sound, ?mirth: *as.* E23; *ds.* ⟨DREA⟩ME E17; *ap.* DRÆMES E26.

DREAMÞURLES   *n.,* sound-hole, i.e., ear: *ap.* *E30.

DREIȝEN   *v.2,* to suffer, endure: *inf.* G6, DRIÆN B36.

DRIHTEN   *m.,* God: *ns.* E12, E43; *?as.* G49; *ds.* E23, G18, G50; *gs.* DRIHTENES B33, C11, E33, E44, F50, G47.   DRIHTENES E1, ⟨DRIH⟩TENES, E45.

DROWE   *v.6,* to attract, draw: *pret. 2s.* F3.

DURE *f.*, door: *ds.* B16, C6.
DURELEASE *adj.*, doorless: *dsn.* B40, E8.

EAREN *n.*, ear: *ap.* EAREN E17, *ÆREN A17.
EARFEÞSIÞ *m.*, misfortune: *as.* *A41, EARUEÞSIÞ A43.
EASTWARD *adv.*, toward the east, in an easterly direction: A31.
ECE I *adj.*, eternal, *asf.* D37; *asn.* ECHE E48. II *pron.*, each, every, each and every: EC D12.
ECHELICHE *adv.*, eternally, forever: E52.
EFRE *adv.*, 1. always, perpetually: D41, D45, D50, E29, F6, F18, F29, F48, G24, EFRE, D1a, ⟨E⟩fre, E49, ÆFFRE B45, ÆFRE B3, B34, C12, D27, ⟨ÆFRE⟩ D33. 2. at any particular time, i.e., with particularizing force: F4. 3. by any means, i.e., with emphasis: ÆFFRE A14.
EFT *adv.*, 1. again, once more: E12. 2. likewise: A27. 3. afterwards: F18.
EFTER *prep.*, 1. following after (in time): C15, C37, D9, D16, F19, ÆFTER D42. 2. because, as a consequence of: G47.
EIȜEN *n.* eye: *ap.* *A17, EȜEN A42, ⟨EIȜEN⟩ D21.
ELE *mn.*, oil, chrism: *ds.* G40.
ENDE *m.*, end: *ns.* D43, E49.
IENDED *v.II*, to end, finish: *pp.* A29.
ENGLES, *m.*, angel: *np.* F38.
ENI *adv.*, any: D34.
EORÞE *f.*, earth, ground, the world: *ns.* F38, EOR⟨ÞE⟩ E4; *ds.* C5, D24, EORÞAN C28.
EORÞLICHE *adj.*, earthly, transitory: *asm.* C8.
ERMING *m.*, wretch: *ns.* D18, E14.

FACEN *adj.*, deceitful, false: *nsf.* G10, FAKEN G17.
FAKENLICHE *adv.*, deceitfully: G21.
FAREN *v.6*, to go, journey, to fare: *inf.* C4, E48, FARENE (with TO) B28. Cf. FERDEN.

FÆDER *m.*, father, God: *ns.* G53; *ds.* G29, *gs.* F41.
⟨FEI⟩ȜE *m.*, the doomed or dead one: *ns.* A30.
FEIRE *adv.*, properly, precisely: G30, G39.
FENGE *v.7*, to succeed to, inherit: *pret. 2s.* *FENGE B29. Cf. ONFOÞ.
FEOLE *adj.*, many: *apm.* ⟨FEOLE⟩ E19; *dpm.* G11.
FEONDE *m.*, 1. foe, enemy: *ds.* *C12; FEOND *np.*, C39; *ap.* D2. 2. fiend, the Devil: *ds.* G10, G21; *?adp.* FEONDES E48.
FEORÞSIÞ *m.*, a going forth, i.e., death: *A27.
FERDEN *v.I*, to undergo, suffer, ?depart: *pret. 3p.* D23, Cf. FAREN.
FINDEN *v.3*, to find: *inf.* C24; *3p.* FIN⟨DEÞ⟩ C41.
FLÆSC *n.*, flesh: *ns.* C40; *ds.* FLÆSCE D1.
⟨FLEOÞ⟩ *v.2*, to go away from, flee: *3p.* A37.
FLET *n.* paved floor of a room or hall: *as.* D10.
IFLUT *v.I*, to convey or move something: *pp.* *A30.
FLOR *m.*, floor: *as.* D10; *ds.* FLORE A30, A36.
FONTSTONE *m.*, baptismal font: *ds.* G37.
FOR I *prep.*, 1. on account of, for the love of: B33, D4, D35. 2. for the sake of, because: B24, F33, G5, G6. II *conj.* (introducing causal clauses) because: A15, A44, B2, etc. Cf. FORE.
FORBINDEÞ *v.3*, to bind up, wrap: *3s.* A42; *pp.* FOR⟨BUN⟩DEN *F17.
FORDF⟨ÆDERES⟩ *m.*, ancestor: *np.* *D23.
FORDUTTE *v.I*, to obstruct, block up, shut: *pp.* (apparently agreeing with p. nouns) E17, E30, FORDUTTED E38.
FORDON *v.AN*, to ruin: *pp.* D32. Cf. DON, UNDON.
FORE *prep.*, for, instead of, on behalf of: *B23, FO⟨RE⟩ B21. Cf. FOR.
FORESEIDE *v.III*, to say beforehand, previously: *pret. 1s.* *F40.

FORHOWEÞ   *v.II*, to despise or reject something: *3s.* A43, ⟨FORH⟩OWEÞ A41.

FORLETEN   *v.7*, to release or let go (someone): *pret. 3p.* G44. Cf. LETTEST.

FORLURE   *v.2*, 1. to lose or forfeit something: *pret. 2s.* G43; *pp.* FORLOREN D37, G51, FORLOR⟨EN⟩ F14.   2. to abandon, leave: *pret. 1s.* FORLEAS G33; *pret. 2s.* D15.   3. to repudiate: *pp.* FORLOREN G38.   4. to remove: *pp.* *FORLOREN B35.

FORMELTEN   *v.3*, to decay: *inf.* C49.

FORNON   *adv.*, before, ahead, still to come: *B8, B44, D40.

FORSCUTTED   *v.I*, to shut completely, stop up: *pp.* E38.

FORÞON   *conj.*, therefore, consequently: A10, FO⟨RÞON⟩ B18.

FOSTER   *?nm.*, bringing up, care, protection: *as.* *G31.

FOSTRIEN   *v.I*, to feed, nourish, bring up a child: *inf.* G54, FOSTREN D2.

FOTAN   *m.*, foot: *dp.* *C3.

FRECLICHE   *adv.*, eagerly, greedily: C40.

IFREOED   *v.I*, to free, liberate: *pp.* B28.

FREOME   *f.*, advantage, good (with the verb DON): *as.* A37.

FREONDEN   *m.*, friend: *dp.* B37, E37, F17.

FRETEN   *v.5*, to devour, consume: *inf.* C39, C40, C41; *pp.* IFRETEN D2. Cf. UNFRETEN.

FROM   *prep.*, from (in terms of position, location): A37, B26, *B35, D31, E6, E11, E33, E37, G8.

FROMWARD   *prep.*, away from: *F25.

FRUMÞE   *mf.*, the beginning of one's life: *ds.* G30.

FUL   *adv.*, completely, entirely: C31, D49, E23, F27, F31, F33, G15, G19.

FULE   I *adj.*, foul: *nsm.* G3, G4; *nsn.* E6; *asn.* C41; *dsf.* G5; *dsn.* E5, G6; *dpm.* G38; *supl.* FULEST E7, *FULES⟨T⟩ (MS. FUWELES) B42. II *adv.* foully: D46.

IFULED   *v.II*, to befoul, desecrate: *pp.* A39, G37. Cf. AFULEST.

FULLE   *adj.*, enough, too much: *dsm.* D35.

IFULLED   *v.I*, 1. to fill *pp.* D48.   2. to fulfil: *inf.* FULLEN D50; *pp.* A24.

FUL⟨LUHT⟩ *mfn.*, the sacrament of baptism: *as.* G38.

FUR   *n.*, fire: *as.* E48; *ds.* FURE D14.

FUSE   *adj.*, eager: *npm.* B15.

GÆDEREDEST   *v.I*, to bring together, gather, accumulate: *pret. 2s.* B34, C12, G13; *pp.* IGÆDERED B5.

GÆRSUME   *f.*, treasure, valuables (collective): *as.* G16, GÆR⟨SUME⟩ *C12; *?ads.* ⟨GÆRSU⟩ME G13.

GETE   *?f.*, (with the verb NIMEN) to pay attention, take pains: *as.* *C13.

GNAWEN   *v.6*, to gnaw: *inf.* C42.

GOD   *m.*, god, God: *ns.*, D36, F36, ? ⟨GOD⟩ Gla; *ds.* GODE D31, E51, G42; *gs.* GODES G31.

GODEN   *adj.*, 1. (as a noun) *?n.* good people: *np.* E51.   2. (as a collective noun) *n.*, goodness, goods, property: *ns.* GODE D41; *as.* GO⟨DE⟩ *D4; *ds.* GODE B21.   3. (as an adj.) good: *dsp.* GODE *D4 (the first one).

GODFÆDERES   *m.*, godfather: *np.* G44.

GODNESSE   *f.*, goodness: *as.* B3.

GOLDFÆTEN   *?n.*, noun golden vessel, or *adj. as a noun*, golden thing: *np.* *B7.

GOLDFOHNE   *adj.*, variegated, shining with gold: *asm.* *C4.

GRÆDILICHE   *adv.*, greedily, covetously, B34.

GREDI   *adj.*, greedy, eager: *nsm.* D33; *npm.* GRÆDIE B13.

GRENNIEN   *v.II*, to bare the teeth, to grimace: *inf.* *D7.

GREONEÞ   *v.II*, to groan, moan: *3s.* A25; *prp.* GREONING A15.

GRIPEN   *v.I*, to grasp, take hold of: *inf.* (with TO) B13.

GRISLICHE   *adv.*, terribly, hideously: D7.

GROMEN   *m.*, anger, rage: *?dp.* D33.

GROS   *v.1.*, (impersonal) to be frightened of: *pret. 3s.* C18.

GRULDE   *v.I*, to offend, enrage: *pret. 3s.* C18.

GULDENE   *adj.*, golden: *?npn.*, *B7.

GULTES   *m.,* guilt, offence: *ap.* E19;
?*adp.* G11.

ӠEAT   *v.2,* to shed, pour forth: *pret. 3s.*
B27.

ӠEO⟨DDE⟩DE (MS Ӡeodďde)   *v.II,* to
speak formally, to sing: *pret. 3s.* *G21.

ӠEORNE   *adv.,* earnestly, zealously: B11,
D13.

ӠERDE   *f.,* staff, rod (for measuring): *ds.*
A33.

ӠET   *adv.,* yet, still, further: C2, D17,
D26, E3, E36, G7.

ӠIF   *conj.,* if (introducing conditional
clauses): A40, G43.

ӠIUEN   *v.5,* to give: *inf.* B21.

HABBEN   *v.III,* 1. to have, possess, own:
inf. A34, D39; ?*2s.* HAUEST C29, G41;
3s. HAUEÞ F16; *pret. 1s.* HA⟨FDE⟩ D34;
pret. 2s. HÆFDEST D27, HEUEDEST
C14, HEFDEST D39.   2. *a finite auxiliary preceded or followed by a pp.: 2s.*
HAUEST G4, G37, D32, D37 (twice); *3s.*
HAUEÞ C19, E38, G3, HAUEF *G26; *3p.* HABBEÞ D24;
pret. 2s. HEFDEST C35, D19; *neg. 2s.*
NAFEST G16, NAFST C14.

HE   *pron. of the 3rd person: nsm.* A3, A5,
*A12, *E23, etc.; *asm.* HINE A33, C19,
E38, F24; *dsm.* HIM A2, A4, A17, etc.;
gsm. HIS A11, A13, A15, etc.; *nsf.* HEO
G16, G17, G18, etc.; *asf.* HEO E5; *dsf.*
HIRE E4, G19, ?C1; *gsf.* HIRE D17,
D26, E3, E36; *nsn.* HIT A6, A7, *A10,
etc.; *asn.* HIT C41, D8, D14, E43, F48,
G43, HIŢ C35, ⟨HIT⟩ D19, F46; *np.*
HEO A38, A40, B6, etc; *ap.* HEO A5,
HAM D13, D24, F7, ⟨HAM⟩ F6, G54,
HI B14, *D22; *dp.* HEOM A39, B12,
B14, C18, C34 (twice), H⟨EOM⟩ D11,
⟨HEOM⟩ C40, HAM B21, B38, C18,
*D13, F8, HAM B38; *gp.* HORE A39,
C45, D5, E42, E44, F9, HOR⟨E.* F11,
⟨HORE⟩ D25.

HEAFOD   *n.,* head: *as.* A38; *ds.*
HEAFDE G40.

HEAUEDPONNE   *f.,* skull, *ds.* D5.

HEARDE   *adj.,* hard, bitter: *asm.*
⟨HEA⟩RDE E34; *dsm.* D35; *dsn.* G22.

HEARPE   *f.,* harp: *as.* E22.

HEIӠE   I *adj.,* high: *gsm.* E39. II *adv.,*
high, high up: HEIE G40.

HEIHNESSE   *f.,* excellence, ?highness,
i.e., heaven: *ds.* F34.

HELDAN   *v.7,* 1. to possess, own, have:
inf. C35; *pp.* HOLDEN G32.   2. to
hold, keep: *pret. 1s.* HEOLD D21; *pp.*
HOLDEN G45.

HELEWEWES   ?*n.,* the end wall of a
building: *np.* *C30.

HELLE   *f.,* hell: *ds.* F32, G26; ?*ads.*
⟨HELL⟩E G5.

HELLEWITE   *n.,* hell pain, torment: *ds.*
B26.

HELP   *m., ?f.,* help, succour: *ns.* E28.

HELPEN   *v.3,* to help, aid, assist: *inf.*
C25; *3p.* HELPEÞ F11.

HEORTE   *f.,* heart: *ds.* D49.

HEOU   *v.7,* to hew, slander, to be cutting: *pret. 2s.* G22.

HEOUENE   *f.,* heaven: *ns.* F38; *as.* B28;
ds. G42.

HER   *adv.,* here: C9, C10, D18.

HERBORWEN   *v.3,* to harbour, shelter:
inf. C23, D3.

IHEREN   *v.I,* 1. to hear: *inf.* E26, E34;
3p. IHEREÞ E31; *pret. 2s.* IHERDEST
E23;   2. to listen to (*with d.*): *IHEREÞ
E17.

HERUNGE   *f.,* that which is heard,
words, sounds: *as.* E31.

HEUI   *adj.,* woeful, sorrowful: *nsf.* A15.

HINEN   *m.,* servant, member of a
household: *np.* C33.

HOLD   *n.,* dead body, corpse: *ns.*
⟨HO⟩LD E6; *as.* C41; *ds.* HOLDE E5.

HOLI   *adj.,* holy: *nsn.* D38; *asf.* HOLIE
E28; *dsm.* HOLIE F43, G40; *dsf.*
HOLIE G45; *apm.* HOLIE E26.

HOLIWATERE   *n.,* holy water: *ds.*
*D12.

HOND   *f.,* hand: ?*as.* *D38; *np.*
HONDEN A39; *dp.* HONDEN A38;
?*adp* HONDEN B7.

HONDLEÞ   *v.II,* to handle: *3p.* A40.

HORD   *n.,* treasure hoard: *ns.* C45; *as.*
D5, *⟨H⟩ORD D49; *gp.* HORDE E7.

IHOTEN   *v.7,* to be named or called
something: *pp.* F34. Cf. BIHETEN.

HOWE   *f.*, care, anxiety: *ads.* C4.

HU   *conj. adv.*, in what manner, to what extent: D23, G2.

HUND   *m.*, hound: *ns.* D47.

⟨HUNEÐ⟩E   *v.1*, to abuse, hate: *pret 3s.* G22.

HUNGRIE   *adj.*, hungry: *npm.* C39.

HUS   *n.*, house, dwelling: *as.* C29; *ds.* HUSE B15, B40, C23, E8.

HWAR   *adv.*, where: B4, B5, B7, B9, B10.

HWI   *adv.*, why, wherefore: D22, G4, HWUI B17.

HWULE   *f.*, while, at the time: B1, C41, D21, HWILE B17, D27.

HWO   *pron. (indefinite)*, whosoever: C13, D8.

IC   *pron. of the 1st person: ns.* A13, F4, F31, etc.; *as.* ME F3, F27, F32, etc.; *ds.* ME F15, F29, F30, G3; *gs.* MIN B8, MINE A14, G29, ⟨MI⟩NE G7; *n. dual* WIT E47, G51, G52, G54; *a. dual* UNC D32, E32, G26; *g. dual* UNKER E28, G51; ⟨U⟩NKER E27; *gp.* URE E12.

ILE   *m.*, hedgehog: *ds.* F21.

IN I   *prep.*, 1. in: C28, C46, I(N) E52, ?I(N) C50. 2. into: E48. II *adv.*, in: C45.

INNE   I. *prep.*, in, within: B1, D21, F32, INNEN B17. II. *adv.*, within, inside: INNE C29.

INTO   *prep.*, into: I(N)TO B28.

KEIƷE *f.*, key: *as.* F16.

KENE   *adj.*, sharp, fierce, keen: *nsf.* G23.

KINEMERKE   *f.*, ?the post-baptismal seal of the cross, ?a mark signifying royalty: *?as.* G41.

KINGES   *m.*, king, God: *gs.* E39.

IKUNDE   *adj.*, see ICUNDE.

LA   *interj.*, a particle emphasizing a question: D18.

LAC   *n.*, see LOC.

LAWE   *f.*, law, practice, ?way of life: *ds.* G46; *ap.* LAWEN G50.

LEAS   *adj.*, false, faithless: *nsm.* B2, D28.

LEDEN   *v.I*, to lead, conduct: *inf.* G46.

LEFEN   *v.I*, to believe: *inf.* D22.

ILEIDE   *v.I*, to put, place, set: *pret. 3s.* *A4, ?⟨LEIDE⟩ *D49.   Cf. UNDERLEID, ALEID.

LEOFLICHE   *adv.*, kindly, lovingly: LEOFLI⟨CHE⟩ B24.

LEORNEDEN   *v.II*, to learn: *pret. 3p.* E18.

LEOUE   *adj.*, dear, precious: *dsm.* G29.

ILERED   *v.I*, to teach, to give instruction: *pp.* G29, ILÆREDE B20.

ILEST   *v.I*, to last, endure, go on: *3s.* D41, ILÆSTEÞ B45; *3p.* ILESTEÞ A14.

LETTEST   *v.7*, to let out, emit: *pret. 2s.* *C17. Cf. FORLETEN.

LIBBE   *v.III*, to live, exist: *1s.* A13.

LICAME   *m.*, body, corpse: *ns.* A28; *as.* A11, B25, *ds.* D17, E3, E36, ⟨LIC⟩AME A9, LICH⟨AME⟩ A45, LIÇAME C2, L⟨ICAME⟩ D26.

⟨LICHE⟩   *n.*, body, corpse, torso: *as.* *A21.

LIKEÞ   *v.II*, to be pleasing to (*with d*): *3s.* C40; *pret. 3s.* LICODE G14, LIKEDE E21.

LIF   *n.*, animate existence, vitality, the span of life: *ns.* A29, E16; *as.* A4, C37, D9, D16, D27, D42, F19, G6, G32, ⟨LIF⟩ C15; *ds.* LIUE B12, LIFE E35.

LIFDAWES   *m.*, the span of life: *np.* A14.

LIFLEAS   *adj.*, lifeless, dead: *ns.* G33.

LIFRE   *f.*, the liver: *as.* C48.

LIHTE   *n.* light, i.e., lung: *ap.* C48.

LIPPEN   *f.*, lip: *ap.* *A18, D6.

LIST   *v.5*, to lie down: *2s.* B38; *3s.* LIÞ A36, G15, LIIÞ C31; *3p.* LIGGEÞ E11, A21; *pret. 2s.* LEIƷE D11.

LISTEN   *mf.*, trick, artifice: *ap.* E18.

LIÞ   *mn.* limb, member: *ns.* E11; *ds.* LIÞE E11.

LOC   *n.*, gift: *as.* B24, LAC B25.

LODLICHE   *adv.*, fiercely, grievously: LOD⟨LICHE⟩ C48.

LOKIENNE   *v.II*, to look: *inf.* F18.

LOND   *n.*, land: *ns.* D38.

LONG   *adj.*, long in duration, i.e., in terms of time: B38, LONGE B12 (but see following entry).

LONGE   *adv.*, for a long time: E25, ⟨LON⟩GE A14, LONG⟨E⟩ D44 (see previous entry).

LORE *f.,* lore, teaching: *as.* *E28; *?ads.* B29, E21, G14, G43.

LOÞ *adj.,* loathsome, horrible: *nsm.* B37, E23, F17; *dsf.* LOÞRE G1; *npm.* LOÞE G18; *npf.* LOÞE G50; *comp.* LOÞRE D11.

LOWE *adj.,* low, not high: *npn.* C30.

LUFE *f.,* love: *ns.* A44; *as.* *B20; *ds.* D4, G1, G45.

LUFEDEST *v.II,* to love, to feel affection for: *pret. 2s.* B2, B9, B35, B43, G49, G50; LUFEDÆST B4, LUFEDE⟨ST⟩ D28; *pp.* ILUFED D15.

LUFT *mn.,* air, sky: *ns.* F38.

LUT I *adj.,* little: *?nsn.* C34. II *adv.,* little, to a small extent: E29.

LUTIƷ *adj.,* crafty, cunning: *nsm.* *B2, LUTI D28.

LUÞER *adj.,* bad, wicked: *nsm.* D27; *npmf.* LUÞERE E18; *dpf.* LUÞERE D29, D32, F14.

LUÞERLICHE *adv.,* wickedly: E35, LU⟨ÞER⟩LICHE B35.

LUÞERNESSE *f.,* wickedness: *ns.* C22.

MA *adv.,* see MUCHEL.

IMAKE *f.,* wife: *ns.* G34.

⟨MA⟩KIEN *v.II,* to make, perform: *inf.* *B20.

MA⟨KUNGE⟩ *f.,* making, doing: *ns.* F41.

MARKES *f.,* a monetary unit equivalent to 160 pennies or 2/3 of a pound sterling: *dp.* B6.

MAÞE⟨ME⟩TE *m.,* food for worms: *ns.* *G4.

MAWE *m.,* stomach, belly: *ns.* C49.

MAWEN *v.,* see MÆI.

MÆI *v.PP.,* to be able or capable of doing something (with a following infinitive): *3s.* C9; *3p.* MAWEN F24; *pret. 2s.* MIHTE⟨ST⟩ D30; *pret. 3s.* MIHTE D8; *pret. 3p.* MIHTEN B22, B24, C24.

MÆNET *v.I,* 1. to bemoan, complain: *3s.* A7. 2. to signify, tell of, mean: *3p.* MÆNEÞ G55. Cf. BIMÆNEN.

ME *pron.,* see MON II.

IMENGED *v.I,* to combine, mix: *pp.* A26.

IMERKED *v.II,* to mark, seal: *pp.* G39.

MESSE *f.,* mass, a celebration of the Eucharistic service: *ds.* *B23.

MEST *adj.,* see MUCHEL.

IMET I *n.,* rule, law: *ns.* A35. II *v.5,* 1. to measure: *3s.* MET A33. 2. to repay, requite: *inf.* IMETEN *E15 (but see following entry).

IMETEN *v.I,* to meet, encounter: *inf.* *E15 (but see previous entry).

MID *prep.,* 1. in conjunction with, in the company of, with: A11, A16, A26, etc.; 2. by means of, by, with: A3, A33, A38, etc.

⟨MIDD⟩ENEARDE *m.,* the world, the earth: *?ds.* A1.

MIHT *f.,* might, strength: *as.* A20.

MIHTE, MIHTEST, MIHTEN *v.,* see MÆI.

MILDELICHE *adv.,* kindly, ?gently: F36.

MILTE *mf.,* spleen: *ns.* *C49.

MILTS⟨E⟩ *f.,* compassion, forgiveness: *as.* F9.

MILTS⟨UNGE⟩ *f.,* compassion, forgiveness: *as.* F15.

MISDEDEN *f.,* misdeed, crime, sin: *ap.* B23, F9.

MO *adv.,* see MUCHEL.

MODES *n.,* wile, trick, ?thought: *ap.* *G48.

MODER *f.,* mother: *ns.* A25, G53.

⟨MO⟩DINESSE *f.,* pride: *ns.* B4.

MOLDE *f.,* earth, ground: *as.* MOL⟨DE⟩ A33; *ds.* A34.

MON I *m.,* a person, a man: *ns.* C9 (the second one); *as.* A3; *ds. ?ap.* *MEN D4; *gs.* MONNES F39; *np.* MEN F8, C16; *ap.* MEN B20; D29, E13; ⟨MEN⟩ D7; *dp.* MONNEN E6. II. *pron.* (indefinite) one, a man, a person: *ns.* A33, C9 (the first one), ME D10.

IMONG *prep.,* among, between: B14.

MONIFOLDE *adj.,* numerous, many: *npm.* B6.

MONSWARE *m.,* perjurer: *ns.* D47.

MORE *adv.,* see MUCHEL.

MORÞDEDEN *f.* deadly sin, crime: *ap.* E15.

MOT *v.PP,* 1. to be allowed or permitted, may: *3s.* A34. 2. to be compelled,

?to desire, wish: *pret. 2s.* MOSTES E26.

MUCHEL I. *adj.*, great, much: *asf.* MUCHELE A23; *dsm.* MUCHELE A3; *supl.* MEST E47, ⟨MEST⟩ E52. II. *adv.* 1. so much, greatly: MUCHEL *B4; *comp.* MORE B34, D20. 2. more (in terms of time), again: *comp.* MA F18, MO G16, MORE E31.

MURIE *adj.*, pleasing, agreeable: *npf.* E15.

MUÞ *m.*, mouth: *ns.* C17, E38; *as.* A42, ⟨MUÞ⟩ F3; MUÞE *ds.* C22, E44, *E45, F5, F15.

NAMMORE I. *pron.*, nothing more, nothing further: NA(M)MORE A34. II *adv.*, no longer, not again: ⟨NAM⟩MARE E39.

NE I *adv.*, no, not: A34, F13, F24, etc.; II *conj.*, nor: C24, E26, E28, E39 (the first one), F22.

NEFRE *adv.*, never, at no time: C11, C25, D43, E49, F13, NEFR⟨E⟩ D39, NEFRE E1, ⟨NEFR⟩E E31, NÆFFRE C6, ⟨N NÆFFRE⟩ B45.

NEIH *prep.*, near, close to: B38; *adv.*, near, close: C31, D49.

NEODE *f.*, need, care: *ap.* F5.

NEOSE *f.*, nose: *as.* A18.

NEOWE *adj.*, new: *asn.* C29.

NIMEN *v.4*, to take, to get possession of: *inf.* *C13, D44. Cf. BINUMEN.

NIÞE *m.*, hatred, spite, ?affliction: *ds.* D35.

NONE I *adj.*, no, not any: C24, E31, F7, F15. NENNE C4. II *adv.*, not, not at all: NON G27.

INOUH I *adj.*, enough, sufficient: *as.* D39. II *adv.*, sufficiently: D47.

NOUHT *adv.*, see NOWIHT

NOWIHT *adv.*, not at all: D19, F22. ⟨NOUHT⟩ G32, *?pron.*, nothing: NOUHT B33.

NU *adv.*, now, at the present time: F16, F32, G5, etc.

O see A.

OF *prep.*, 1. from, out of, of: *A9, A34, B15, etc.

OFEODEST *v.AN*, to acquire, obtain: *pret. 2s.* E35. Cf. AGON.

OFER *prep.*, 1. over, across, through: C27, C44. 2. beside, next to, over: B10.

OFERMETE *m.* gluttony: *ds.* D35.

OFFERED *v.I*, to frighten: *pp.* D8.

OFFRIAN *v.I*, to offer, i.e., to offer an oblation: *inf.* B24.

⟨OFTES⟩IÞES *adv.*, many times, frequently: *A12.

OHTEST *v.PP.*, to have, possess: *2s.* C8; *pret. 3s.* AHTE E2, E29.

ON *prep.*, 1. on, upon: A13, A36, B27, etc. 2. in: A4, F43, G15, etc. 3. among: ?*⟨O⟩N C12. 4. at: O⟨N⟩ D7.

ONE *num.*, one (used adjectively): *dsf.* A33; *dsn.* F46.

ONFOÞ *v.7*, to receive, accept: *3s.* F12; *3p.* E44, ⟨ON⟩FOÞ F9. Cf. FENGE.

ONFULLED *v.I*, to fill up, to sate: *pp.* D33. Cf. IFULLED.

ON3EAN *adv.*, again: *C6. See A3AN.

ONHOR⟨DED⟩ *v.II*, to hoard up, to store: *pp.* C35.

ONLICN⟨ESSE⟩ *f.*, likeness, image: *?as.* F50.

ONSCUNEDEST *v.II*, to shun, avoid: *pret. 2s.* B3.

OPENE *adj.*, open: *apn.* D21.

ORE *f.*, grace, mercy: *as.* F8.

ORLEASE *adj.*, 1. dishonourable, base, ?poor: *dpm.* C25. 2. base, cruel, pitiless: *npm.* C43.

⟨OÞ⟩ *conj.*, until: ⟨OÞ⟩ E12.

OÞES *m.*, oath: *ap.* G38.

OÞRE *pron.*, other (used substantively): *ap.* E20, G12.

OWEN *adj.* own, i.e., possession: *nsn.* C45.

⟨PA⟩NEWES *m.*, penny: *ap.* *B5.

PARADIS *?f.*, paradise: *as.* D37.

PIKES *m.*, a pointed tool, pick: *np.* F27, F32.

PILES *m.*, a pointed object, spine, needle: *np.* F21, PIL⟨ES⟩ F24; *dp.* F22.

PINIEN *v.II*, to torture, torment: *inf.* F33; *3s.* PINEÞ A11; *pp.* IPINED F31.

PREOSTEN *m.,* priest, presbyter: *dp.*
F7.
PRICKE *mf.,* prick, pain: *ds.* A11.
PRIKIEN *v.II,* to pierce, prick, sting:
inf. F32, ⟨PRI⟩KIEN F24; *3p.*
P(RI)KIEⱣ F22, F27; *prp.* PRIKIENDE
F21.
PRICKUNGE *f.,* pricking: *ds.*
P(RI)CKUNGE F31.
PSALM see SALM.
PUNDES *n.,* pound, i.e., 240 pennies:
np. B5.

QUALEHOLDE *n.,* "torture-body": *gp.*
*B42.

READE *adj.,* red: *dsn.* B27.
REOWLICHE I *adj.,* wretched,
grievous: *nsm.* *C15, D9,
RE⟨OWLICHE⟩ D16, REOULIC
*F19. II *adv.,* pitifully, wretchedly: C7.
REPIE *v.II,* to refer to, to touch: *1s.*
G28.
RESTE *f.,* rest, repose: *as.* C24, F12.
RESTEN *v.I,* to rest, repose: *inf.* F13.
RICHE *adj.,* great, of high rank: *nsf.*
*A43.
RIDEN *v.1,* to ride: *inf.* C7, RIDÆN
*C5.
RI⟨F⟩E (MS: RIPE) *adj.,* rife, abundant:
nsf. *C22.
RIHT I *n.,* justice, law, truth: *as.* B3.
II *adj.,* lawful, fair, just: *nsn.* RIHTE
A35; *dsf.* ⟨R⟩IHTERE G46; *gsn.*
RIHTES E20, G12. III *?adv.,* correctly:
*A38.
⟨RIH⟩TLICHE *adv.,* correctly, exactly:
A35. Cf. RIHT III.
RODE *f.,* rood, cross: *ds.* B27.
ROF *m.,* roof: ns. C31: *ds.* ROUE C24.
ROTIEN *v.II,* to rot, putrefy: *inf.* E9.
RUGLUNGE *adv.,* backwards: *C5.
RUNGEN *v.3* (OE I), to ring: *pp.* *E27;
? adj.

SAKE *f.,* strife, sedition, a lawsuit: *as.*
D45.
SALM *m.,* psalm: *ds.* PSALME E40,
G19; (*used adjectivally*) ds. *?m.* SALME
C20.

SALMSONGE *m.* psalm: *ds.* B22.
SÆPE *m.,* hole, pit: *ds.* B40, SEAPE E8.
SCAL *v.PP.,* 1. to be obliged to, to have
to (*as an auxiliary followed or preceded by an
inf.*) *1s.* B36, *G5, G8; *2s.* SCALT B39,
C5, D1, D2, D3, D7, E9, E14, E34,
⟨SCAL⟩T C4; *3s.* SCAL C49, C50,
SCHAL A9; *3p.* SCULEN C38, E42,
E47, SCU⟨LEN⟩ E32, ⟨SCULE⟩N E51;
pret. 1s. SCEOLDE G32; *2s.*
SCEOLDEST G42, SCOLDEST C28,
G45, ⟨SCOLDE⟩ST G53; *pret. 3s.*
SCOLDE D43; *pret. 3p.* SCOLDEN
G51, G52, G54. 2. to be obliged to,
to have to (*with an elided verb of motion*):
? *3p.* SCULEN A2; 3. to pertain to,
to be proper to: ? *3p.* *ŞCULEN A2.
ISCEAFT *mf.,* created being, creature:
ns. ISCEAFT F35; *ap.* ISCEAFTE F47,
ISCEÆFTAN A2.
SCEARP *adj.,* 1. sharp, bitter: *nsf.* G23.
2. *n.* (*used substantively*) sharpness: *ns.*
SCEARPE F25, SCERPE F29.
ISCEND *v.I,* to corrupt, injure: *pp.* IS-
CEND D36, ISC⟨END⟩ D25.
ISCEARPEN *v.,* see ISCOP.
SCERP *adj.,* see SCEARP.
SCERPEⱣ *v.II,* to become sharp: *3s.*
A18.
ISCOP *v.6,* to shape, create: *pret. 3s.*
F47; *pp.* ISCEAPEN F34.
SCOREDE *v.I,* to jut out, to point: *pret.*
3s. F29.
SCORTEⱣ *v.II,* to become short: *3s.*
A19. Cf. ASCORTED.
SCRIFT *m.,* penance: *as.* F10.
SCRINCKEⱣ *v.3,* to shrink, shrivel up:
3s. A18.
SEAPE see SÆPE.
SECHEⱣ *v.I,* to seek, to look for: *3p.* F8;
pret. 1s. SOUHTE B19.
SEGGEN *v.III,* 1. to say, tell, reveal: *inf.*
E42, SIGGEN F7, ⟨SEG⟩GEN C9;
1s. SEGGE G27; *3s.* SÆIⱣ A13, C2,
D17, SEIⱣ D26, E3, E36, E40; *3p.*
SEGGEⱣ F11, F35, SIGGEⱣ G34; *pret.
3s.* SEIDE F45; *pp.* ISEID B30, C20,
ISÆID G19.
SELLIC *adj.,* strange, marvellous: (*used
substantively*) ns. *G27.

SEMDEST *v.I,* to load, burden: *pret. 2s.* B18.

SEN⟨DEN⟩ *v.I,* to send: *inf.* C33; *pp.* ISEND D31.

ISENE *adj.,* easy to see, clear: *nsn.* E40.

ISEIƷE *v.5,* to see, to look on; *?pret. 2s. ?subj. pret. 2s.* D22; *subj. 3s.* D8. Cf. BISIHP.

SEORUHFUL *adj.,* full of sorrow, grief: *nsm.* B18, E16; *nsf.* SEORHFUL A15; *asm.* SEORUHFULE A8, SEORUHFULNE B19; *apn.* SORHFULLE D25.

SEORUHLICHE *adv.,* sorrowfully, in a sorrowful manner: A22.

SEORUWE *f.,* sorrow, care: *ns.* B8; *ds.* SEORWE A16; *dp.* SEORUWEN A27; *gp.* E47.

SEOPPEN I *adv.,* afterwards; A33, F9. II *conj.,* after, when, since: A40, D15, G33, G49.

SEOUENE *num.,* 1. seven (*used substantively*): *np.* F40; 2. the ordinal, seventh (*used adjectively*): *nsmf.* SE⟨QUEPE⟩ F35.

ISET *v.I,* to occupy, set, fix: *pp.* F26. Cf. UTSET

⟨SIBBE⟩ *fn.* kinsmen, relation: *np.* B10.

SIDWOWES *n.,* sidewall: *np.* C30.

SETE *v.5,* to sit: *pret. 2s.* C26; *pret. 3p.* SETEN B10.

SIP *m.,* fate, fortune, time, i.e., occasion, departure, i.e., death: *ns.* A16, C15, C37, D9, D16, F19, ⟨SIP⟩ D42; *as.* A8, G6; *?ads.* A29.

SIPIEN *v.II,* to go, travel, depart: *inf.* G8, SIPIAN E51, SI⟨PIEN⟩ E47; *3p.* SIPIEP F10.

SLEPTEST *v.I (OE 7),* to sleep: *pret. 2s.* E24.

SO I *adv. conj.,* so, as, consequently, thus: A26, A27, F30, etc. II *adv.,* 1. as, in such wise, so: B19, F21, G25, ⟨SO⟩ G16, G36, SWO B4. 2. (with HU) howsoever: G2. 3. (SO SO) just as: G55, ⟨SO PEO⟩ G34. 4. (with HWO) whosoever: D8.

SOFTE *n.,* softness: *ns.* F23, F28.

SOFTLICHE *adv.,* gently, calmly: A5.

ISOLD *v.I,* to give, deliver: *pp.* *D38.

ISOM⟨NEDE⟩ *v.II,* to unite, join together, *pret. 3s.* A5.

SONE *adv.,* soon, directly, forthwith: A31, A37, A41, C7, G33.

SOR *adj.,* sore, painful: *nsm.* A5.

SORE *adv.,* painfully, with much suffering: C18, F24, F27, F31, F33.

SORI *adj.,* full of grief or sorrow: *nsm.* B10; *asm.* A8; *adsm.* A29.

SORILICHE *adv.,* in a sorrowful manner: A28, D17, D26, E3, G8, SORILI-CHE C2, ⟨SORIL⟩ICHE E36, SORLICHE A9, A45, ⟨SORILICH⟩E G28.

SORIMOD *adj.,* dejected, sad: *nsm.* E16.

SOP I *n.,* truth: *ns.* C20; *?as.* SOPE G28. II *adj.,* true, just: *nsn.* B30, G19; *asm.* SOPNE F10; *adsf.* SOPE F12. See SOPE.

SOPE *adv.,* truthfully: ? G28.

SOUHTE *v.* see SECHEP.

SOULE *f.,* soul: *ns.* A9, A45, D17, D26, E3, F12, F34, F39, SOWLE, A28, E36, SOWLE C2, SOUL⟨E⟩ B36; *as.* A4; *np.* ⟨SO⟩ULE E42; *?ap.* ⟨SOULE⟩ F11.

SOULEHUS *n.,* the body: *ns.* A22.

SPEKINDE *v.5,* to speak, say: *prp.* G16, G25.

STIF *adj.,* stiff, rigid: *nsm.* A31.

STILLE *adv.,* quietly, silently: A21, E11, G15.

STIROPE *m.,* stirrup: *ds.* *C3.

STONDEN *v.6,* to stand: *inf.* C3.

ISTREIHT *v.I,* to stretch out, lay prostrate: *pp.* A31.

ISTREONES *n.,* property, treasure: *gs.* E20, G12.

SUKE *v.2,* to suck, draw: *?subj. s.* SUKE F1.

SULFEN *pron.,* self: *C27, F23, SULUEN F28.

SUNE *m.,* son, Christ: *?as.* *F47.

SUNFULE *adj.,* sinful, guilty: *npm.* F27, ⟨SUNFU⟩LE F8.

SUNNE I *f.,* sin, guilt: *as.* B22, D25; *ds.* B18, D48, F26, F33, G5, *G24; *ap.* SUNNEN F11; *dp.* *SUNNE⟨N⟩ (MS. SUNNE) F20.

SWEFEDE *v.II,* to put to sleep, lull: *pret. 3s.* E24.

SWEIȜE   m., sound, melody: ds. E24.
SWETE   n. sweetness: ns. B45, D40.
SWETNESSE f., sweetness: ns. B44; ds. B43.
SWOPEN   v.7, to sweep: inf. D10.
SWOTE   adv., sweetly: E24.
SWUÞE   adv., very much, exceedingly: A39, B11, B25, B43, D46.

TÆCHEÞ   v.I, to prescribe, direct: 3s. A35. Cf. BITÆIHT.
TEAM   m., family, children: ns. G51.
TEMAN   v.I, to bring forth, engender: inf. G51, G52.
TEONE   m.?f., insult, reproach: as. *C17, C19.
TEOREÞ   v.I, to fail, weary: 3s. A20.
TO   I prep., to, into, for, as: A2, A45, *E10, etc.; II adv., too, excessively: B12, B38, C34, D44, *G13.
TOCUME   v.4, to come, arrive: subj. 2s. E4. Cf. CUMEN.
TO⟨DÆL⟩EÞ   v.I, 1. to separate, divide: 3p. A28. 2. to rend, destroy: inf. TODELEN C47, pp. TODÆLED D24. Cf. IDÆLEN.
⟨TO⟩FERDE   v.I, to depart, go: pret. 1s. G30. Cf. FERDEN.
ITOLDE   v.II, to count, reckon: pp. B6.
TORENDEN   v.I, to rend apart, tear in pieces: inf. C48.
TEÞ   m. tooth: np. G9.
TOUWAR⟨D⟩   prep., towards, in the direction of: F29.
TRUKEÞ   v.II, to fail, run short: 3s. A20. Cf. ATRUKED.
TUHTE   v.I, to draw, pull, seduce: ?pret. 3s. E22 (twice), E29.
TUNGE   f., tongue: ns. G9, ⟨TUN⟩GE G15; as. A19.

ÞA   adv. conj., see ÞO.
ÞAUH   conj., although, even if: G27, G28.
ÞÆR   adv. conj., there, where: A5, B39, B41, PER E49, F8, G6, ⟨ÞER⟩ E49.
ÞÆROF   adv., thereof: B33, C11.
ÞÆRTO   adv., thereto: G48.
ÞE   pron., 1. as a demonstrative adj. or article with a following noun: nsm. A27, A28 (the first one), A30, D49, F36 (the second one); asm. ÞENE A8, A11, A41, etc., ?ÞEO C17; dsm. ÞEN A30, A36, A45, etc.; gsm. ÞÆS A42, F39, F41, etc.; nsf. ÞEO A25, A26, A44 (the first one), etc.; ÞE A28 (the second one), D17, E36 (the second one); asf. ÞEO A7, A44 (the second one), F16, etc., ÞA A33, ?ÞE D37, ?A18, ?A19; dsf. ÞÆRE A34, C5, C6, ⟨ÞÆRE⟩ B43; gsf. does not occur; nsn. ÞET A22, A25, A29, etc., ?ÞE A36; asn. ÞET A5, D10, E48, G31; dsn. ?⟨Þ⟩EN G40; gsn. ÞÆS A24; npm. ÞEO C16, C43, F27, F32, ⟨ÞEO⟩ C39; apn. ÞA G22, ÞEO ?A2, C23, ?D12, ?E18 (the second one), E26; dpm. ÞAM C25; npf. ÞEO E32, E42; apf. ÞEO ?A2, ?E18, E27, G50, ÞA ?A18; npn. ÞE A21, ?B10, C30 (the first one), E11, ÞEO B5, ?B7, ?F35, ?F40; apn. ÞA ?A17 (twice). 2. as a demonstrative pron.: ÞET ?A9, *E6 (the first one), *ÞÆRE B26. 3. as a relative pron.: ÞE A2, A23, A41, etc., ÞET A6, A13, B21, etc., ÞEO *A37, B7, B43, etc., ÞA E18. 4. with a comparative form, i.e., "the": ÞE G16 (the first one), ⟨ÞE⟩ C16 (the first one), D11. 5. adv. conj., see ÞO, ÞET.
ÞE⟨ARF⟩   v.PP, to need, to have occasion to (preceding an infinitive): 1s. F13; 2s. ÞEARFT C6, ⟨ÞEA⟩RFT C3.
ÞEN   conj., than: D20.
ÞEOW   ?m., slave: ns. B32.
ÞEOWDOME   m., slavery, servitude: ds. B29.
ÞER,   adv. conj., see ÞÆR.
ÞERINNE   adv., therein: A23.
ÞERMES   m., gut, entrail: ap. C47.
ÞERON   adv., thereon: D11.
ÞET   adv.conj., that, so that: A14, A39, F4, etc.
ÞICKE   I adj., thick, dense: nsm. F22. II adv., thickly, abundantly: F20.
ÞING   n. (with ALLE) everything: np. F45; ap. F42.
ÞES   pron. (demonstrative), this: nsm. C9; dsf. ÞISSE E35; ?nsn. ÞIS F40 F41; dsn. ÞISSEN F42; npn. ÞEOS G55.
ÞO   adv. conj., then, when: B28, ÞA D22, D26, ÞE E3, E36 (the first one).

⟨ÞO⟩LEDE   *v. II,* to suffer, endure: *pret. 3s.* *D44.

ÞONNE   *adv. conj.,* then, therefore, when: A6, A22, A28, etc.

ÞU   *pron. of the 2nd person: ns.* F3, F5, F6, etc.; *as.* ÞE B14, B15, B16, etc. *ds.* ÞE F1, F3, F4, etc.; *gs.* ÞIN F3, F19, *C36, etc., *ÞIIN E38, ÞINE F5 (twice), F13, F14, etc., ÞINES B32, ÞIRE B16. Neither plural nor dual forms occur.

ÞUNCHEÞ   *v. I,* to appear, seem (*impersonal with d.*): *3s.* A39, C34, ⟨ÞUN⟩CHEÞ B38, ⟨ÞUNC⟩HEÞ C1; *pret. 3s.* *ÞUÞTE B12.

ÞURH   *prep.,* through, by means of, as a consequence of: *F10, F12, F14, etc., ÞURUH G43, G45.

ÞUS   *adv.,* thus, in this way: A14, A24, F19, etc.

ÞUÞTE   *v.,* see ÞUNCHEÞ.

UFEL   *adj.,* bad, ill, wicked: *nsf.* A44; *supl.* WURST D30, F30.

UNBLISSE   *f.,* sorrow, affliction: *np.?s.* *A44.

UNC, UNKER   *pron.,* see IC.

UNDER   *prep.,* under, beneath: C24, G42.

UNDERLEID   *v. I,* to prop, support: *pp.* C26. Cf. ILEID, ALEID.

UNDON   *v. AN,* to open, loosen: *inf.* E39. Cf. DON, FORDON.

UNFRETEN   *v. 5,* uneaten, undevoured: *pp.* D6. Cf. FRETEN.

UNHEI3E   *adj.,* low: *npn.* C30.

UNHOL   *adj.,* evil, ?sick: *ap.?f,* *D3.

UNIFOUH   *n.,* excess: *as.* D39.

⟨U⟩NLEÞE   *f.,* misery, suffering: *as.* *G32.

UNNEAÞE   *adv.,* hardly, scarcely: D34.

UNRIHT   *n.,* sin, vice, evil: *as.* D28, U⟨N⟩RIHT B2.

UNSEIHTE   *adj.,* hostile, quarrelsome: *nsm.* *D45.

UNWURÞ   *adj.,* contemptible, worthless: *nsm.* B37. Cf. WURÞEST.

UP   *adv.,* up: E14.

UT⟨SE⟩T   *v. I,* to place outside: *pp.* C6. Cf. ISET.

UT   *adv.,* out, outside: B15, B16, *C17, C45, D14.

WA   *f.?m. and interj.,* see WO.

WADAN   *v. 6,* to go, move, advance: *inf.* C46.

WALAWA   *interj.,* oh!, alas!: F4, WEILA C10, G3, WEILE B19, ⟨WEI⟩LAWEI C14.

WALE   *?mf.,* slave, servant: *as.* G2.

WALKEÞ   *v. 7,* to move around, roll, toss: *3s.* A12.

WAS, WERE   *v.,* see BEON.

WATE⟨R⟩   *n.,* water: *ns.* F39.

WAXEN   *v. 7,* to flourish, grow: *inf.* C38.

WÆDE   *f.,* robe, garment, covering: *np.* B9; *?gds.* E10.

WÆLDEÞ   *v. I,* to have control or power over: *3p.* B41.

IWEARÞ   *v. 3,* to become, be made, to get: *pret. 1s.* G2; *pret. 3s.* F37; *pret. ?subj. 3s.* WURÞE G25; *imp.s.* IWU⟨RÞE⟩ F45; *pp.* *IWORÞEN F45, IWURÞEN F46.

WEASIÞES   *m.,* time of woe, ?troubles: *ap.* *G7.

WEDLOWE   *m.,* violator of an agreement, traitor: *ns.* D47.

WEILA, WEILE, WEILAWEI   *interj.,* see WALAWA.

WEL *adv.,* well, abundantly: B9, E21, G14, ⟨WEL⟩ E22.

WEN⟨DEN⟩   *v. I,* to turn, direct: *inf.* A38; *3s.* WENDEÞ A12; *pp.* IWEND F23, *F25, F28, F30. See WENDEST.

WENDEST   *v. I,* to expect, imagine, believe: *pret. 2s.* C36, D17, D43.

WEOLE   *m.,* prosperity, riches, weal: *ns.* C36; *as.* C8, C14, *a.?ds.?p.* WEOLEN B16; *gs.?p.* WEOLAN *B32; *np.* *WEOLÆN C10.

WEOPINDE   *v. 7,* to weep, complain: *prp.* A10.

WEOWE, WOWE   *f.m. and adj.,* see WO.

WERKE   *n.,* deed, action: *ds.* D30.

WIDE   *adv.,* widely, far and wide: C46.

WIELES   *n.,* wile, stratagem: *ap.* G48.

WIF   *n.,* wife, woman: *ns.* A41, A43.

WIHTE   *?f.,* creature, thing: *ap.* *D3.

WILLE   *m.,* desire, mind, pleasure, will:

ns. G24, IWILL G3; *as.* C11, D50, ⟨WILLE⟩ E1; *ds.* WILLÆN B33.

⟨WINBOW⟩E *m.,* vine: *ads.* *G36.

WIND *n.,* wind: *ns.* F39.

WINDEÞ *v.3,* to wind, curl: *3p.* C43. Cf. BIWUNDEN.

WISDOME *m.,* 1. learning, wisdom: *ds.* *E43, F43. 2. the second person of the Trinity: *ds.* *F48.

WISEÞ *v.II,* to direct, guide: *3s.* F48.

WISLICHE *adv.,* truly, certainly: E43, F48, WISLI⟨CHE⟩ F37.

WIT *pron.,* see IC.

IWIT *n.,* understanding, consciousness: *as.* A20.

IWITEÞ *v.I,* to depart, leave, lose: *3s.* A10; *pp.* IWITEN C9, IWITAN C36.

WIÞ *prep.,* 1. with, beside: B20. 2. against: C16. 3. against, from: D13.

WIÞINNE I *adv.,* within: D48 *WIÞINE F26. II *prep.,* within, inside: WIÞI(N)NEN D46.

WIÞSOKE *v.6,* to renounce, abandon: *pret. 2s.* G47.

WIÞUTEN *adv.,* without, outside: *B14.

WO I *f.?m.,* woe, misery, affliction: *ns.* WA G25; *as.* G3, WEOWE A7, ⟨WOA⟩ B1, ⟨WEO⟩WE B36. II *adj.,* evil, nasty: *apm.* WOWE E19; *dpm.* WOWE G11. III *interj.* woe!, alas!: A13, ?WA F4.

IWOLD *n.,* might, power, possession: *as.* C8, E29, ⟨IWO⟩LD E2.

WOLDEST *v.AN,* 1. to will, desire: *?pret. 2s.* ⟨WOL⟩DEST G2; *pret. 3s.* WOLDE G32. 2. will, shall (*accompanying an inf. as a sign of the future*): *1s.* WULLE G7; *3s.* WULE D10; *3p.* WULLEÞ C39, C40, C42, C46, D5, D12, F32; *neg. 3p.* NULLEÞ A38, C13, C33, N⟨ULLEÞ⟩ D6. 3. (*accompanying an inf., perhaps as a sign of the subj.*) to be used to, would: *pret. 2s.* D50, WOLD⟨EST⟩ F6; *neg. 2s.* NOLDEST *F5, F7, F15, etc.; *pret. 3s.* NOLDE D44, ⟨NOL⟩DE C11.

⟨WOM⟩BE *f.,* belly: *ns.* D36; C46.

WONEÞ *v.II,* to complain, bewail, bemoan: *3s.* A12, WOANEÞ A25, ⟨WOAN⟩EÞ A7; *prp.* WONIENDE A10. WOANING A15.

WORDE *n.,* word, speech: *ds.* D30, F37, F46, G22.

WOT *v.PP,* to know, to observe: *3s.* E43.

W⟨OWES⟩ *m.,* wall: *ap.* *D12. Cf. HELEWEWES, SIDWOWES.

WRECCHES I *m.,* wretch, outcast: *ap.* G22, WRECCHEN C23; *dp.* WRE⟨CCHE⟩N C25. II *adj.,* wretched, miserable: *nsf.* WRECCHE A44, WRÆCCHE B36; *nsn.* WRECCHE A41, WRÆCCHE A29; *asm.* WRECCHE G6; *asn.* WRECCHE C15, C37, D9, D16, F19, WRECCE D42.

WRÆNCHES *m.,* stratagem, trick: *ap.* G48.

IWRITEN *v.1,* to write: *pp.* F43. Cf. AWRITEN.

WROUHTE, WROHTEN *v.,* see WURCHEN.

WULDER *n.* glory, splendour: *ns.* D36; *gp.* WULD⟨RE⟩ E52.

WUNIEN *v.II,* 1. to dwell, live: *inf.* E52, WUNIENNE D18 (with TO), ⟨WU⟩NIEN C28; *3p.* WUNIEÞ D24; *pret. 1s.* WUNEDE B1; *pret. 3s.* WUNEDE A23. 2. to be accustomed to: *pp.* IWUNEDE *E10.

WUNNE *f.,* joy, delight, pleasure: *as.* A23.

WUNUNGE *f.,* space for dwelling, habitation: *as.* D34.

WURCHEN *v.I,* to work on, make, create: *inf.* D5, WURCHEN E1; *pret. 2s.* ⟨WROHTEST⟩ B1; *pret. 3s.* IWROUHTE E16, F36, F42; *pret. 3p.* WROHTEN D25.

WURMES *m.,* worm, insect: *np.* B41, C38, D24, WUR⟨MES⟩ C43; *?ap.* ⟨WUR⟩MES D1; *dp.* WURMEN C28.

WURPE *v.3* to cast, throw: *pret. 2s.* C27.

WURST *adj.,* see UFEL.

WURÞE, IWURÞEN *v.,* see WEARÞ.

WURÞEST *adj.,* worthy, honoured: *supl.* B41. Cf. UNWURÞ.

WURÞLICHE *adv.,* worthily, honourably: G36.

BIBLIOGRAPHY

1. EDITIONS, REVIEWS OF EDITIONS.

(a) *Editions*

Buchholz, Richard, ed. *Die Fragmente der Reden der Seele an den Leichnam in zwei Handschriften zu Worcester und Oxford.* Erlangen, 1890; rpt. Amsterdam: Rodopi, 1970.

Hall, Joseph, ed. *Selections from Early Middle English: 1130–1250.* 2 vols. Oxford: Clarendon Press, 1920. Text (I, 2–4) and notes (II, 228–40) for Fragments A and B.

Haufe, Ernst ed. *Die Fragmente der Rede der Seele an den Leichnam in der Handschrift er Cathedrale zu Worcester.* Greifswald, 1880.

Hauffe [*sic*], Ernst. "Zu den Reden der Seele in der Worcester-HS." *Anglia,* 4 (1881), 237.

Kaiser, Rolf, ed. *Medieval English: An Old English and Middle English Anthology.* 3rd ed. Berlin: Rolf Kaiser, 1958, p. 208. Lines 36–45 of Fragment A and all of Fragment B.

Phillipps, Sir Thomas, ed. *A Fragment of Ælfric's Grammar and Glossary and a Poem on the Soul and Body.* London, 1838.

Ricciardi, Gail Dana Dauterman, ed. "The Grave-bound Body and Soul: A Collective Edition of Four Related Poems from *The Vercelli* and *Exeter Books,* Bodley and Worcester Manscripts." Diss. University of Pennsylvania, 1976.

Singer, S. W., ed. *The Departing Soul's Address to the Body: A Fragment of a Semi-Saxon Poem Discovered among the Archives of Worcester Cathedral by Sir Thomas Phillipps, Bart., with an English Translation.* London: Luke James Hansard, 1845.

(b) *Reviews*

Holthausen, Ferdinand. "Zu Alt- und mittelenglischen Dichtungen." *Anglia,* 14 (1892), 302–22. Notes to *Die Fragmente der Reden der Seele an den Leichnam,* Richard Buchholz, ed., on p. 321.

Kaluza, Max. Rev. of *Die Fragmente der Reden der Seele an den Leichnam,* Richard Buchholz, ed., among other works. *Literaturblatt für germanische und romanische Philologie,* 12 (1891), 12–16. See especially pp. 15–16.

Wissmann, Th. Rev. of *Die Fragmente der Rede der Seele an den Leichnam,* Ernst Haufe, ed. *Literaturblatt für germanische und romanische Philologie,* 2 (1880), 92–94.

Zupitza, Julius. Rev. of *Die Fragmente der Reden der Seele an den Leichnam,* Richard Buchholz, ed. *Archiv für das Studium der neueren Sprachen und Literaturen,* 85 (1890), 78–83.

2. OTHER WORKS CITED IN THE TEXT.

Ackerman, Robert W. "'The Debate of the Body and the Soul' and Parochial Christianity." *Speculum,* 37 (1962), 541–65.

Allen, Michael J. B., and Daniel G. Calder, trans. *Sources and Analogues of Old English Poetry: The Major Latin Texts in Translation.* Cambridge: D. S. Brewer, 1976. Translations of the Batiouchkof homily, pp. 41–44, and Sermons 49 and 58 of the *"Sermones ad Fratres,"* pp. 44–7 and 48–50.

Ångström, Margareta. *Studies in Old English MSS with Special Reference to the Delabialization of y(< u + i) to i.* Diss. Uppsala: Almquist and Wiksells, 1937.

Assmann, Bruno, ed. *Angelsächsische Homilien und Heiligenleben. Bibliothek der angelsächsischen Prosa,* III. Kassel: Georg H. Wigand, 1889, pp. 164–69. In particular pp. 167–9, ll. 76–141.

Atkinson, Robert, ed. *The Passions and the Homilies from* Leabhar Breac: *Text, Translation, and Glossary.* The Royal Irish Academy Todd Lecture Series, Vol. II. Dublin: Royal Irish Academy, 1887, pp. 266–73. Homily 36, "On the soul's exit from the body"; translation, pp. 507–14.

Batiouchkof, Théodor. "Le Débat de l'Ame et du Corps." *Romania,* 20 (1891), 1–55 and 511–78. The first part deals with the development of the address form, the second part with the debate form; pp. 576–78, an edition of the Batiouchkof homily.

Benskin, Michael, and Margaret Laing. "Translations and *Mischsprachen* in Middle English Manuscripts." In *So Many People Languages and Tonges: Philological Essays in Scots and Mediaeval English Presented to Angus McIntosh.* Ed. Michael Benskin and M. L. Samuels. Edinburgh, 1981, pp. 55–106.

Bethurum, Dorothy. "The Connection of the Katherine Group with Old English Prose." *JEGP,* 34 (1935), 553–64.

———. "The Form of Ælfric's Lives of Saints." *SP,* 29 (1932), 515–33.

Blake, N. F. "Rhythmical Alliteration." *MP,* 67 (1969), 118–24.

Bliss, A. J. *The Metre of* Beowulf. 1958: rpt. Oxford: Basil Blackwell, 1962.

Bossy, Michel-André. "Medieval Debates of Body and Soul." *Comparative Literature,* 28 (1976), 144–63.

Bosworth, Joseph. *An Anglo-Saxon Dictionary.* Ed. and rev. T. Northcote Toller. Oxford: Clarendon Press, 1898.

Brown, Carleton, ed. *English Lyrics of the Thirteenth Century.* Oxford: Clarendon Press, 1932. Two versions of *The Latemest Day,* pp. 47–54, and *Shroud and Grave,* p. 31.

Bruce, J. D. "A Contribution to the Study of 'The Body and the Soul' Poems in English." *MLN,* 5 (1890), 385–401. An assessment of the relationship of the English poems to one another and a review of the scholarship up to that time.

Brunner, Karl. *Altenglische Grammatik nach der angelsächsischen Grammatik Eduard Sievers neuarbeitet.* Halle: Max Niemeyer, 1942; rev. 1951.

Cable, Thomas. *The Meter and Melody of* Beowulf. Urbana, Ill.: University of Illinois Press, 1974.

Campbell, Alistair. *Old English Grammar.* Oxford: Clarendon Press, 1959.

Clark, Ardath Sue McKee, ed. "'Seinte Maregrete' and 'Body and Soul': An Edition from the Trinity College, Cambridge MS: B 14.39 with Variant Texts in Parallel." Diss. University of Michigan, 1972. "Body and Soul," i.e. "In a thestri stude."

Clark Hall, John R. *A Concise Anglo-Saxon Dictionary.* 4th ed., with a supplement by Herbert D. Merritt, 1960; rpt. Cambridge: University Press, 1969.

Crawford, S. J. "The Worcester Marks and Glosses of the Old English Manuscripts in the Bodleian, together with the Worcester Version of the Nicene Creed." *Anglia,* 52 (1928), 1–25.

Cross, J. E. "*Ubi Sunt* Passages in Old English — Sources and Relationships." *Vetenskaps-Societetens i Lund Årsbok* (1956), pp. 25–44.

d'Ardenne, S. R. T. O., ed. *Þe Liflade ant te Passiun of Seinte Iulienne.* Liège, 1936; rpt. EETS (O.S.), no. 248. London: Oxford University Press, 1961.

du Méril, Edélestand Pontas. *Poésies populaires latines antérieures au douzième siècle.* Paris: Brockhaus et Avenarius, 1843. According to Northrup (see below), du Méril's edition of *Vision of St. Philibert* is the best available.

Dudley, Louise. "An Early Homily on the 'Soul and Body' Theme." *JEGP,* 8 (1909), 225–53. A parallel edition and discussion of "*Sermones ad Fratres in Eremo*" 69, the Batiouchkof homily, and the relevant portions of the Napier and Thorpe homilies, pp. 226–35.

———. *The Egyptian Elements in the Legend of the Body and Soul.* Bryn Mawr

College Monographs, Vol. VIII. Bryn Mawr, Penn., 1911.

————. " 'The Grave'." *MP,* 11 (1914), 429-42. A discussion of its relation to *SA.*

Everett, Dorothy. *Essays on Middle English Literature.* Ed. Patrick Kean,
1955; rev. Oxford: Clarendon Press, 1959.

Ferguson, Mary Heyward. "The Debate between the Body and the Soul:
A Study in the Relationship between Form and Content." Diss. Ohio
State University, 1965.

————. "The Structure of the Soul's Address to the Body in Old English."
JEGP, 69 (1970), 72-80.

Fisiak, Jacek. *A Short Grammar of Middle English, Part One: Graphemics,
Phonemics, and Morphemics.* London: Oxford University Press, 1968.

Floyer, John Kestell. *Catalogue of Manuscripts Preserved in the Chapter Library
of Worcester Cathedral.* Ed. and rev. Sidney Graves Hamilton. Oxford:
James Parker, 1906.

Förster, Max, ed. *Die Vercelli-Homilien: I–VIII Homilie. Bibliothek der
angelsächsischen Prosa,* XII. 1932; rpt. Darmstadt: Wissenschaftliche
Buchgesellschaft, 1964. Homily IV, pp. 72-107, in particular pp.
84-103, ll. 131-339.

Friedlander, Carolynn Van Dyke. "Early Middle English Accentual
Verse." *MP,* 76 (1979), 219-30.

Funke, Otto. "Some Remarks on Wulfstan's Prose Rhythm." *ES,* 43
(1962), 311-18.

Furnivall, F. J., ed. *Political, Religious, and Love Poems.* EETS (O.S.),
no. 15, 1866; rev. London: Oxford University Press, 1903; rpt. 1965.

Godden, Malcolm, ed. *Ælfric's Catholic Homilies: The Second Series.* EETS
(S.S.), no. 5. London: Oxford University Press, 1979.

Heningham, Eleanor Kellogg, ed. *An Early Latin Debate of the Soul and
Body Preserved in MS. Royal 7 a III in the British Museum.* New York, 1939.

————. "Old English Precursors to the 'Worcester Fragments'." *PMLA,*
55 (1940), 291-307. "Worcester Fragments," i.e., *Soul's Address.*

Holthausen, Ferdinand, ed. *Vices and Virtues (Part I).* EETS (O.S.), no.
89. London: N. Trübner, 1888.

Horn, Wilhelm. *Beiträge zur Geschichte der englischen Gutturallaute.* Berlin:
Wilhelm Gronau, 1901.

Jordan, Richard. *Handbook of Middle English Grammar: Phonology.*
Heidelberg, 1925, rev. 1934. Trans. and rev. Eugene Joseph Crook.
Janua Linguarum, Series Practica, 218. The Hague: Mouton, 1974.

Keller, Wolfgang. *Die litterarischen Bestrebungen von Worcester in angelsächsischer
Zeit.* Quellen und Forschungen zur Sprach- und Kulturgeschichte der

germanischen Völker, 84. Strassburg: Karl J. Trübner, 1900.

Ker, Neil Ripley. *Catalogue of Manuscripts Containing Anglo-Saxon.* Oxford: Clarendon Press, 1957.

————. "The Date of the 'Tremulous' Worcester Hand." *Leeds Studies in English,* 6 (1937), 28-29.

————. *English Manuscripts in the Century after the Norman Conquest: The Lyell Lectures, 1952-53.* Oxford: Clarendon Press, 1960.

————. *Medieval Libraries of Great Britain: A List of Surviving Books.* 2nd ed. Royal Historical Society Guides and Handbooks, no. 3. London: Royal Historical Society, 1964.

Kleinert, Gustav. *Über den Streit zwischen Leib und Seele: Ein Beitrag zur Entwicklungsgeschichte der 'Visio Fulberti'.* Halle, 1980.

Krapp, George Philip, ed. *The Vercelli Book.* The Anglo-Saxon Poetic Records, Vol. II. New York: Columbia University, 1932. *Soul and Body I,* pp. 54-59.

————, and Elliott Van Kirk Dobbie, eds. *The Exeter Book.* The Anglo-Saxon Poetic Records, Vol. III. New York: Columbia University, 1936. *Soul and Body II,* pp. 174-78.

Kuhn, Sherman M. "Was Ælfric a Poet?" *PQ,* 52 (1973), 543-62.

Kurath, Hans, and Sherman Kuhn, eds. *Middle English Dictionary: A-P.* Ann Arbor: University of Michigan Press, 1956, etc.

————. *Middle English Dictionary: Plan and Bibliography.* Ann Arbor: University of Michigan Press, 1954.

Lampe, G. W. H. *The Seal of the Spirit.* London: Longmans, Green, 1951.

Lehmann, Winfred P. *The Development of Germanic Verse Form.* 1956; rpt. New York: Gordian Press, 1971.

Linow, Wilhelm, ed. *Þe Desputisoun bitwen þe Bodi and þe Soule.* Erlanger Beiträge zur englischen Philologie, I. Erlangen and Leipzig: A. Deichert (Georg Böhme), 1889.

Lipp, Frances Randall. "Ælfric's Old English Prose Style." *SP,* 66 (1969), 689-718.

Mack, Frances, ed. *Seinte Marherete.* EETS (O.S.), no. 193. London: Oxford University Press, 1934; rpt. 1958.

McIntosh, Angus. "Early Middle English Alliterative Verse." In *Middle English Alliterative Poetry and its Literary Background: Seven Essays.* Ed. David Lawton. Cambridge: D. S. Brewer, 1982, pp. 20-33.

————. "The Relative Pronouns *þe* and *þet* in Early Middle English." *English and Germanic Studies,* 1 (1947), 73-87.

————. *Wulfstan's Prose: The Israel Gollancz Memorial Lecture for 1948;* rpt. Folcroft Press, 1970.

Mellinkoff, Ruth. "Riding Backwards: Theme of Humiliation and Symbol of Evil." *Viator: Medieval and Renaissance Studies,* 4 (1973), 153–76.

Migne, J. P., gen. ed. "Sermones ad Fratres in Eremo Commorantes, et quosdam alios." In *Patrologiae Cursus Completus: Series Latina,* Vol. 40. Paris, 1845, cols. 1233–1358. In particular Sermons 48, cols. 1328–32, 49, cols. 1332–34, 56, cols. 1339–41, 58, cols. 1341–42, and 69, cols. 1355–57.

Moffat, Douglas. "The Worcester *Soul's Address to the Body:* An Examination of Fragment Order." *Papers on Language and Literature,* 20 (1984), 123–40.

Moore, Samuel, Sanford Brown Meech, and Harold Whitehall. "Middle English Dialect Characteristics and Dialect Boundaries: Preliminary Report of an Investigation Based Exclusively on Localized Texts." In *Essays and Studies in English and Comparative Literature by Members of the English Department of the University of Michigan.* Ann Arbor: University of Michigan Press, 1935, pp. 1–60.

Morris, Richard, ed. *Old English Homilies of the Twelfth Century.* EETS (O.S.), no. 53. London: N. Trübner, 1873, pp. 173–84.

Mossé, Fernand. *A Handbook of Middle English.* Trans. James A. Walker. Baltimore: Johns Hopkins, 1952.

Murray, James A. H., Henry Bradley, W. A. Craigie, and C. T. Onions, eds. *The Oxford English Dictionary,* 12 vols. 1933; rpt. Oxford: Clarendon Press, 1961.

Mustanoja, Tauno F. *A Middle English Syntax, Part I (Parts of Speech).* Mémoires de la Société Néophilologique de Helsinki, 23. Helsinki: Société Néophilologique, 1960.

Napier, Arthur, ed. *Wulfstan: Sammlung der ihm zugeschriebenen Homilien nebst Untersuchungen über ihre Echtheit.* Sammlung englischer Denkmäler in kritischen Ausgaben, 4, 1. Abteilung, 1883; rpt. Berlin: Weidmann, 1966, pp. 134–43. In particular p. 140, l. 9 to p. 141, l. 25.

Noble, James Erwin. "Layamon's *Brut* and the Continuity of the Alliterative Tradition." Diss. University of Western Ontario, 1981.

Northrup, Clark Sutherland. "*Dialogus inter Corpus et Animam:* A Fragment and a Translation." *PMLA,* 16 (1901), 503–25.

Oakden, J. P. *Alliterative Poetry in Middle English.* 2 vols. Manchester, 1930, 1935; rpt. Archon Press, 1968.

Paris, Gaston. Rev. of *Über den Streit von* [sic] *Leib und Seele,* by Gustav Kleinert. *Romania,* 9 (1880), 311–14.

Pearsall, Derek. *Old and Middle English Poetry.* The Routledge History of English Poetry, I. London: Routledge and Kegan Paul, 1977.

Pope, John C., ed. *Homilies of Ælfric: A Supplementary Collection.* Vol. I.

EETS (O.S.), no. 259, London: Oxford University Press, 1967. In particular pp. 105-36 on Ælfric's rhythmical prose.

———. *The Rhythm of* Beowulf: *An Interpretation of Normal and Hypermetric Verse-Forms in Old English Poetry.* 1942; rpt. New Haven: Yale University Press, 1966.

———. *Seven Old English Poems.* Indianapolis: Bobbs-Merrill, 1966, pp. 97-138.

Reichl, Karl, ed. *Religiöse Dichtung im englischen Hochmittelalter: Untersuchung und Edition der Handschrift B.14.39 des Trinity College in Cambridge.* Münchener Universitäts-Schriften, Band 1. München: Wilhelm Fink, 1973, pp. 339-65. An edition of one version (with variants) of *In a Thestri Stude.*

Robbins, Rossell Hope. "Signs of Death in Middle English." *MS,* 32 (1970), pp. 282-98.

Rock, Daniel. *The Church of our Fathers: A New Edition in Four Volumes,* Ed. G. W. Hart and W. H. Frere. London: John Murray, 1905.

Schipper, Jakob. *A History of English Versification.* Oxford: Clarendon Press, 1910, pp. 64-79.

Schlemilch, Willy. *Beiträge zur Sprache und Orthographie spätaltengl. Sprachdenkmäler der Übergangszeit (1000-1150).* Studien zur englischen Philologie, 34, 1914.

Schroeer, Arnold, ed. "The Grave." *Anglia,* 5 (1883), 289-90.

Serjeantson, Mary S. "The Dialects of the West Midlands in Middle English." *The Review of English Studies,* 3 (1927), 54-67, 186-203, 319-31.

Short, Douglas D. "Aesthetics and Unpleasantness: Classical Rhetoric in the Medieval English Lyric *The Grave.*" *SN,* 48 (1976), 291-9.

Silverstein, Theodore. *Visio Sancti Pauli: The History of the Apocalypse in Latin together with Nine Texts.* London: Christophers, 1935.

Slay, D. "Some Aspects of the Technique of Composition of Old English Verse." *Transactions of the Philological Society,* 1952, pp. 1-14.

Stanley, E. G. "Layamon's Antiquarian Sentiments." *Medium Aevum,* 38 (1969), 23-37.

Stratmann, Francis Henry. *A Middle English Dictionary: A New Edition.* Rev. Henry Bradley. London: Oxford University Press, 1891.

Sundby, Bertil. *Studies in the Middle English Dialect Material of the Worcestershire Records.* Bergen: Norwegian Universities Press, 1964.

Thorpe, Benjamin, ed. *Ancient Laws and Institutes of England.* The Commissioners' Report on the Public Record of England, Vol. II, 1840, pp. 394-400. In particular pp. 396-98.

Toller, T. Northcote. *An Anglo-Saxon Dictionary: Supplement.* 1921. Rev. Alistair Campbell, 1955; rpt. Oxford: Oxford University Press, 1972.

Turville-Petre, Thorlac. *The Alliterative Revival.* Cambridge: D. S. Brewer, 1977, pp. 1–17.

Utley, Francis Lee. "Dialogues, Debates, and Catechisms." In *A Manual of Middle English Writings: 1050–1500.* Vol. III. Ed. Albert E. Hartung. New Haven: The Connecticut Academy of Arts and Sciences, 1972. Pp. 691–95, a discussion of the English 'body and soul' literature; pp. 845–62, a bibliography of English 'body and soul' literature.

————. Rev. of *An Early Latin Debate,* E. K. Heningham, ed. *MLQ,* 2 (1941), 503–05.

Van Os, Arnold Barel. *Religious Visions: The Development of the Eschatological Elements in Mediaeval English Religious Literature.* Amsterdam: H. J. Paris, 1932.

Varnhagen, Hermann, ed. "Das altfranzösische Gedicht '*Un Samedi par Nuit.*'" Erlanger Beiträge zur englischen Philologie, I, 1. Anhang. Erlangen and Leipzig: A. Deichert (Georg Böhme), 1889.

————. "Zu mittelenglischen Gedichten." *Anglia,* 2 (1879), 225–55. A brief discussion of "body and soul" literature in Middle English and an edition of one version of the *Desputisoun,* now superseded by the Linow edition.

Visser, F. Th. *An Historical Syntax of the English Language.* 4 vols. Leiden: E. J. Brill, 1963, 1966, 1969, 1973.

Vogel, Sister Mary Ursula. *Some Aspects of the Horse and Rider Analogy in "The Debate between the Body and the Soul."* Washington: Catholic University, 1948. "The Debate between the Body and the Soul," i.e., the *Desputisoun.*

Von Glahn, Nikolaus. *Zur Geschichte des grammatischen Geschlechts im Mittelenglischen vor dem völligen Erlöschen des aus dem Altenglischen ererbten Zustandes,* Anglistische Forschungen, 53. Heidelberg: Carl Winters, 1918.

Walther, Hans. *Das Streitgedicht in der lateinischen Literatur des Mittelalters.* Quellen und Untersuchungen zur Lateinischen Philologie des Mittelalters, V, 2. Abteilung. Munich: C. H. Beck, 1920. Thus far the definitive discussion of debate literature in the Middle Ages.

Wenzel, Siegfried. *Verses in Sermons: "Fasciculus Morum" and its Middle English Poems.* Cambridge, Mass.: Medieval Academy of America, 1978.

Willard, Rudolph. "The Address of the Soul to the Body." *PMLA,* 50 (1935), 957–83. An edition of two OE homiletic exempla and a discussion of the concept of visitations by the soul to the body after death.

————. *Two Apocrypha in Old English Homilies.* Beiträge zur englischen Philologie, 30. Leipzig, 1935; rpt. Johnson Reprint, 1967. A discussion, with texts, of the three questions the soul asks of its angelic or demonic companions after death.

Woolf, Rosemary. *The English Religious Lyric in the Middle Ages.* Oxford: Clarendon Press, 1968. Especially the chapters on the theme of death.

Wright, Thomas, ed. *The Latin Poems Commonly Attributed to Walter Mapes.* London, 1841; rpt. Hildesheim: Georg Olms, 1968. Versions of *Vision of St. Philibert*, pp. 95–106, *"Un Samedi par Nuit,"* pp. 321–33, the *Desputisoun*, pp. 334–39 and pp. 340–46, and *"In a thestri Stude,"* pp. 346–59.

Young, Patrick *Catalogus Librorum Manuscriptorum Bibliotecae Wigorniensis, Made in 1622-23.* Ed. and introd. Ivor Atkins and Neil R. Ker. Cambridge: University Press, 1944.

Zupitza, Julius. "Das Nicaeische Symbolum in englischer Aufzeichnung des 12. Jahrhunderts." *Anglia*, 1 (1878), 286–87.

————. "Zu 'Seele und Leib.'" *Archiv für das Studium der neueren Sprachen und Literaturen*, 91 (1891), 369–404. An edition of an OE "body and soul" passage in prose, a comparison of the late Middle English translation of *Vision of St. Philibert* to an edition of one of the Latin versions, and a comparison of the Batiouchkof, Napier, and Thorpe homilies largely superseded by Dudley's "An Early Homily on the 'Body and Soul' Theme."

This book was designed and typeset

in Baskerville II

with specially adapted

early English characters

by

Medieval & Renaissance Texts & Studies

Binghamton, New York